ADVANCES IN MICROBIOLOGY

APPLICATIONS AND SIGNIFICANCE

ENV BOOKS SERIES

ADVANCES IN MICROBIOLOGY

APPLICATIONS AND SIGNIFICANCE

Editor

Dr. Pawan Kumar 'Bharti'

Society for Environment, Health
Awareness of Nutrition & Toxicology (SEHAT)
B-225/5D, Top Floor, Subhash Gali, Road No. 7, Block B
Ashok Nagar, Shahdara
Delhi-110 093
(India)

DPH

DISCOVERY PUBLISHING HOUSE PVT. LTD.
INDIA

Published by:

Namit Wasan

DISCOVERY PUBLISHING HOUSE PVT. LTD.
4383/4B, Ansari Road, Darya Ganj
New Delhi-110 002 (India)
Phone : +91-11-23279245; 23253475; 43596065
E-mail : discoverybooksindia@gmail.com
discoverypublishinghouse@gmail.com
namitwasan9@gmail.com
web : www.discoverypublishinggroup.com

***First Edition:* 2019**

ISBN: 978-93-86841-97-1

Advances in Microbiology: ***Applications and Significance***

Printed at:
Infinity Imaging Systems
Delhi

PREFACE

Microbiology is the study of all living organisms that are too small to be visible with the naked eye. This includes bacteria, archaea, viruses, fungi, prions, protozoa and algae, collectively known as 'microbes'. These microbes play key roles in nutrient cycling, biodegradation/biodeterioration, climate change, food spoilage, the cause and control of disease, and biotechnology. Thanks to their versatility, microbes can be put to work in many ways: making life-saving drugs, the manufacture of biofuels, cleaning up pollution, and producing/processing food and drink.

Microbiologists study microbes, and some of the most important discoveries that have underpinned modern society have resulted from the research of famous microbiologists, such as Jenner and his vaccine against smallpox, Fleming and the discovery of penicillin, Marshall and the identification of the link between *Helicobacter pylori* infection and stomach ulcers and zur Hausen, who identified the link between papilloma virus and cervical cancer.

Microbiology research has been, and continues to be, central to meeting many of the current global aspirations and challenges, such as maintaining food, water and energy security for a healthy population on a habitable earth.

Microbiology is the study of microorganisms, those being unicellular (single cell), multicellular (cell colony), or acellular (lacking cells). Microbiology encompasses numerous sub-disciplines including virology, parasitology, mycology and bacteriology.

The present book updates the recent research advancements in the field of microbiology, microbial degradation of materials, secondary metabolites, antibiotics, pathogens, endophytic microbes and pseudomonas species.

Thanks are due to publisher and contributors from various institutions and universities.

The book will be helpful for the researchers, academia working in the field of basic microbiology, microbial degradation of materials, secondary metabolites, antibiotics, pathogens, endophytic microbes and pseudomonas species.

Editors
(envbooks@gmail.com)

CONTENTS

Advances in Microbiology: *Applications & Significance* Pages 1-11
Edited by: Dr. Pawan Kumar 'Bharti'
ISBN: 978-93-86841-97-1
Edition: 2019
Published by: Discovery Publishing House Pvt. Ltd., New Delhi (India)

1 Introduction

Microbiology is the study of microscopic organisms, such as bacteria, viruses, archaea, fungi and protozoa. This discipline includes fundamental research on the biochemistry, physiology, cell biology, ecology, evolution and clinical aspects of microorganisms, including the host response to these agents.

Microbiology

Micro-organisms and their activities are vitally important to virtually all processes on Earth. Micro-organisms matter because they affect every aspect of our lives – they are in us, on us and around us.

Microbiology is the study of all living organisms that are too small to be visible with the naked eye. This includes bacteria, archaea, viruses, fungi, prions, protozoa and algae, collectively known as 'microbes'. These microbes play key roles in nutrient cycling, biodegradation/biodeterioration, climate change, food spoilage, the cause and control of disease, and biotechnology. Thanks to their versatility, microbes can be put to work in many ways: making life-saving drugs, the manufacture of biofuels, cleaning up pollution, and producing/processing food and drink.

Microbiologists study microbes, and some of the most important discoveries that have underpinned modern society have resulted from the research of famous microbiologists, such as Jenner and his vaccine against smallpox, Fleming and the discovery of penicillin, Marshall and the identification of the link between *Helicobacter pylori* infection and stomach ulcers, and zur Hausen, who identified the link between papilloma virus and cervical cancer.

Microbiology research has been, and continues to be, central to meeting many of the current global aspirations and challenges, such as maintaining food, water and energy security for a healthy population on a habitable earth. Microbiology research will also help to answer big questions such as 'how diverse is life on Earth?', and 'does life exist elsewhere in the Universe'?

Microbiology is the study of microorganisms, those being unicellular (single cell), multicellular (cell colony), or acellular (lacking cells). Microbiology encompasses numerous sub-disciplines including virology, parasitology, mycology and bacteriology.

Eukaryotic microorganisms possess membrane-bound cell organelles and include fungi and protists, whereas prokaryotic organisms—all of which are microorganisms—are conventionally classified as lacking membrane-bound organelles and include Bacteria and Archaea. Microbiologists traditionally relied on culture, staining, and microscopy. However, less than 1% of the microorganisms present in common environments can be cultured in isolation using current means. Microbiologists often rely on molecular biology tools such as DNA sequence based identification, for example 16s rRNA gene sequence used for bacteria identification.

Viruses have been variably classified as organisms, as they have been considered either as very simple microorganisms or very complex molecules. Prions, never considered as microorganisms, have been investigated by virologists, however, as the clinical effects traced to them were originally presumed due to chronic viral infections, and virologists took search—discovering "infectious proteins".

The existence of microorganisms was predicted many centuries before they were first observed, for example by the Jains in India and by Marcus Terentius Varro in ancient Rome. The first recorded microscope observation was of the fruiting bodies of moulds, by Robert Hooke in 1666, but the Jesuit priest Athanasius Kircher was likely the first to see microbes, which he mentioned observing in milk and putrid material in 1658. Antonie van Leeuwenhoek is considered a father of microbiology as he observed and experimented with microscopic organisms in 1676, using simple microscopes of his own design. Scientific microbiology developed in the 19th century through the work of Louis Pasteur and in medical microbiology Robert Koch.

Definition of Microbiology

Microbiology is the study of microorganisms, which are unicellular or cell-cluster microscopic organisms. This includes eukaryotes such as fungi and protists and prokaryotes such as bacteria and certain algae. Viruses are also included. Microbiology subdivided into divisions including bacteriology, virology, mycology, parasitology and others. A scientist who specializes in the area of microbiology is called a microbiologist. Microbiology can be divided into several subdisciplines, including:

Microbial physiology: The study of how the microbial cell functions biochemically. Includes the study of microbial growth, microbial metabolism and microbial cell structure.

Microbial genetics: The study of how genes are organised and regulated in microbes in relation to their cellular functions. Closely related to the field of molecular biology.

Molecular Microbiology: The study of the molecular biology and genomics of microorganisms.

Medical microbiology: The study of the role of microbes in human illness. Includes the study of microbial pathogenesis and epidemiology and is related to the study of disease pathology and immunology.

Veterinary microbiology: The study of the role in microbes in veterinary medicine or animal taxonomy.

Environmental microbiology: The study of the function and diversity of microbes in their natural environments. Includes the study of microbial ecology, microbially-mediated nutrient cycling, geomicrobiology, microbial diversity and bioremediation. Characterisation of key bacterial habitats such as the rhizosphere and phyllosphere.

Evolutionary microbiology: The study of the evolution of microbes. Includes the study of bacterial systematics and taxonomy.

Industrial microbiology: The exploitation of microbes for use in industrial processes. Examples include industrial fermentation and wastewater treatment. Closely linked to the biotechnology industry. This field also includes brewing, an important application of microbiology.

Aeromicrobiology: The study of airborne microorganisms.

Food microbiology: The study of microorganisms causing food spoilage.

Pharmaceutical microbiology: the study of microorganisms causing pharmaceutical contamination and spoillage.

General Microbiology

Microbial Biodegradation, Bioremediation and Biotransformation Interest in the microbial biodegradation of pollutants has intensified in recent years as mankind strives to find sustainable ways to cleanup contaminated environments. These bioremediation and biotransformation methods endeavour to harness the astonishing, naturally occurring, microbial catabolic diversity to degrade, transform or accumulate a huge range of compounds.

Environmental Microbiology The study of the composition and physiology of microbial communities in the environment i.e. the soil, water, air and sediments covering the planet. Can also include the microorganisms living on or in the animals and plants that inhabit these areas.

Oral Microbiology The study of the microorganisms that inhabit the mouth and in particular those involved in the two major dental diseases: caries and periodontal disease. Oral bacteria include streptococci, lactobacilli, staphylococci, corynebacteria, and various anaerobes in particular bacteroides.

Plant Pathogenic Bacteria Bacteria pathogenic for plants are responsible for devastating losses in agriculture. Plant pathogenic bacteria impact innumerable and valuable agricultural crops, causing hundreds of millions of dollars in damage each year. The use of antibiotics to control such infections is restricted in many countries due to worries over the evolution and transmission of antibiotic resistance.

Bacteria

Acinetobacter the genus Acinetobacter is a group of Gram-negative, non-motile and non-fermentative bacteria belonging to the family Moraxellaceae. They are important soil organisms where they contribute to the mineralisation of, for example, aromatic compounds. Acinetobacter are able to survive on various surfaces (both moist and dry) in the hospital environment, thereby being an important source of infection in debilitated patients. These bacteria are innately resistant to many classes of antibiotics. In addition, Acinetobacter is uniquely suited to exploitation for biotechnological purposes.

Bacillus Bacillus subtilis is one of the best understood prokaryotes in terms of molecular biology and cell biology. Its superb genetic amenability and relatively large size have provided powerful tools to investigate a bacterium in all possible aspects. Recent improvements in technology have provided novel and amazing insights into the dynamic structure of this single cell organism. The organism is a model for differentiation, gene/protein regulation and cell cycle events in bacteria.

Clostridium The genus Clostridium comprises a heterogeneous group of anaerobic spore-forming bacteria, including prominent toxin-producing species, such as C. difficile, C. botulinum, C. tetani and C. perfringens, in addition to well-known non-pathogens like solventogenic C. acetobutylicum. Clostridia produce a range of different clostridial toxins including two of the most potent biological toxins known to affect humans.

Corynebacteria Corynebacteria are a diverse group Gram-positive bacteria found in a range of different ecological niches such as soil, vegetables, sewage, skin, and cheese smear. Some are important pathogens while others are of immense industrial importance.

Cyanobacteria Cyanobacteria are a fascinating and versatile group of bacteria of immense biological importance. Thought to be amongst the first organisms to colonize the earth, these bacteria are the photosynthetic ancestors of chloroplasts in eukaryotes such as plants and algae. In addition they can fix nitrogen, survive in very hostile environments (e.g. down to -60°C), are symbiotic, have circadian rhythms, exhibit gliding mobility, and can differentiate into specialized cell types called heterocysts. This makes them ideal model systems for studying fundamental processes such as nitrogen fixation and photosynthesis.

Gram-positive Bacteria Gram-positive bacteria are generally divided into the Actinobacteria and the Firmicutes. The Actinobacteria include some of the most common soil bacteria and some pathogens, such as Mycobacterium, Corynebacterium.

Helicobacter pylori Helicobacter pylori causes peptic ulcers, gastritis and gastric cancer. The bacterium infects up to 50% of the human population. H. pylori has very unique characteristics, such as microaerophily and nitrogen metabolism.

Lactobacillus Lactobacillus is a genus of Gram-positive facultative anaerobic or microaerophilic bacteria. In humans they are symbiotic and are found in the gut flora. Lactobacillus species are used for the production of yogurt, cheese, sauerkraut, pickles, beer, wine, cider, kimchi, chocolate and other fermented foods, as well as animal feeds such as silage.

Legionella Legionella is the genus of bacterium that causes Legionnaires' Disease also known as Legionellosis. These bacteria are commonly found in aquatic habitats where they can survive and multiply in different protozoa enabling the bacterium to be transmissible and pathogenic to humans.

Mycobacterium Mycobacterium is a genus of Actinobacteria, given its own family, the Mycobacteriaceae. The genus includes pathogens known to cause serious diseases in mammals, including tuberculosis and leprosy. Mycobacteria are aerobic and nonmotile bacteria (except for the species Mycobacterium marinum which has been shown to be motile within macrophages) that are characteristically acid-alcohol fast. Mycobacteria do not contain endospores or capsules and are usually considered to be Gram-positive bacteria.

Pasteurellaceae The Pasteurellaceae family comprises a large and diverse family of Gram-negative bacteria with members ranging from important pathogens such as Haemophilus influenzae to commensals of the animal and human mucosa. Members of the family Pasteurellaceae cause a wide variety of diseases in humans and animals.

Pseudomonas The bacterial genus Pseudomonas includes the opportunistic human pathogen P. aeruginosa, plant pathogenic bacteria, plant beneficial bacteria, ubiquitous soil bacteria with bioremediation capabilities and other species that cause spoilage of milk and dairy products. P. aeruginosa can cause chronic opportunistic infections that have become increasingly apparent in immunocompromised patients and the ageing population of industrialised societies.

Staphylococcus Species of Staphylococcus are important pathogens that cause a variety of diseases in humans and animals. In particular, they cause hospital acquired infections and antibiotic resistant strains (MRSA) cause major problems in hospitals.

Treponema Treponema pallidum is a gram-negative spirochaete bacterium. There are at least four known subspecies: T. pallidum pallidum, which causes syphilis; T. pallidum pertenue, which causes yaws; T. pallidum carateum, which causes pinta; and T. pallidum endemicum, which causes bejel.

Vibrio cholerae Vibrio cholerae is the causative agent of cholera and belongs to a group of organisms whose natural habitats are the aquatic ecosystems. The strains that cause cholera epidemics have evolved from non-pathogenic progenitor strains by acquisition of virulence genes, and V. cholerae represents a paradigm for this evolutionary process.

Fungi

Candida Candida species are important human pathogens that are best known for causing opportunist infections in immunocompromised hosts (e.g. transplant patients, AIDS sufferers, cancer patients). Infections are difficult to treat and can be very serious: 30-40% of systemic infections result in death. The sequencing of the genome of C. albicans and those of several other medically-relevant Candida species has provided a major impetus for Candida comparative and functional genomic analyses. These have provided a fascinating insight into the molecular and cellular biology of these fungi and these should pave the way for the development of more sensitive diagnostic strategies and novel antifungal therapies.

Pathogenic Fungi Pathogenic fungi are fungi that cause disease in humans or other organisms. The study of pathogenic fungi is referred to as medical mycology. Although fungi are eukaryotic organisms many pathogenic fungi are also microorganisms.

Viruses

Animal Viruses The study of animal viruses is important from a veterinary viewpoint and many of these viruses causes diseases that are economically devastating. Many animal viruses are also important from a human medical perspective.

Bluetongue Virus Bluetongue virus (BTV), a member of Orbivirus genus within the Reoviridae family causes serious disease in livestock (sheep, goat, cattle). Partly due to this BTV has been in the forefront of molecular studies for last three decades and now represents one of the best understood viruses at the molecular and structural levels.

Coronavirus Coronaviruses are positive-strand, enveloped RNA viruses that are important pathogens of mammals and birds. This group of viruses cause enteric or respiratory tract infections in a variety of animals including humans, livestock and pets.

Bacteriophage: The New Phage Biology from genomics to applications. Bacterial viruses, or bacteriophages, are estimated to be the most widely distributed and diverse entities in the biosphere. From initial research defining the nature of viruses, to deciphering the fundamental principles of life, to the development of the science of molecular biology, phages have been 'model organisms' for probing the basic chemistry of life. With more recent advances in technology, most notably the ability to elucidate the genome sequences of phages and their bacterial hosts, there has been a resurgence of interest in phages as more information is generated regarding their biology, ecology and diverse nature. Phage research in more recent years has revealed not only their abundance and diversity of form, but also their dramatic impact on the ecology of our planet, their influence on the evolution of microbial populations, and their potential applications. This review focuses on this new post-genomic era of phage biology, from information emerging from genomics and metagenomics approaches through to applications in agriculture, human therapy and biotechnology.

Foot and Mouth Foot-and-mouth disease virus (FMDV) is the prototypic member of the Aphthovirus genus in the Picornaviridae family. This picornavirus is the etiological agent of an acute systemic vesicular disease that affects cattle worldwide.

Cytomegalovirus Cytomegaloviruses are members of the herpesvirus group and can infect humans and other primates. Between 50-80% of adults in developed countries and up to 100% in developing countries are infected with human cytomegalovirus. Infection causes problems in immunocompromised hosts including AIDS victims or patients undergoing organ and stem cell transplantation and congenital infection can cause birth defects in the child. Development of an effective vaccine has high priority.

Epstein-Barr Virus Epstein-Barr virus (EBV) is a human gamma herpes virus that remains one of the most successful viral parasites known to man. It is the etiological agent of infectious mononucleosis and is the major biological cofactor contributing to a number of human cancers including B-cell neoplasms (e.g. Burkitt's lymphoma, Hodgkin's disease and immunoblastic lymphomas), certain forms of T-cell lymphoma, and some epithelial tumours (e.g. nasopharyngeal carcinomas and gastric carcinomas).

Papillomavirus Papillomaviruses are oncogenic DNA tumour viruses that infect humans and animals. Human papillomavirus is one of the most common causes of sexually transmitted infection in the world and can also cause cancer. Papillomavirus research has been revolutionised in recent years with the advent of new technologies such as organotypic raft cultures, virus-like particles and transgenic mice.

Bacteriophage

Phage Bacterial viruses, or bacteriophages, are estimated to be the most widely distributed and diverse entities in the biosphere. From initial research defining the nature of viruses, to deciphering the fundamental principles of life, to the development of the science of molecular biology, phages have been 'model organisms' for probing the basic chemistry of life. With more recent advances in technology, most notably the ability to elucidate the genome sequences of phages and their bacterial hosts, there has been a resurgence of interest in phages as more information is generated regarding their biology, ecology and diverse nature. Phage research in more recent years has revealed not only their abundance and diversity of form, but also their dramatic impact on the ecology of our planet, their influence on the evolution of microbial populations, and their potential applications.

Gram-positive Bacteria

Gram-positive Bacteria are generally divided into the Actinobacteria and the Firmicutes. The Actinobacteria include some of the most common soil bacteria and some pathogens, including Mycobacterium, Corynebacterium, Bacillus, Staphylococcus.

Bacillus Bacillus subtilis is one of the best understood prokaryotes in terms of molecular biology and cell biology. Its superb genetic amenability and relatively large size have provided powerful tools to investigate a bacterium in all possible aspects. Recent improvements in technology have provided novel and amazing insights into the dynamic structure of this single cell organism. The organism is a model for differentiation, gene/protein regulation and cell cycle events in bacteria.

Clostridium The genus Clostridium comprises a heterogeneous group of anaerobic spore-forming bacteria, including prominent toxin-producing species, such as C. difficile, C. botulinum, C. tetani and C. perfringens, in addition to well-known non-pathogens like solventogenic C. acetobutylicum. Clostridia produce a range of different clostridial toxins including two of the most potent biological toxins known to affect humans.

Corynebacteria Corynebacteria are a diverse group of Gram-positive bacteria found in a range of different ecological niches such as soil, vegetables, sewage, skin, and cheese smear. Some are important pathogens while others are of immense industrial importance.

Lactobacillus Lactobacillus is a genus of Gram-positive facultative anaerobic or microaerophilic bacteria. In humans they are symbiotic and are found in the gut flora. Lactobacillus species are used for the production of yogurt, cheese, sauerkraut, pickles, beer, wine, cider, kimchi, chocolate and other fermented foods, as well as animal feeds such as silage.

Mycobacterium Mycobacterium is a genus of Actinobacteria, given its own family, the Mycobacteriaceae. The genus includes pathogens known to cause serious diseases in mammals, including tuberculosis and leprosy. Mycobacteria are aerobic and nonmotile bacteria (except for the species Mycobacterium marinum which has been shown to be motile within macrophages) that are characteristically acid-alcohol fast. Mycobacteria do not contain endospores or capsules and are usually considered to be Gram-positive bacteria.

Staphylococcus Species of Staphylococcus are important pathogens that cause a variety of diseases in humans and animals. In particular, they cause hospital acquired infections and antibiotic resistant strains (MRSA) cause major problems in hospitals.

Gram-negative Bacteria

Many species of Gram-negative bacteria are pathogenic. Medically relevant Gram-negative include Acinetobacter, Helicobacter pylori, Legionella, Pasteurellaceae, Pseudomonas, Treponema, Vibrio cholerae.

Acinetobacter The genus Acinetobacter is a group of Gram-negative, non-motile and non-fermentative bacteria belonging to the family Moraxellaceae. They are important soil organisms where they contribute to the mineralisation of, for example, aromatic compounds. Acinetobacter are able to survive on various surfaces (both moist and dry) in the hospital environment, thereby being an important source of infection in debilitated patients. These bacteria are innately resistant to many classes of antibiotics. In addition, Acinetobacter is uniquely suited to exploitation for biotechnological purposes.

Cyanobacteria Cyanobacteria are a fascinating and versatile group of bacteria of immense biological importance. Thought to be amongst the first organisms to colonize the earth, these bacteria are the photosynthetic ancestors of chloroplasts in eukaryotes such as plants and algae. In addition they can fix nitrogen, survive in very hostile environments (e.g. down to -60°C), are symbiotic, have circadian rhythms, exhibit gliding mobility, and can differentiate into specialized cell types called heterocysts. This makes them ideal model systems for studying fundamental processes such as nitrogen fixation and photosynthesis.

Helicobacter pylori Helicobacter pylori causes peptic ulcers, gastritis and gastric cancer. The bacterium infects up to 50% of the human population. H. pylori has very unique characteristics, such as microaerophily and nitrogen metabolism.

Legionella Legionella is the genus of bacterium that causes Legionnaires' Disease also known as Legionellosis. These bacteria are commonly found in aquatic habitats where they can survive and multiply in different protozoa enabling the bacterium to be transmissible and pathogenic to humans.

Pasteurellaceae The Pasteurellaceae family comprises a large and diverse family of Gram-negative bacteria with members ranging from important pathogens such as Haemophilus influenzae to commensals of the animal and human mucosa. Members of the family Pasteurellaceae cause a wide variety of diseases in humans and animals.

Pseudomonas The bacterial genus Pseudomonas includes the opportunistic human pathogen P. aeruginosa, plant pathogenic bacteria, plant beneficial bacteria, ubiquitous soil bacteria with bioremediation capabilities and other species that cause spoilage of milk and dairy products. P. aeruginosa can cause chronic opportunistic infections that have become increasingly apparent in immunocompromised patients and the ageing population of industrialised societies.

Treponema Treponema pallidum is a gram-negative spirochaete bacterium. There are at least four known subspecies: T. pallidum pallidum, which causes syphilis; T. pallidum pertenue, which causes yaws; T. pallidum carateum, which causes pinta; and T. pallidum endemicum, which causes bejel.

Vibrio cholerae Vibrio cholerae is the causative agent of cholera and belongs to a group of organisms whose natural habitats are the aquatic ecosystems. The strains that cause cholera epidemics have evolved from non-pathogenic progenitor strains by acquisition of virulence genes, and V. cholerae represents a paradigm for this evolutionary process.

Borrelia The genus Borrelia, in the spirochete phylum, is not closely related to any other bacteria and has a highly unusual genome composed of a linear chromosome and multiple circular and linear plasmids that appear to be in a constant state of rearrangement, recombination, and deletion. The determination of the genome sequence of Borrelia strains has facilitated tremendous advances in understanding this genus at the molecular and cellular level as well as the pathogenesis of Lyme disease and relapsing fever.

Branches

The branches of microbiology can be classified into pure and applied sciences, or divided according to taxonomy, as is the case with bacteriology, mycology, protozoology and phycology. There is considerable overlap between the specific branches of microbiology with each other and with other disciplines, and certain aspects of these branches can extend beyond the traditional scope of microbiology.

Applications

While some fear microbes due to the association of some microbes with various human diseases, many microbes are also responsible for numerous beneficial processes such as industrial fermentation (e.g. the production of alcohol, vinegar and dairy products), antibiotic production and act as molecular vehicles to transfer DNA to complex organisms such as plants and animals. Scientists have also exploited their knowledge of microbes to produce biotechnologically important enzymes such as Taq polymerase, reporter genes for use in other genetic systems and novel molecular biology techniques such as the yeast two-hybrid system.

Bacteria can be used for the industrial production of amino acids. Corynebacterium glutamicum is one of the most important bacterial species with an annual production of more than two million tons of amino acids, mainly L-glutamate and L-lysine. Since some bacteria have the ability to synthesize antibiotics, they are used for medicinal purposes, such as Streptomyces to make aminoglycoside antibiotics.

A variety of biopolymers, such as polysaccharides, polyesters and polyamides, are produced by microorganisms. Microorganisms are used for the biotechnological production of biopolymers with tailored properties suitable for high-value medical application such as tissue engineering and drug delivery. Microorganisms are used for the biosynthesis of xanthan, alginate, cellulose, cyanophycin, poly (gamma-glutamic acid), levan, hyaluronic acid, organic acids, oligosaccharides and polysaccharide, and polyhydroxyalkanoates.

Microorganisms are beneficial for microbial biodegradation or bioremediation of domestic, agricultural and industrial wastes and subsurface pollution in soils, sediments and marine environments. The ability of each microorganism to degrade toxic waste depends on the nature of each contaminant. Since sites typically have multiple pollutant types, the most effective approach to microbial biodegradation is to use a mixture of bacterial and fungal species and strains, each specific to the biodegradation of one or more types of contaminants.

Symbiotic microbial communities confer benefits to their human and animal hosts health including aiding digestion, producing beneficial vitamins and amino acids, and suppressing pathogenic microbes. Some benefit may be conferred by eating fermented foods, probiotics (bacteria potentially beneficial to the digestive system) or prebiotics (substances consumed to promote the growth of probiotic microorganisms). The ways the microbiome influences human and animal health, as well as methods to influence the microbiome are active areas of research.

Research has suggested that microorganisms could be useful in the treatment of cancer. Various strains of non-pathogenic clostridia can infiltrate and replicate within solid tumors. Clostridial vectors can be safely administered and their potential to deliver therapeutic proteins has been demonstrated in a variety of preclinical models.

REFERENCES

https://www.nature.com/subjects/microbiology

https://microbiologysociety.org/about/what-is-microbiology-.html

http://www.highveld.com/microbiology/micro.html

https://en.wikipedia.org/wiki/Microbiology

Advances in Microbiology: *Applications & Significance* Pages 12-17
Edited by: Dr. Pawan Kumar 'Bharti'
ISBN: 978-93-86841-97-1
Edition: 2019
Published by: Discovery Publishing House Pvt. Ltd., New Delhi (India)

2

Psychrophilic *Pseudomonas spp.* in Antarctic Freshwater Lake

[1]Dr. Pawan Kumar 'Bharti'

ABSTRACT

Environmental monitoring and assessment was carried out during the 30th Indian Scientific Expedition to Antarctica (ISEA) at Larsemann Hills area in Ingrid Christenson coast. Surface water samples were collected from two lakes on Stornes Peninsula in mid-January 2011 and analysed for the physico-chemical parameters, major elements and trace metals. Lake waters were slightly acid, free from any colour, odour and turbidity, with dissolved oxygen close to saturation. Total dissolved solids were rather similar in both lakes, up to 71 mg/l and the dominant elements were Cl and Ca. Several minor and trace elements were very low or under detection limits. Total organic carbon was ca 0.7 mg C/l in both lakes and PO_4 was at 0.002 mg/level in one lake.

Total bacterial count was 1.6×10^3 cfu/ml in lake ST-2 and lower in other lake while psychrophilic bacterial count was 1.6×10^2 cfu in the former lake. Also a Pseudomonas spp. was detected in the ST-2 lake sample. Ecological studies of aquatic ecosystem of freshwater lakes indicated the suitable condition for the growth and survival of Pseudomonas species in a lake at Stornes Peninsula, Larsemann Hills over east Antarctica. The present study shows that the selected site may be an ideal habitat for the discovery of new species of Pseudomonas bacteria.

Key words: Antarctic lake, Pseudomonas, Psychrophillic bacteria, Stornes Peninsula, Aquatic Ecology

Introduction

High altitude lakes of Antarctica continent represent a relatively unique ecosystem in general; however, they remain less intensely studied than lowland lakes, mainly because of their remoteness and the short summer open-water period (Bhat *et al.,* 2011). Nevertheless, Antarctic lakes are sensitive reference systems of global climatic change and other human impacts

1 Antarctica Laboratory, R & D Division, Shriram Institute for Industrial Research, 19, University Road, Delhi-110007, India

(Schimidt and Psenner, 1992). In fact, although remote high altitude lakes are in general protected from direct human impacts, in the last few decades they have been increasingly affected by airborne contaminants, such as acids and nutrients (Rogora *et al.*, 2006), organic pollutants and heavy metals (Carrera *et al.*, 2002). Due to the extreme environmental conditions (low temperature, strong radiations, mostly low buffering capacity and low nutrient level) these ecosystems have a relatively simple food web and react more rapidly and more sensitively to environmental changes than other lakes (Psenner, 2002). Even minor impacts are able to significantly affect the physical and chemical properties of soft water high altitude lakes, to induce changes in species composition and abundance of the biota and to cause accumulation of trace substances in higher trophic organisms (Hofer *et al.*, 2001; Bharti and Gajananda, 2013). In spite of the socio-economic and ecological importance of these lakes, better knowledge of several ecological aspects is needed for better understanding of their relationships with the environmental variables. These lakes have received little attention so far in terms of their limnology, diversity, conservation and water management, but they are becoming increasingly important due to the possible consequences of the global climate change.

Material and Methods

Study Area

The Larsemann Hills is an ice-free area of approximately 50 km^2, located halfway between the Vestfold Hills and the Amery Ice Shelf on the south-eastern coast of Prydz Bay, Princess Elizabeth Land, East Antarctica (69°30′S, 76°19′58″E). The ice-free area consists of two major peninsulas (Stornes and Broknes), four minor peninsulas, and approximately 130 islands. The Larsemann Hills area contains more than 150 lakes at different Islands and peninsulas.

Environmental monitoring and impact assessment studies were carried out during the austral summers of various Indian Scientific Expeditions to Antarctica since 2003. We analyzed the physicochemical parameters and the ionic constituents of water samples from two lakes on Stornes during 2010-11 during the construction of the third Indian Antarctic research station Bharti.

Sampling

Stornes Peninsula of Larsemann Hills in east Antarctica was selected as a sampling site for the present study. Water samples were collected from two selected lakes of Stornes Peninsula during 30th Indian Scientific Expedition to Antarctica (ISEA) and analysed for the physico-chemical parameters, microbiological parameters, major elements and trace metal in surface lake water. Water samples were collected from two selected small lakes and analysed for the physico-chemical parameters, major and trace elements in surface lake water. The location map of study area is given in the Figure 2.1.

Two sampling points were selected at various locations, namely ST-1 and ST-2. Geo-coordinates and basic details of both sampling points are given in Table 2.1.

Analytical Methods

Some of the physico-chemical characteristics of water including temperature, color, pH were determined *in situ* by mercury thermometer, visual observation and digital pH meter respectively, while dissolved oxygen, turbidity and total dissolved solids were analyzed using Orion onsite water quality monitoring kit. Physico-chemical parameters were analysed using standard methodology (APHA, 2005; Trivedi and Goel, 1984). The concentrations of metals were measured using Inductively Coupled Plasma Optical Emission spectroscopy (ICP-OES).

Results and Discussion

Lake water was found to be free from any colour, odour or turbidity. pH of both samples were close to neutral, 6.7 and 6.8. Total hardness of water samples was found to be 14 mg/l and 13 mg/l respectively for ST-1 and ST-2 and alkalinity was 4 mg/l and 5 mg/l respectively for ST-1 and ST-2. Total dissolved solids of ST-1 and ST-2 lakes were recorded as 71 mg/l and 64 mg/l respectively, whereas dissolved oxygen was recorded 10.8 mg/l and 13.2 mg/l for ST-1 and ST-2 respectively. Total organic carbon of both samples was found to be 0.7 mg/l.

Chlorides and calcium were found to be the dominant constituents among the lake water contents. Chloride was found to be 32 mg/l and 31 mg/l, while calcium was 3.6 mg/l and 1.3 mg/l at in ST-1 lake and ST-2 lake, respectively. Magnesium was found to be 1.3 mg/l at ST-1 lake and was nil in ST-2 lake. Boron was 0.007 mg/l at ST-2 lake site and nil in ST-1 lake. Iron was found to be 0.02 mg/l in ST-1 lake water, while it was found below detection limit in ST-2 lake water.

Fluoride (0.1 mg/l in ST-1 lake), aluminum (0.006 mg/l in ST-1 & 0.007 mg/l in ST-2 lake) and manganese (0.003 mg/l at ST-2) were found in minor quantities Sulphate (1.0 mg/l) and phosphate (0.002 mg/l) were detected in sample ST-1 only.

Of trace metals cadmium was below detection level in both samples. Similar trend was observed for copper, mercury, selenium, arsenic, lead, zinc & chromium metals. Few metals are biologically essential to living organisms in trace quantities in aquatic ecosystems. These trace metals may re-circulate from sediment and became available for biota (Campbell *et al.*, 1988).

Results of studies on microbiological parameters of lake water samples are given in Table 2.4. Total bacterial count was found to be less than 1 cfu and 1.6 × 10^3 cfu in ST-1 and ST-2 lake water samples, while psychrophillic counts were found to be 66 cfu and 1.6×10^2 cfu in ST-1 and ST-2 respectively. No growth was observed for MPN coliform in any of the samples. Salmonnela and Staphylococcus were also found to be absent in both of the lake water sample, while Pseudomonas spp. was found in ST-2 lake water sample. The above given physico-chemical parameters, metal content and other variables provide favorable conditions to microbial community especially to Pseudomonas spp.

High dissolved oxygen content in lake water always support to aquatic organisms. This is indeed very good and healthy condition for any aquatic ecosystem. Selected lake water sample are almost pesticide free and radiation contamination free. Lake water samples were found free from harmful pathogens and have an abundant psychrophillic bacterial population in both lake water. Due to bacterial community in both of the lakes, water may be harmful for drinking purposes. Total dissolved solids are also very low, so the raw lake water can be considered as drinking water, but in case of emergency only. The presence of Pseudomonas spp. in ST-2 lake indicates the survival of new bacterium and its new strain in Antarctic lake water under subzero conditions. However, many strains were isolated by Reddy *et al.* (2004) from cyanobacterial mat from Antarctica, but the selected location of Stornes peninsula has a potential to have some new strains of Pseudomonas in freshwater lake of Antarctica.

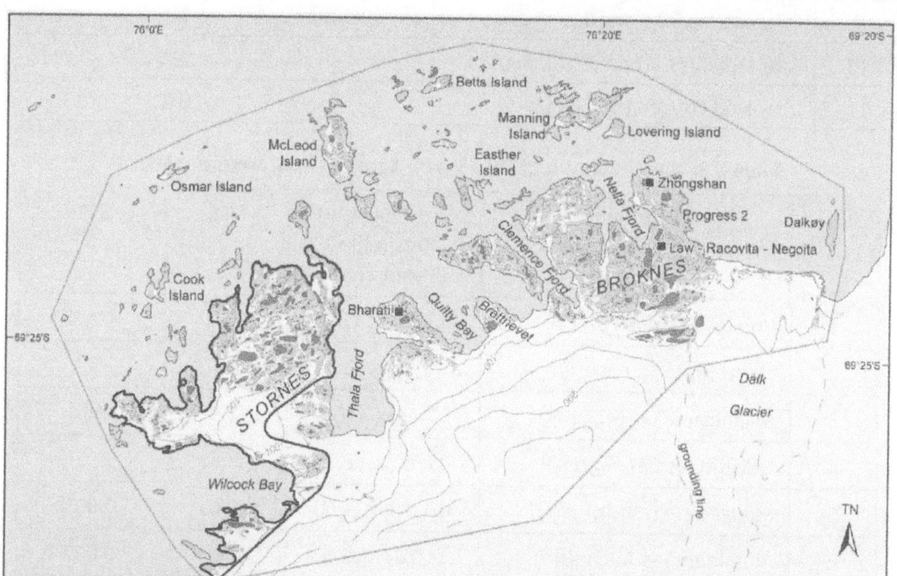

Fig. 2.1: Location Map of Stornes peninsula in Larsemann Hills, East Antarctica

Table 2.1: Location of Lake Water Sampling points at Stornes Peninsula

Sl.No.	Sample ID	Date	Latitude (S)	Longitude (E)	Altitude (m)	Temperature (°C)
1.	ST1	15.01.2011	69° 26' 45.4"S	76° 07' 02.6"E	29	1.0
2.	ST2	15.01.2011	69° 21' 18.8"S	76° 07' 36.0"E	31	1.8

Table 2.2: Physico-chemical Parameters of Lake Water at Stornes Peninsula

Sl.No.	Parameter	IS: 10500-1991 Desirable (Permissible)	ST1	ST2
1.	Colour, Hazen unit	5, Max.	<5	<5
2.	Odour	Unobjectionable (UO)	UO	UO
3.	Turbidity, NTU	5, Max. (10)	<1	<1
4.	pH	6.5-8.5	6.8	6.7
5.	Total hardness (as $CaCO_3$), mg/l	300, Max. (600)	14	13
6.	Dissolved Solids, mg/l	500, Max. (2000)	71	64
7.	Chloride (as Cl), mg/l	250, Max. (1000)	32	31
8.	Alkalinity (as $CaCO_3$), mg/l	200 Max.(600)	4	5
9.	Sulphate (as SO_4), mg/l	200, Max.	1	<1
10.	Total Organic Carbon (TOC), mg/l	-	0.735	0.711
11.	Dissolved Oxygen (DO), mg/l	-	10.8	13.2

Table 2.3: Metal Content of Lake Water Samples at *Stornes peninsula*

Sl.No.	Parameter	IS: 10500-1991 Desirable (Permissible)	ST1	ST2
1	Iron (as Fe), mg/l	0.3, Max. (1.0)	0.02	<0.01
2	Fluoride (as F), mg/l	1.0, Max. (1.5)	0.1	<0.1
3	Magnesium (as Mg), mg/l	30, Max. (100)	1.3	Nil
4	Calcium (as Ca), mg/l	75, Max. (200)	3.6	1.3
5	Manganese (as Mn), mg/l	0.1, Max. (0.3)	<0.01	0.003
6	Aluminum (as Al), mg/l	0.2, Max	0.006	0.007
7	Boron (as B), mg/l	1, Max (5)	<0.001	0.007

Table 2.4: Microbial Community in Lake Water Samples at *Stornes peninsula*

Sl.No.	Sample ID.	ST-1	ST-2
1.	Total Bacterial Count/ml (As per guidelines of IS : 5402-2002, Reaff 2007)	Less than 1 cfu	1.6×10^3
2.	Psychrophillic Count/ml (As per guidelines of IS: 1479 p-3, 1977, Reaff: 2003)	66 cfu	1.6×10^2
3.	MPN Coliform /100 ml (As per guidelines of IS:1622-1981, Reaff : 2003) Ed 2.4 (2003-05)	No growth observed	No growth observed
4.	Salmonella/ 25 ml (As per guidelines of IS: 5887 (p-3) 1999 Reaff: 2005)	Absent	Absent
5.	Staphylococcus aureus/25ml (As per guidelines of IS : 5887 P-2 1976 Reaff : 2005)	Absent	Absent
6.	Pseudomonas spp./10ml (As per guidelines of IS:13428, Amn.D, 2005)	Absent	Present

REFERENCES

APHA (2005): Standard Methods for the Examination of Water and Wastewater. *21st Ed. American Public Health Association, APHA, AWWA, WEF, Washington, D. C.* pp. 1170.

Bhat. F.A., Yousuf, A.R., Aftab, A., Arshid, J., Mahdi, M. D., and Balkhi M. H. (2011). International Journal of Biodiversity and Conservation 3(10), 501-511.

Bharti, P. K. and Gajananda, Kh. (2013). Environmental Monitoring and Assessment in Antarctica, In: Environmental Health and Problems (Eds.- Bharti, P. K. and Gajananda, Kh.), Discovery Publishing House, Delhi, 178-186 pp.

Carrera. G., Fernandez, P., Grimalt, J.O., Ventura. M., Camarero. L, Catalan, J., Nickus, U., Thies, H. and Psenner R. (2002), Environ. Sci. Technol. 36, 2581-2588.

Campbell, P.G.C., A. G. Lewis, P. M. Chapman, A. A. Crowder, W. K. Fletcher, B. Imber, S. N. Luoma, P. M. Stokes, and M. Winfrey (1988): Biologically Available Metals in Sediments. Publication No. NRCC 27694, *National Research Council of Canada,* Ottawa, Canada.

Hofer. R., Lackner, R., Kargl, J., Thaler, B., Tait, D., Bonetti, L., Vistocco, R., and Flaim G. (2001). Water, Air and Soil Pollution 125, 189-200.

Psenner, R. (2002). In: Global Environmental Change in Alpine Region: New Horizons in Environmental Economics (Steininger K.W., Weck-Hannemann H. eds.). Edward Eldgar, Cheltenham, UK, 271 pp.

Reddy GS, Matsumoto GI, Schumann P, Stackebrandt E, Shivaji S. (2004). Int J Syst Evol Microbiol 54 (3), 713-19.

Rogora. M., Mosello, R., Arisci, S., Brizzio, M.C., Barbieri, A., Balestrini, R., Waldner, P., Schmitt, M., Stahli, M., Thimonier, A., Kalina, M., Puxbaum, H., Nickus, U., Ulrich, E., and Probst A. (2006). Hydrobiologia 562, 17-40.

Schmidt, R. and Psenner, R. (1992). Documenta Ist. Ital. Hydrobiol 32, 31-57.

Trivedi, R. K. and Goel, P. K. (1984): Chemical and Biological Methods for Water Pollution Studies. *Enviro Media Publication, Karad.* p. 225.

Advances in Microbiology: *Applications & Significance* **Pages 18-37**
Edited by: Dr. Pawan Kumar 'Bharti'
ISBN: 978-93-86841-97-1
Edition: 2019
Published by: Discovery Publishing House Pvt. Ltd., New Delhi (India)

3 Microbial Secondary Metabolites as Novel Antimicrobial Compounds

[1]Harpreet Kaur, [2]Priyanka Chandra and [3]Daljit Singh Arora

Introduction

A disease is an impairment of the normal state of an organism or any of its components that hinders the performance of vital functions. It may be attributed to one or many factors e.g. malnutrition, industrial hazards, climate, specific infective agents (e.g. viruses, bacteria, fungi, protozoa, helminthes), inherent defects of the body (e.g. various genetic and immunologic anomalies) or combination of these. Infectious diseases are major hazard all over the world causing premature deaths (Pinner *et al.*, 1996). Chemotherapy started with vaccination discovered by Edward Jenner but the term chemotherapy was originally coined by Paul Ehrlich who discovered the first effective chemotherapeutic agent-arsphenamine/salvarsan, which opened the door to future developments in chemotherapy and antibiotics. Discovery and development of sulfonamides was followed by a golden period (1935-1970) with flurry of discoveries of antibiotics leading to more than a dozen classes of antibiotics including sulphonamides, β lactams, aminoglycosides, chloramphenicol, tetracycline, macrolides, trimethoprim, rifamycins, quinolones and glycopeptides. It was the discovery of the most beneficial secondary metabolite i.e. penicillin from *Penicillium notatum* by Alexander Fleming in 1929, which revolutionized the field of modern medicine. Since then, a lot of compounds possessing antibiotic activity have been isolated from different fungi. In general naturally occurring substances are distinguished from the synthetic compounds by the name of antibiotics. Natural products are chemical compounds obtained as a result of primary or secondary metabolism of living organisms (Bentley, 1997). The primary metabolites such as nucleic acids, fatty acids, polysaccharides and proteins) are present in all biological systems whereas secondary metabolites are diverse chemical compounds with varied biological functions. An important part of the natural products, the

[1,3] Department of Microbiology, Guru Nanak Dev University, Amritsar-143005, India
[2] ICAR-Central Soil Salinity Research Institute, Karnal, Haryana -132001, India

group of smaller molecular secondary metabolites of microorganisms usually exhibits some kind of biological activities. Vast majority of clinically relevant compounds, including antibacterial, antifungal, and antitumor have been derived from natural products (Yue-Zhong Shu, 1998). They represent the greatest single contribution of drug therapy for the health care of increasing population of the world and provide effective control against many microbial pathogens. Various biotic entities like actinomycetes, plants, mushrooms, animals etc have been proved to be potential sources for various bioactive compounds which help to fight different diseases. But as the increasing population is becoming resistant to many commercially available antibiotics leading to the emergence of many fatal diseases, so there is a real need to find and expand the spectrum of such sources which can help in finding novel compounds to resolve the problem posed by resistance or to expand the spectrum of the existing antimicrobial sources. Fungi are well known source of bioactive compounds and the research for isolation of novel fungal metabolites that blossomed more than 40 years ago is still very active now. At present, the search for new producers of biologically active compounds that help them to survive and adapt to their surroundings can be expected in these fungi with the greatest probability (Gloer, 1995; Grabley *et al.*, 1999). Microbes have made a phenomenal contribution to the health and well being of people throughout the world. They produce a number of secondary metabolites which are an integral part of the pharmaceuticals currently available in the market (Demain and Sanchez, 2009). Soil holds an enormous biodiversity that can be screened for antibiotic producers. Because of huge expenditure on synthetic molecules with effective antimicrobial properties, natural products are still a worth promise (Newman and Cragg, 2007). Fungi are important sources of secondary metabolites and they continue to provide new chemical entities with novel biological activities (Baker and Alvi, 2004). They have been a rich source of compounds for therapeutic applications including antibacterial (Rancic *et al.*, 2006; Lucas *et al.*, 2007; Takahashi *et al.*, 2009), antifungal (Nicoletti *et al.*, 2007; Omura *et al.*, 2008), antiviral (Nishihara *et al.*, 2000), immunosuppressants and cholesterol-lowering agents (Grabley *et al.*, 1992; Kwon *et al.*, 2002). Although many fungi have been listed, to possess antimicrobial activity, still there is a need to explore more such organisms to meet the problem of emerging strains of resistant microorganisms and to expand the spectrum of suitable organisms which can be useful to meet the requirements of potent antimicrobials.

The present book chapter focus on the development of novel antimicrobial compounds from microbial sources or to find the novel microorganisms which can further be useful for providing different metabolites of various pharmaceutical importance's. Nature is a great repository of such organisms which can be tapped for various uses.

Antimicrobials from Plants

Medicinal plants are rich repository of various bioactive molecules that serve as natural plant defense mechanisms against invasion by microorganisms, insects or for combating infectious or parasitic agents or generated in response to stress conditions (Cowan, 1999). Traditionally, a number of herbs are recommended for various ailments and reported for their carminative, stomachic, anti-inflammatory, antioxidant, antihypoglycemic, antihypertensive, antispasmodic, gastric acid suppressive etc. (Eguale and Giday, 2009). Various reports are available on antimicrobial potential of the plants from all over the world (Arora and Kaur, 1999; Rojas *et al.*, 2006; Sharker and Shahid, 2010).

Flavonoids, is a class of aromatic compounds commonly found in fruit, vegetables etc. Flavonoids have been reported to possess bioactivities, *viz.*, anti-inflammatory (Okwu, 2004), antiallergic (Mills and Bone, 2000); anticancer; antiulcer (Vidari *et al.*, 2003); antibacterial (Xu and Lee, 2001; Ozcelik *et al.*, 2008) and antiviral properties (Li *et al.*, 2002). Many plant extracts such as *Terminalia chebula, Mahonia bealei, Rabdosia rubescens, Rubus chingii, Scutellaria baicalensis, Magnolia officinalis* and *Rosa rugosa* were reported by Miyasaki *et al.*, (2013) for antimicrobial activity against *Acinetobacter baumanniii.* Compounds such as Ellagic acid, norwogonin and chebulagic acid isolated from plant extracts of *Rosa rugosa, Scutellaria baicalensis* and *Terminalia chebula* have been reported to have antimicrobial activity against *Acinetobacter baumanniii.*

In another report, the active compound isolated from *Acalypha indica* showed better activity than standard antibiotic Clotrimazole (Solomon *et al.*, 2005).

Plants derived phytoconstituents such as tannins, saponins also have potential antimicrobial (Funatogawa *et al.*, 2004; Yang *et al.*, 2006), antiviral (Mengoni *et al.*, 2002); antiprotozoal (Wallace, 2004); antioxidant; chemo preventive (Mujoo *et al.*, 2001) and hypoglycemic properties (Yoshikawa *et al.*, 2001).

Besides so many biological properties of medicinal plants their commercial usage is still under question. Medicinal plants consist of several chemicals which may either act alone or in a synergistic manner. It is not easy to track these synergistic interactions since the underlying mechanism has not yet been completely explored. Mostly plants based medicines are locally restricted and downstreaming process is more studied in case of microorganisms which help in commercial production of the antimicrobial agents. As, a lot of medicinal plants have been studied for their biological activities but antibiotics have been used for quick relief from any ailment. Herbs had been in use since time immemorial but in case of severe infections, such as bouts of mastitis and UTI's; which require quick relief; antibiotics such as erythromycin and ciprofloxacin play an important role. When it comes to disease causing bacteria, we live in a world where bacteria continually evolve resistance to older remedies and even older antibiotics. Microbial secondary metabolites are one of the major sources of anti-bacterial, anti-fungal, antitumor, anti-virus and immunosuppressive agents for clinical use. Present challenges in microbial pharmaceutical development are the discovery of novel secondary metabolites with significant biological activities. Novel antibiotics such as ceftriaxone, clarithromycin and augmentin must enter the spectrum of the already existing antimicrobial agents to fight against various diseases caused by drug resistant microorganisms such as MRSA, VRSA, VRE etc (Parra-Ruiz *et al.*, 2010). The interest of the pharmaceutical industries have been directed towards the synthesis of various bioactive metabolites (Demain, 2002) such as cholesterol lowering drugs, e.g., statins (Nicholls *et al.*, 2007), anticancer drugs e.g. bleomycin, dactinomycin, doxorubicin and staurosporin (Minotti *et al.*, 2004). A lot of studies have been carried out to search biologically active compounds from microbial sources like actinomycetes, bacteria and fungi. Thus we can say that microbial world possesses a vast pool of antimicrobial compounds which has been successfully exploited, but a major limitation is that only less than 1% of the microbial world having been explored yet.

Antimicrobials from Actinomycetes

Actinomycetes are filamentous bacteria notably characterized by their antibiotic producing ability. Some of the antibiotics produced by actinomycetes are neomycin, erythromycin, streptomycin and tetracycline (Arasu *et al.*, 2008). The actinomycetes, particularly, *Streptomyces*, has been widely used for the production of antimicrobial agents. Right from the discovery of streptomycin from *Streptomyces griseus*, a lot many actinomycetes have been screened for antimicrobials till date. Attimarad *et al.*, (2012), isolated two antibacterial compounds from marine actinomycetes, 7-demethoxy rapamycin; antimicrobial compound with broad spectrum antimicrobial activity was isolated from *Streptomyces hygroscopicus* BDUS 49 (Parthasarathi *et al.*, 2012). Actinomycetes provide a rich source of compounds for therapeutic applications including antibacterial (Sibanda *et al.*, 2010), antifungal ; antiviral, immunosuppressant and cholesterol-lowering agents (Kumari *et al.*, 2013). A lot of actinomycete strain from different environment have been isolated and screened for antimicrobial activity. Seven actinomycetes strains isolated from soil of Gwalior were shown to possess antimicrobial activity against *Escherichia coli*, Methicillin resistant *Staphylococcus aureus* and Vancomcin resistant *Enterococci* (Singh *et al.*, 2012). Some actinomycetes have been isolated from Himalayan soil and were found to possess better antimicrobial potential against *Staphylococcus aureus*, *Escherichia coli*, *Pseudomonas aeruginosa*, *Bortrytis cinera* and *Trichophyton mentagrophytes* (Duraipandiyan *et al.*, 2010).

Researchers not only worked on soil but marine environments are also the rich source of actinomycetes having various biological activities. In another report, some actinomycete strains, isolated from marine environment, were found to be active against various pathogenic microorganisms such as *Bacillus subtilis Staphylococcus* species, *Vibrio fischeri, Pseudomonas* species, *Proteus vulgaris, Klebsiella pneumoniae* revealed to be the potent antimicrobial source (Valli *et al.*, 2012). Similarly several endophytic strains also rich in bioactive compounds with different biological activities have been reported. An endosymbiotic actinomycete strain showed antibacterial potential against various human clinical and reference strains like *Micrococcus luteus,* haemolytic *Streptococcus, Klebsiella pneumoniae, Staphylococcus epidermidis, Proteus mirabilis, Escherichia coli, Enterococcus faecalis, Pseudomonas aeruginosa* and *Staphyloccus aureus* (Gandhimathi *et al.*, 2008).Various compounds have been isolated from actinomycetes with various biological activities. Novel pyridinum compound isolated from marine actinomycetes, *Amycolatopsis alba* var. nov. isolated from Visakhapatnam coast of Bay of Bengal, India, also showed better antibacterial activity (Dasari *et al.*, 2012). Kitouni *et al.*, (2005), isolated different actinomycete strains from north–east of Algeria which showed antimicrobial potential. Actinomycetes isolated from water and sediments of Lake Tana, Ethiopia displayed an immense antimicrobial potential against *Escherichia. coli, Pseudomonas aeruginosa, Salmonella typhi, Klebsiella pneumoniae,* and *Staphylococcus aureus* (Gebreyohannes *et al.*, 2013).

Although this natural source has a lot of potential to be used for various biological activities but for the search of newer antimicrobials we can look for more microorganisms which can be easily identified first on the morphological basis so that its further selection as a novel antimicrobial source could be easy which in case of actinomycetes is difficult to identify at initial stages of growth.

Antimicrobial from Bacteria

Bacteria are ubiquitous in nature and holds several biotechnological and pharmaceutical applications. The polypeptide antibiotics such as polymyxin and bacitracin) are reportedly produced by *Bacillus polymyxa* and *Bacillus subtilis* respectively. Likewise, *Bacillus cereus* is a well known producer of zwittermicin. Researchers are also making efforts to expand the range of bacteria that can be tapped for antibiotic research. Secondary metabolites from various bacterial species are well reported for their biological activities such as antibacterial (Devi *et al.*, 2011); antioxidant activity (Amaretti *et al.*, 2013). A lot of compounds have been isolated from bacteria showing different biological activities including antiviral (Kamei *et al.*, 1988). "*Pseudoalteromonas flavipulchra* JG1 produces a protein PfaP and a range of small-molecule compounds with inhibitory activities against *Vibrio anguillarum*" (Yu *et al.*, 2012). Not only from soil, marine environment also possess such potential source of antimicrobial agents Likewise, bacteria of *Bacillus, Paenibacillus* and *Saccharothrix* genera, isolated from *Anadara broughtonii* inhabiting possessed broad spectrum antibacterial activity (Romanenko *et al.*, 2008). Wilson *et al.*, (2009) studied one hundred and four marine isolates possessing antimicrobial activity by cross dilution assay against *S.aureus, P.aeruginosa, E.coli,* and two strains of *Shewanella* spp.

In another report, *Pseudomonas fluroscence* (H40, H41) and *Pseudomonas aeruginosa* (H51); the bacterial species associated with sponge, was found to possess better antibacterial activity against some resistant strains: multi drug resistant *Klebsiella pneumonia and* vancomycin resistant *Enterococcus faecium. Bacillus pumilus* Pc 31 and Pc 32, *Pseudovibrio dentrificans* Mm 37 strain were active against gram positive bacteria (Santos *et al.*, 2010). Members of heterotrophic bacteria *Firmicutes, Gammaproteobacteria, Actinobacteria* and *Alphaproteobacteria* isolated from Park Bay sediments showed antimicrobial potential against *Escherichia coli, Proteus mirabilis, Pseudomonas aeruginosa, Shigella boyodii, Salmonella typhi,Staphylococcus aureus, Staphylococcus epidermidis, Klebsiella pneumoniae, Vibrio vulnificus* and *Vibrio harveyi* (Nithya and Pandian, 2010). Thousands of spp. of lactic acid bacteria (LAB) and their metabolites isolated from various sources have been studied for antimicrobial potential. Antimicrobial activity of several strains of lactic acid bacteria (LAB) isolated from Genestoso variety of cheese, possessed antibacterial activity against the five reference varieties of *Enterococcus faecalis, Staphylocccus aureus, Lactobacillus planatarum, Clostridium tyrobutyrium,* and *Listeria monocytogenes.* The evaluation of antimicrobial activities of *Lactobacillus sakei, Pediococcus acidilactici, Pediococcus pentosaceus* was performed by Cizeikiene *et al.*, 2013 inhibiting the growth of pathogenic bacteria belonging to *Bacillus, Pseudomonas, Listeria* and *Escherichia* genera in various degrees. These bacterial strains also showed fungicidal activities against fungi and yeast such as *Fusarium culorum, Penicillium chryosogenum, Aspergillus fumigatus, Aspergillus versicolor, Penicillium expanusm, Aspergillus niger* and *Candida perapsilosis.* A lot many compounds have been purified from various bacterial isolates isolated from different sources possessing antimicrobial activity. Various compounds like "3 hydroxy decanoic acid, 5-oxododecanoic acid and 3-hydroxy-5 dodecenoic acid" were isolated from *Lactobacillus planatrum* having a potential antifungal activity (Ryu *et al.*, 2014). Proteinaceous substance produced by *Lactobacillus paracasei* sub sp. *paracasei* possessed bactericidal and fungistatic activities against *Bacillus subtilis, Helicobacter pylori,* several *Lactbacillus debrueckii* species and yeast strains *Candida pseudointermedia, Candida blankii, Candida albicans* and *Saccharomyces cerevisiae* (Atanassova *et al.*, 2003). A novel antimicrobial peptide produced by *Breviacillus laterosporus* isolated and purified from the soil of mango plants showed a broad range of antimicrobial activity against test organisms used (Zhao *et al.*, 2012).

Thirty one aerobic and three anaerobic lactic acid bacteria isolated from unfermented and fermenting cassava leaves and roots and showed antimicrobial potential against indicator bacteria *Escherichia coli, Salmonella enterica* serotype *typhimurium, Bacillus cereus* and *Staphylococcus aureus* (Anyogu *et al.,* 2014). Four strains of lactic acid bacteria viz. KT2W2G, KT2W2L, TS9S17 and TS9SI9 isolated from mangrove forest in Southern Thailand produced bacteriocin like inhibitory substance (BLIS) and showed an inhibition zone against *Lactobacillus sakei* subsp. *sakei, Listeria monocytogenes* and *Brochothrix thermosphacta* by agar well diffusion assay (Hwanhlem *et al.,* 2014). Several bacterial isolates obtained from honeys (New Zealand), possessed broad spectrum antibacterial potential against microorganisms such as *Bacillus cereus, Bacillus subtilis, Escherichia coli, Listeria monocytogenes,* and *Salmonella enteritidis* (Lee *et al.,* 2008).

Endophytic strains from various sources are also known to be a rich source for many compounds possessing antimicrobial activity. An endophytic bacterium *Bacillus loliquefaciens* isolated from mangrove was found to be antagonistic to some fungal and bacterial pathogens (Hu *et al.,* 2010). Thus a number of bacteria have been shown as the potential sources for various antimicrobial products, still there is a need to explore more microorganisms which can easily reach to downstreaming process for the commercial production of antibiotics. Morphological screening of bacteria at flask level is difficult while in case of fungi we can identify the genus apparently while looking at the colony and further we can easily identify the contamination of another microorganism at flask level. Screening of fungi for antimicrobials can be easier by looking at its morphology.

Antimicrobials from Fungi

Fungi is a diverse group of eukaryotic organisms that include yeasts and molds. This kingdom differs from plants, animals, protists, and bacteria due to a fact that fungal cells have chitineous cell walls in contrast to cellulose- containing cell walls of plants and some protists. "Fungi have a worldwide distribution, and grow in a wide range of habitats, including extreme environments such as deserts or areas with high salt concentrations or ionizing radiation as well as in deep sea sediments. Some can survive the intense cosmic radiations encountered during space travel". Soil fungi play an important role as major decomposers in the soil ecosystem. They also provide mankind with very useful pharmaceutical products, such as antibiotics and other valuable substances, including organic acids, enzymes, pigments and secondary metabolites used in the food industry and fermentation. In addition, many soil fungi are biological control agents for plant pathogens and insect pests. Most common genera of fungi found in soil are *Alternaria, Aspergillus Cephalosporium,*

Botrytis, Fusarium, Penicillium, Rhizopus, Verticillium, Trichoderma, Cladosporium, Gliocladium, Monilia, Pythium, Mucor, Chaetomium etc. The present study concerns the isolation of fungi from soil with an objective to expand the spectrum of such fungi for the isolation of biologically active compounds which can be useful antimicrobials. *Aspergillus* (sac fungi) comprises a diverse group of both beneficial and pathogenic species which occurs predominately in soil and marine habitats. "Some common species include *Aspergillus fumigatus,* responsible for the highest number of human deaths from fungi, "*Aspergillus flavus*", a destructive agricultural pest, and *Aspergillus nidulans,* an important model organism" (Gibbons and Rokas, 2013. *Aspergillus* is a well known genus which produces various bioactive metabolites for ensuring its survival, fitness and reproduction and are of significant importance in fields of genetics, bioengineering, ecology, and biochemistry. Despite such importance, a lot more remains untapped from this diverse genus (Nutzmann *et al.,* 2011).

Many bioactive metabolites from *Aspergillus* spp. were reported in literature, proving its worth for medical applications such as cholesterol lowering agent; lovastatin, antibiotic penicillin and aflatoxin (Gibbons and Rokas, 2013).

Antimicrobials from *Aspergillus* sp.

"A complex and fascinating aspect of fungal development is the production of secondary metabolites. These compounds, frequently associated with sporulation processes, are considered part of the chemical arsenal required for niche specialization and have garnered intense interest by virtue of their biotechnological and pharmaceutical applications" (Demain and Fang, 2000) including antimicrobial, antitumor, immunosuppressant and antihypercholesterolemic, activities (Quang *et al.,* 2002). In a study on fungal biodiversity, "nearly 1.5 million fungal species exist on Earth, with only 5% identified" (Blackwell, 2011).

Genus *Aspergillus owes the credit for the production of large number of* secondary metabolites, due to its versatile metabolic versatility, making it an important part of medical, industrial and commercial fields (Pel *et al.,* 2007).

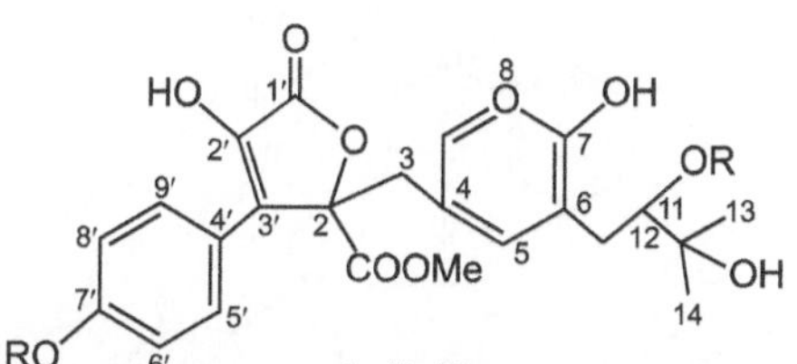

1 R–H
1a R–Ac

1

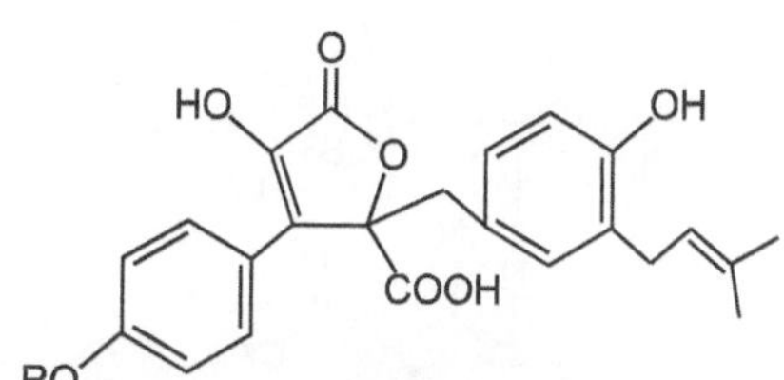

1 R–H
1a R–Ac

2

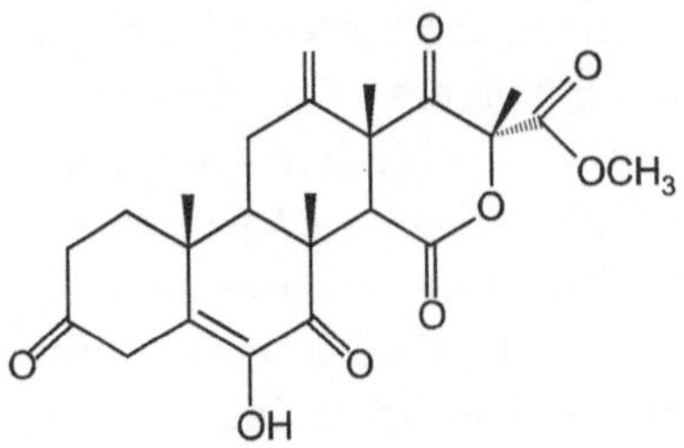

3

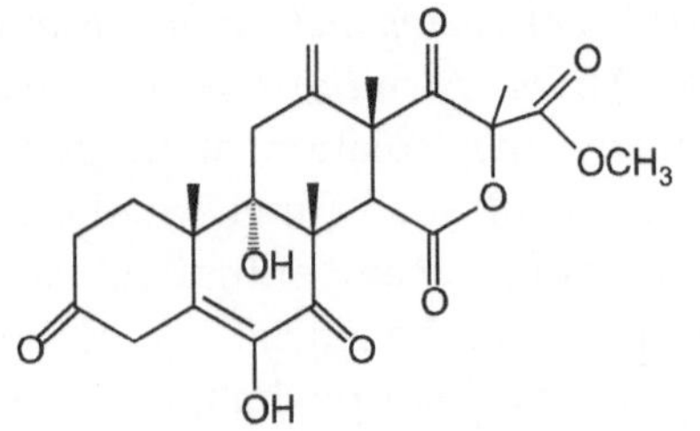

4

Fig. 3.1 : Structure elucidation of compounds isolated from *Aspergillus* sp

Three compounds from an *Aspergillus* sp., *viz.*, butyrolactone I, terretonin A and terretonin B (Figure 3.1) reported antimicrobial activity against *Erwinia carotovora, Pseudomonas syringae* pv *syringae, Xanthomonas arboricola* pv *juglandis, Clavibacter michiganensis* 807 (Gram-positive bacteria) and *Agrobacterium tumefaciens* A348 (Gram-negative bacteria).

Diverse antimicrobial activity was found in the crude extract of *Aspergillus fumigatus* where the ten compounds (Figure 3.2) namely " linoleic acid (1); R (–)- glycerol monolinoleate (2); bis-dethio–(bis methyl-thio)-gliotoxin; FR-49175 (3); fumiquinazoline–F (4); fumiquanzoline–D (5); (Z-Z)-N,N–[1-[(4-Hydroxy phenyl)-methylene]-2-[(4-Hydroxyphenyl)-methylene]-1,2-ethanediyl]-bis-formamide (6), pyrazoline-3-one trimer (7), Tricho-9-ene-2α, 3α, 11α, 16-tetraol (8), 2-deoxy-thymidine (9); and cerebroside (10)" against eleven microbial test strains (Shaaban *et al.*, 2013).

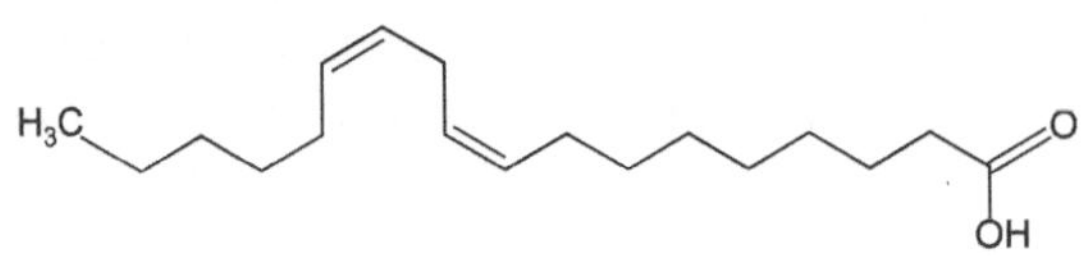

1

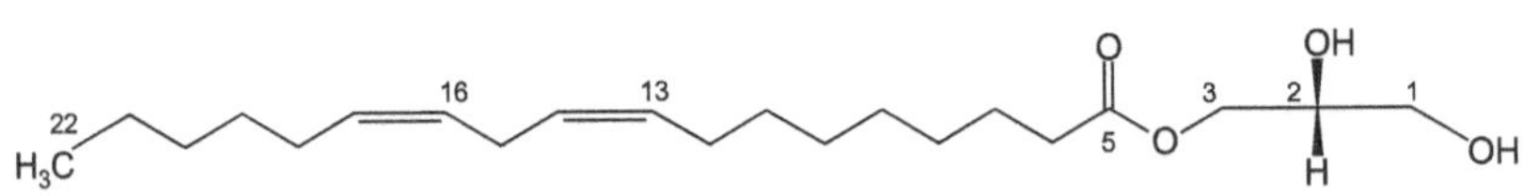

2

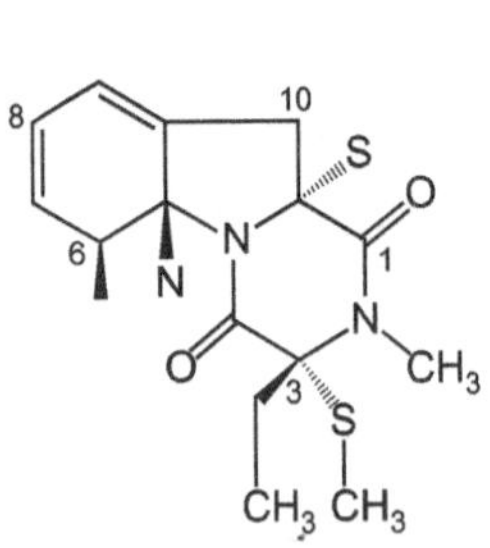

3

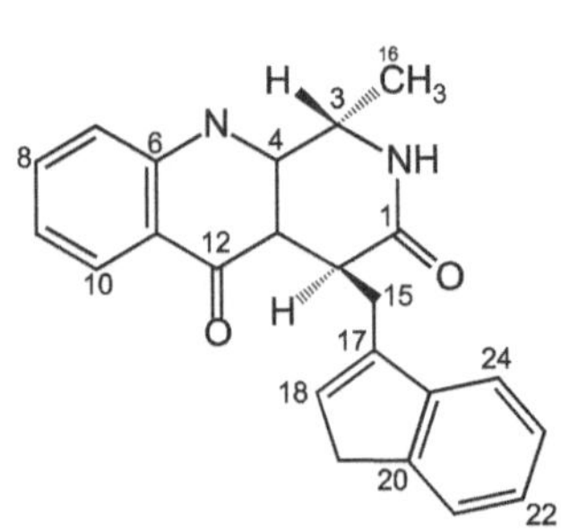

4

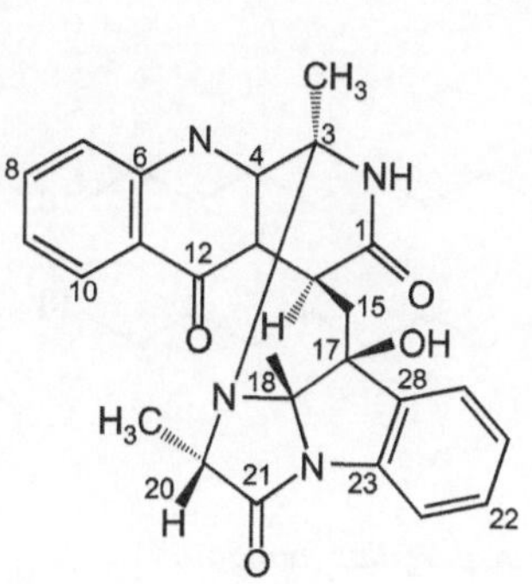

5

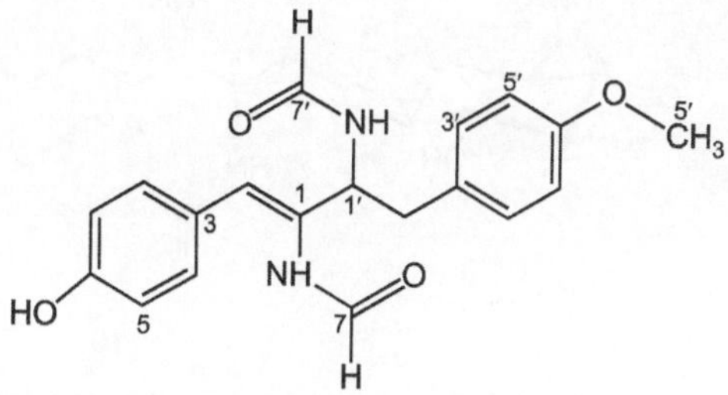

6

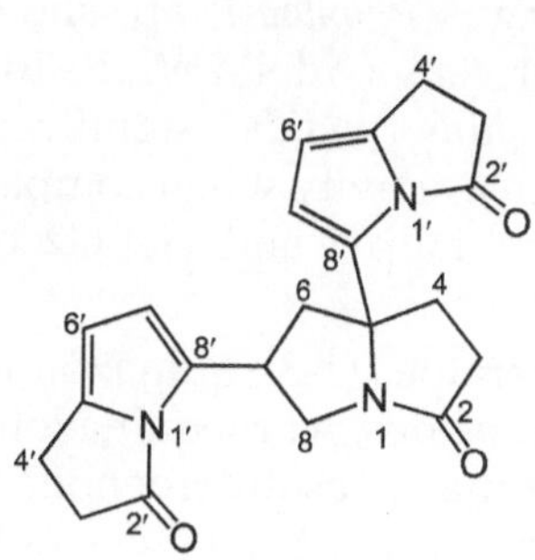

7

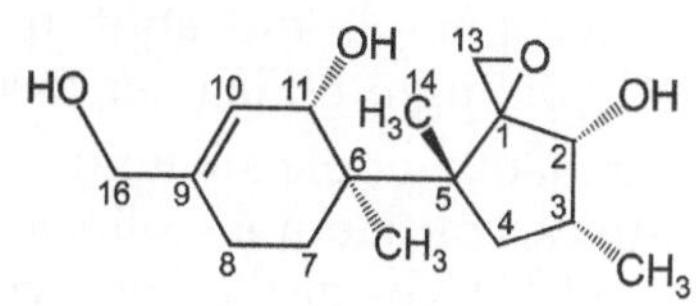

8

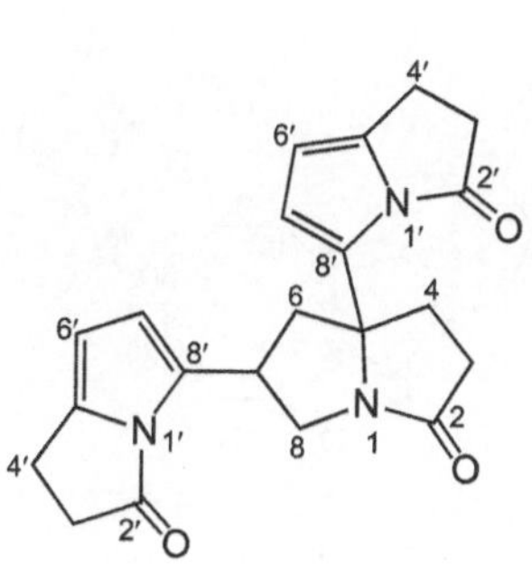

7

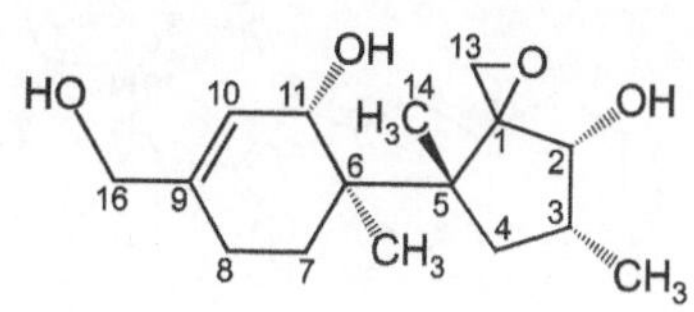

8

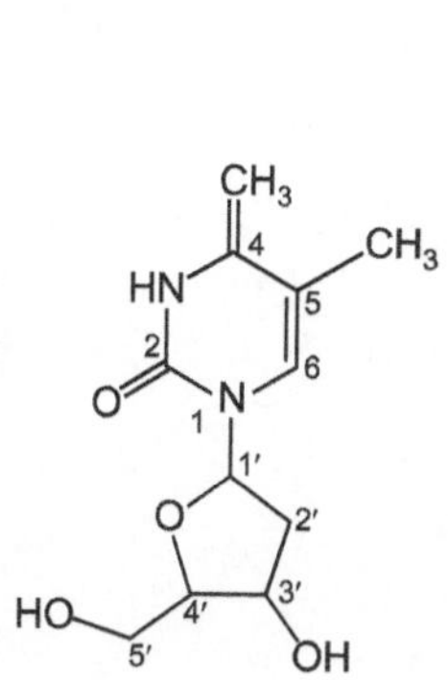

9

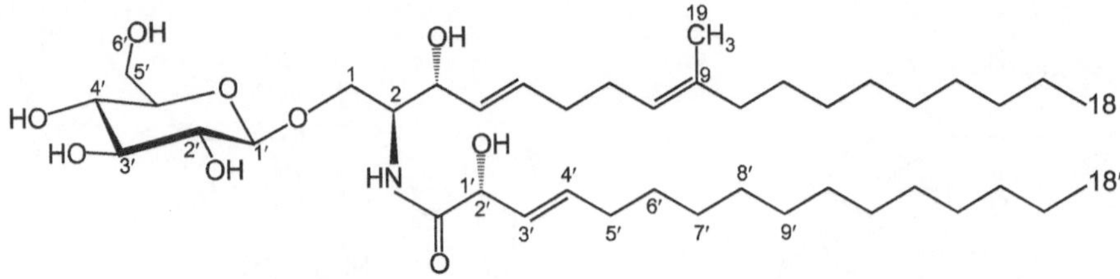

10

Fig. 3.2: Structure of some compounds isolated from *Aspergillus fumigatus*

Two new compounds obtained through microbial transformation of Sch-64235 which is produced by the endophytic fungus *Phomopsis* sp. showed better IC_{50} value against colonic epithelial cancer cells (Adelin *et al.*, 2012). Dihydroxymethyl pyranone isolated from *Aspergillus candidus* significantly showed potent antifungal activity, high antioxidative activity when compared with α-tocopherol, and antitumor activity against HEp-2 and HepG2 cells with IC_{50} of 7μg/ml (Elaasser *et al.*, 2011).

Prenylated indole alkaloids (Figure 3.3), carneamides (1-3), quinazolinone derivatives, carnequina-zolines (5-7), aryl c-glycosides, carnequinazolines (5-7), aryl C-lycosides, carnemycin (8,9) and a drimane sesquiteroenoid (10) from *Aspergillus carneus* (Trichomoeae) have been shown to possess potent antimicrobial activities. These were also examined for their cytotoxic activities (Zhuravleva *et al.*, 2012)

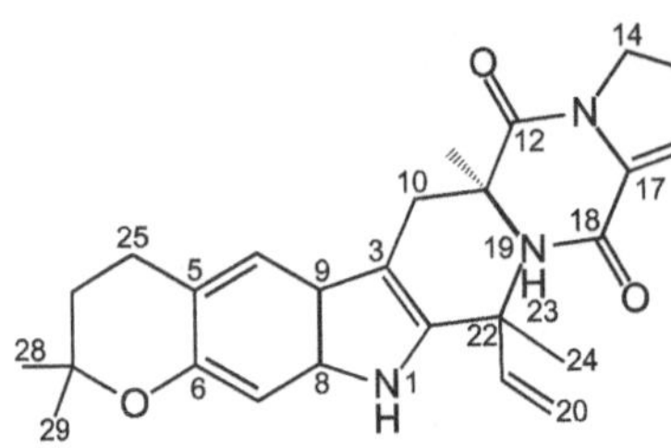

1
1a, 20,21, 25, 26-Tetrahydro-1

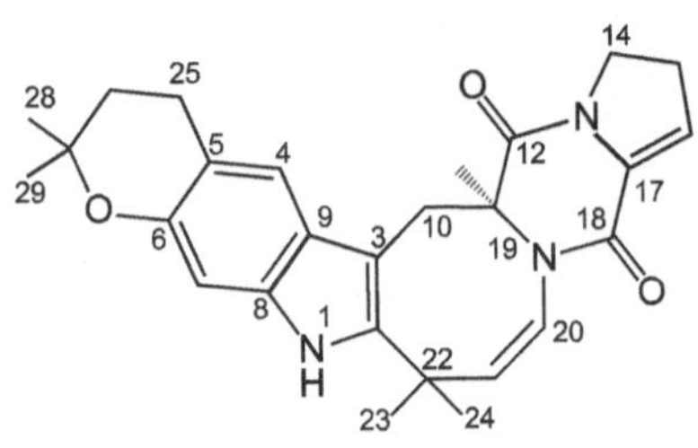

2

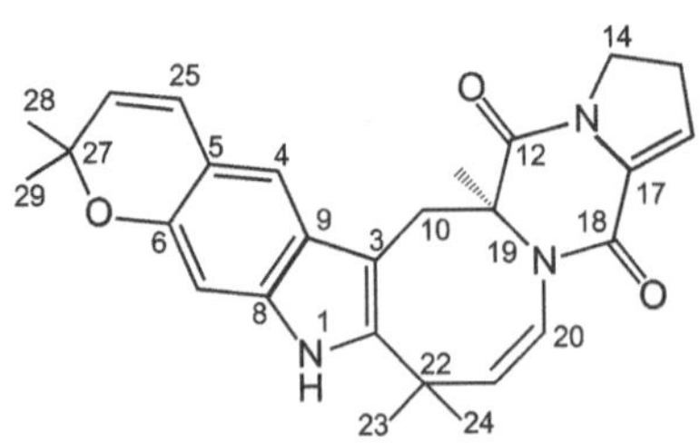

1
4 20,21, 25, 26-Tetrahydro-3

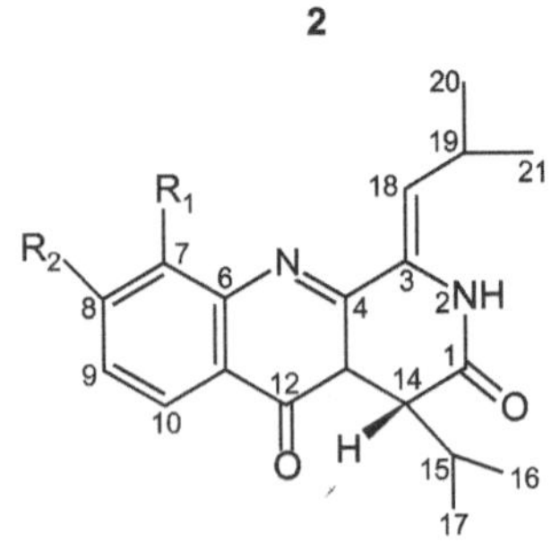

5 R_1 = H, R_2 = H
6 R_1 = OH, R_2 = H
7 R_1 = OH, R_2 = OH

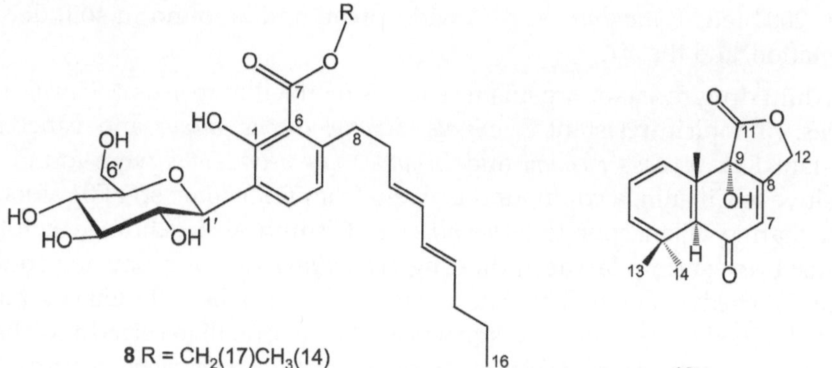

8 R = $CH_2(17)CH_3(14)$
9 R = $CH_3(17)$

10

Fig. 3.3: Structure of some compounds isolated from *Aspergillus carneus*

Similarly many more compounds have been isolated from *Aspergillus* till date having various biological activities. In a study, *Aspergillus janus* was reported to produce two compounds; janoxepin (1) and brevicompanine B (2) which possessed anti malarial activity against *Plasmodium falciparum* with IC_{50} values of 28 and 35 mg/ml, respectively. Three new cyclopentapeptides; versicoloritides, orcinol tetramer, tetracinol and two new lactones together with known metabolites: diorcinol, glyantryine and cordyol C; obtained from extracellular culture broth of *Aspergillus versicolor* were active against *Staphylococcus aureus, Escherichia coli, Enterobacter aerogens, Bacillus subtilis, Pseudomonas aeruginosa* and *Candida albicans* and proved to be better antimicrobial agents (Zhuang *et al.*, 2011). Similarly lists of endophytic strains have been known to produce various compounds with antimicrobial activity. An endophyitc fungus, *Aspergillus fumigatus* CY018 isolated from *Cynodon dactylon*, produced novel metabolites such as asperfumoid (1) and aspertumin (2) with potent antifungal activity against *Candida albicans* (Liu *et al.*, 2004).

Similarly, bioactive secondary metabolites isolated from *Aspergillus ochraceus* identified as Campholene aldehyde, Lucenin-2 and 6-Ethyl oct-3-yl-2-ethylhexyl ester showed potential antimicrobial activity against human pathogens like *Klebsiella, Pseudomonas, Staphylococcus aureus* and *Micrococcus* (Meenupriya and Thangaraj, 2011).

Antimicrobials from *Penicillium* sp

Members of the *Penicillium* spp. are filamentous fungi. It was the discovery of wonder drug penicillin that revolutionized the field of antibiotics and directed the interest of the researchers towards natural resources having different biological activities. Since then, a lot of bioactive compounds were purified from different fungi including *Penicillium janczewskii, Penicillium canescens* (Furtado *et al.*, 2005), *Penicillium sclerotiorium, Penicillium janthinellum, Penicillium citrinum* (Takahashi *et al.*, 2008) and *Myrothecium cinctum* (Kobayashi *et al.*,

1998, 2004) etc. *Penicillium* spp. is widespread and is found in soil, decaying vegetation, and the air.

Multi drug resistant organisms such as methicillin resistant *Staphylococcus aureus*, rifampicin-resistant *S. aureus*, *Staphylococcus aureus* and vancomycin resistant *Enterococcus faecium* and *Cryptococcus neofromans* were found to be sensitive to Citrinin, a compound isolated from *Penicillium* sp FF01 associated with marine Fijian sponge *Melophlus* sp. Citrinin also exhibited cytotoxity against brine shrimp larvae, indicating *Penicillium* sp as a promising source of natural bioactive metabolites (Subramani *et al.*, 2013) Six different compounds were obtained from *Penicillium* spp. isolated from Brazilian cerrado soil having broad spectrum antimicrobial activity against *Listeria monoytogenes* ATCC 19115, *Streptococcus pyogenes* ATCC 19615, *Salmonella typhimurium* ATCC 13311, *Candida albicans* ATCC 18804 and *Bacillus cereus* ATCC 11778 making these compounds, a suitable starting compounds for biotechnological use as a new drug lead (Petit *et al.*, 2009). Not only *Penicillium* spp isolated from soil have been evaluated for their different biological activities but the endophytic strains have also been screened for their biological potential.

A strain of *Penicillium* sp. isolated from *Mauritia flexuosa* roots has been reported to produce seven antimicrobial compounds namely glandicoline B (1), ergosterol (2), brassicasterol (3), ergosterol peroxide (4), cerevisterol (5), mannitol (6) and 1-O-α-D-glucopyranoside (7) (Figure. 4) (Koolen *et al.*, 2012).

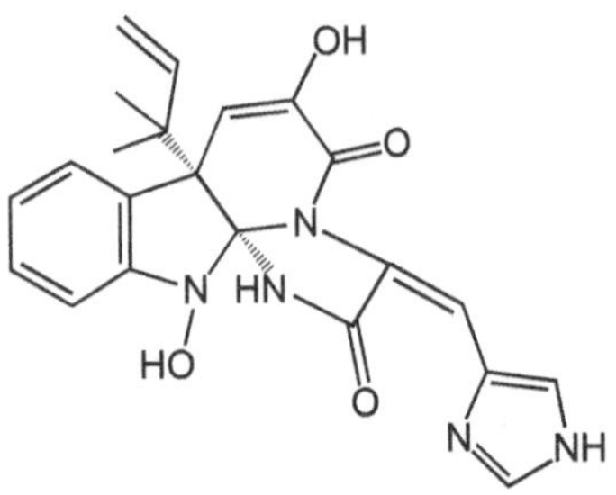

1

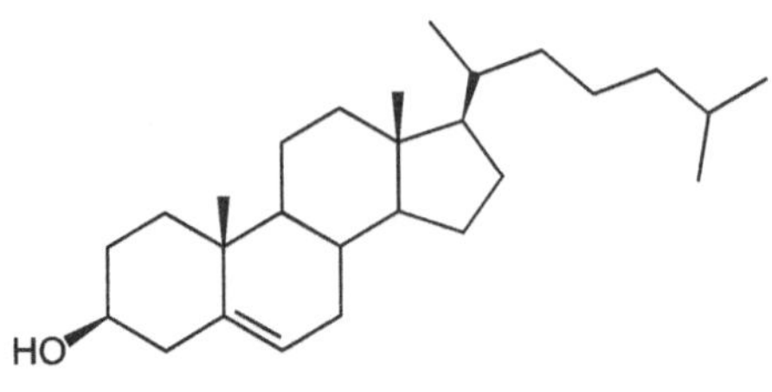

2

3

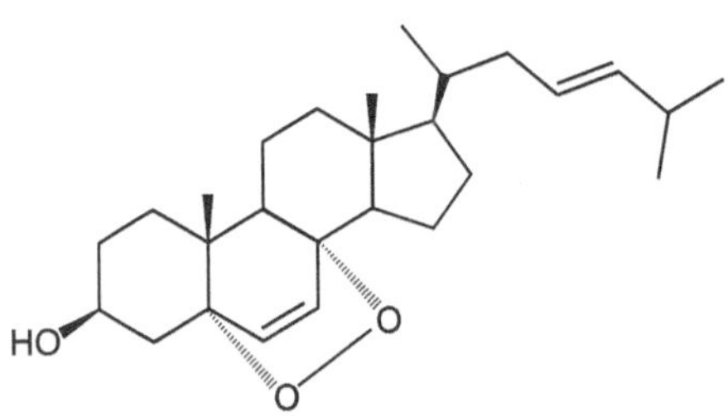

4

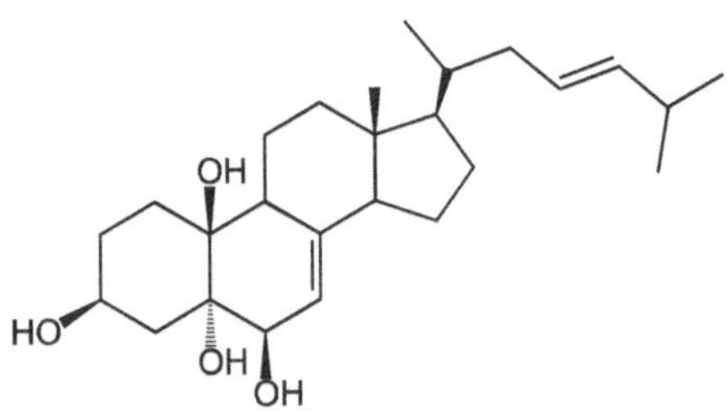

5

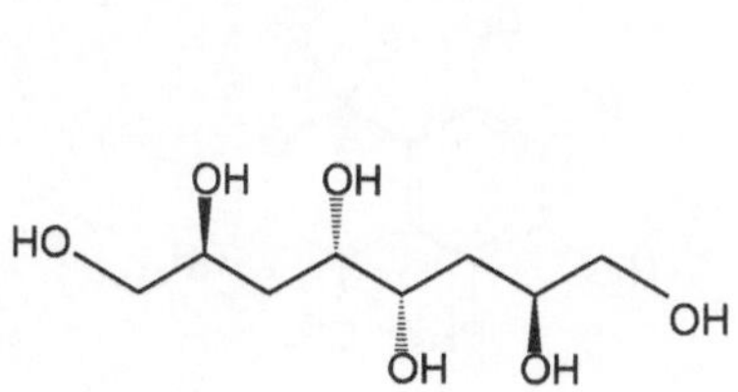

6

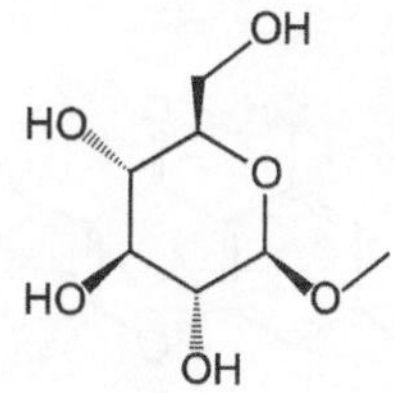

7

Fig. 3.4: Structure of some compounds isolated from *Penicillium* sp.

Two endophytic *Penicillium* spp. isolated from *Aristolochia macrophylla* leaves produced six metabolites: Orcinol, Cyclo(L-Pro–L-Val), Uracil, 4-Hydroxymellein, 8-Methoxymellein and 5-Hydroxymellein exhibited potential bioactivity against fungi such as *Cladosporium cladosporioides* and *Cladosporium sphaerospermum* and also possess acetylcholinestrase inhibitory activity.

The most common *Penicillium citrinum* spp islolated from various sources have been screened and different compounds have been isolated having antimicrobial activity. Such potential was found in a sea derived fungus *Penicillium citrinum* which produced five novel polyketides along with thirteen different known compounds, having better antimicrobial potential with minimum inhibitory concentration of 16 μg/ml against *Staphylococcus aureus,* methicillin-resistant *Staphylococcus aureus* and *Candida albicans* (Figure 5). Not only antimicrobial but the various compounds have been studied for their insecticidal properties. Nine new yaequinolones with insecticidal properties have been reported from *Penicillium* sp. FKI-2140.

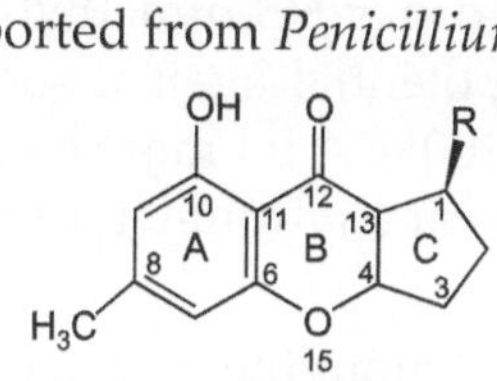

1. R = OCH$_3$

2. R = OCH$_2$CH$_3$

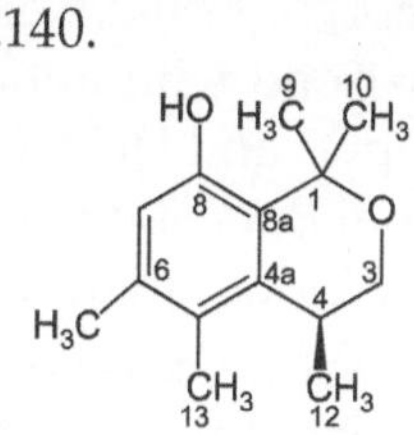

3

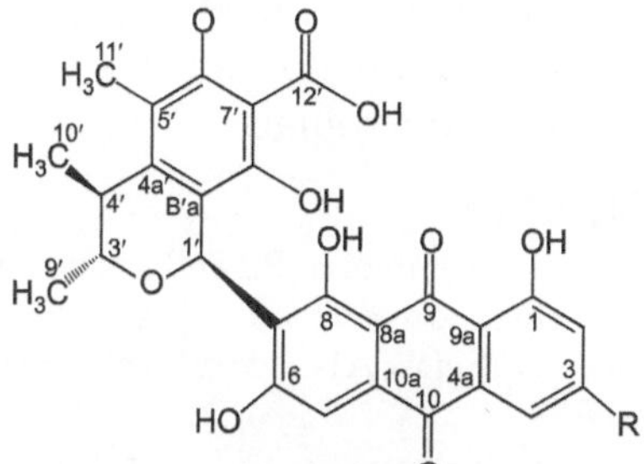

4. R = CH$_3$

5. R = CH$_2$OH

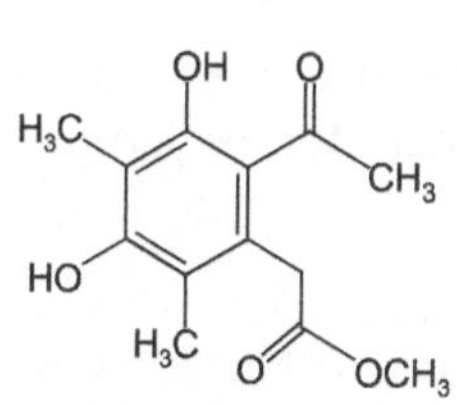

6

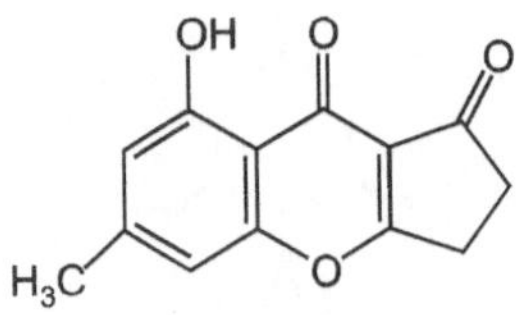

7

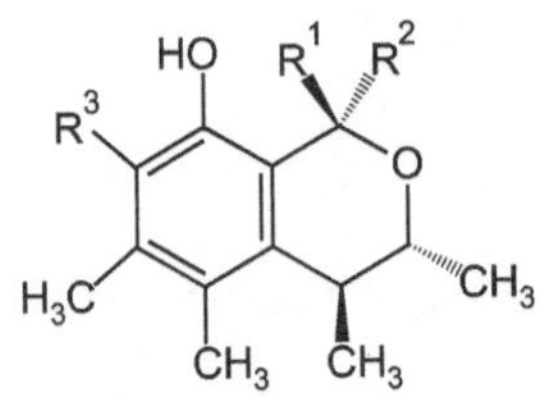

3

8. $R^1 = R^2 = R^3 = H$
9. $R^1 = CH_2COCH_3$, $R^2 = H$, $R^3 = CO_2H$
10. $R^1 + R^2 = {=}O$, $R^3 = CH_3$
18. $R^1 = R^2 = H$, $R^3 = CO_2H$

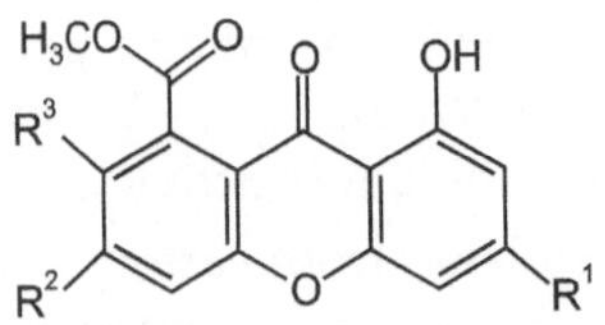

11. $R^1 = CH_3$, $R^2 = R^3 = H$
12. $R^1 = CH_2OH$, $R^2 = R^3 = H$
13. $R^1 = CH_3$, $R^2 = H$, $R^3 = OH$
14. $R^1 = CH_2OH$, $R^2 = OH$, $R^3 = H$

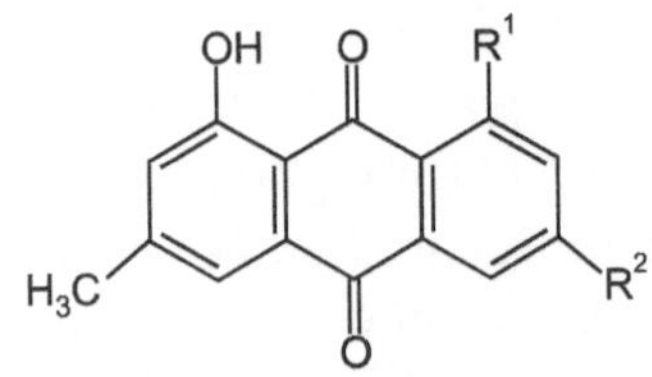

15. $R^1 = OH$, $R^2 = CH_3$, $R^3 = H$
16. $R^1 = R^3 = OH$, $R^2 = CH_3$
17. $R^1 = R^3 = OH$, $R^2 = CH_2OH$

Fig. 3.5. Structure of some compounds 1-18 isolated from *Penicillium citrinum* PSU-F51

Likewise, another *Penicillium* sp. from *Huperzia serrata* produced a novel compound, viz., (2S)-2,3-dihydro-7-hydroxy-6,8-dimethyl-2-[(E)-prop-1-enyl]- chroman-4-one with anticancerous potential against some cancer cell lines such as HepG2 and HeLa (Yang *et al.*, 2006). A lot more compounds have been isolated from *Penicillium* sp from different environments but a lot remain untapped from various environments.

As bacterial resistance is spreading throughout the world, especially in all health care associated pathogens revealing the steadily decreasing potencies of prevalent antibiotics (Gould, 2008). So there is a need to explore more microorganisms which may help in isolating some novel biologically active compounds and to expand the spectrum of suitable organisms which can be useful to meet the requirements of potent antimicrobials.

REFERENCES

Adelin, E., Martin, M. T., Bricot, M. F., Cortial, S., Retailleau, P., and Ouazzani, J. (2012). Biotransformation of Natural Compounds: Unexpected Thio Conjugation of Sch-642305 with 3-mercaptolactate Catalyzed by *Aspergillus niger* ATCC 16404 cells. *Phytochemistry* 84:135-140.

Amaretti, A., di Nunzio, M., Pompei, A., Raimondi, S., Rossi, M. and Bordoni, A. (2013). Antioxidant Properties of Potentially Probiotic Bacteria: *in vitro* and *in vivo* Activities. *Applied Microbiology and Biotechnology* 97: 809-817.

Anyogu, A., Awamaria, B., Sutherland, J. P. and Ouoba, L. I. I. (2014). Molecular Characterisation and Antimicrobial Activity of Bacteria Associated with Submerged Lactic Acid Cassava Fermentation. *Food Control* 39: 119-127.

Arasu, M.V., Duraipandiyan, V., Agastian, P. and Ignacimuthu, P.S. (2008). Antimicrobial Activity of *Streptomyces* spp. ERI-26 Recovered from Western Ghats of Tamil Nadu. *Journal de Mycologie Médicale* 18: 147—153.

Arora, D.S., and Kaur, J. (1999). Antimicrobial Activity of Spices. *International Journal of Antimicrobial Agents* 12: 257-262.

Atanassova, M., Choiset, Y., Dalgalarrondo, M., Chobert, J. M., Dousset, X., Ivanova, I., and Haertle, T. (2003). Isolation and Partial Biochemical Characterization of a Proteinaceous Anti-bacteria and Anti-yeast Compound Produced by *Lactobacillus Paracasei subsp. paracasei* Strain M3. *International Journal of Food Microbiology* 87: 63-73.

Baker, D.D. and Alvi, K.A. (2004). Small Molecule Natural Products: New Structures, New Activities. *Current Opinion in Biotechnology* 15: 576-583.

Bentley, R. (1997). Microbial Secondary Metabolites Play Important Roles in Medicine; Prospects for Discovery of New Drugs. *Perspectives* in *Biology* and *Medicine* 40: 364-94.

Blackwell, M. (2011). The Fungi: 1, 2, 3… 5.1 Million Species? *American Journal of Botany* 98: 426-438.

Cizeikiene, D., Juodeikiene, G., Paskevicius, A., and Bartkiene, E. (2013). Antimicrobial Activity of Lactic Acid Bacteria against Pathogenic and Spoilage Microorganism Isolated from Food and their Control in Wheat Bread. *Food Control* 31: 539-545.

Cowan, M. M. (1999). Plant Products as Antimicrobial Agents. *Clinical Microbiology Reviews*. 12: 564-582.

Dasari, V. R., Muthyala, M. K., Nikku, M. Y. and Donthireddy, S. R. (2012). Novel Pyridinium Compound from Marine Actinomycete, *Amycolatopsis alba* var. *nov.* DVR D4 Showing Antimicrobial and Cytotoxic Activities *in vitro*. *Microbiological Research* 167: 346-351.

Demain, A. and Sanchez, S. (2009). Microbial Drug Discovery: 80 years of Progress. *Journal of Antibiotics* 62: 5-16.

Demain, A. L. (2002). Prescription for an Ailing Pharmaceutical Industry. *Nature biotechnology* 20: 331-331.

Demain, A. L. and Fang, A. (2000). The Natural Functions of Secondary Metabolites. In History of Modern Biotechnology I. pp. 1-39.

Devi, P., Rodrigues, C., Naik, C. G. and D'Souza, L. (2012). Isolation and Characterization of Antibacterial Compound from a Mangrove-endophytic fungus, *Penicillium chrysogenum* MTCC 5108. *Indian Journal of Microbiology* 52: 617-623.

Duraipandiyan, V., Sasi, A. H., Islam, V. I., Valanarasu, M., and Ignacimuthu, S. (2010). Antimicrobial Properties of Actinomycetes from the Soil of Himalaya. *Journal of Medical Mycology* 20: 15-20.

Eguale, T. and Giday, M. (2009). *In vitro* Anthelmintic Activity of Three Medicinal Plants against *Haemonchus contortus*. *International Journal of Green Pharmacy* 3: 29.

Elaasser, M. M., Abdel-Aziz, M. M., and El-Kassas, R. A. (2011). Antioxidant, Antimicrobial, Antiviral and Antitumor Activities of Pyranone Derivative Obtained from *Aspergillus candidus*. *Journal of Microbiology and Biotechnology Research* 1: 5-17.

Funatogawa, K., Hayashi, S., Shimomura, H., Yoshida, T., Hatano, T., Ito, H. and Hirai, Y. (2004). Antibacterial Activity of Hydrolyzable Tannins Derived from Medicinal Plants against *Helicobacter pylori*. *Microbiology and Immunology* 48: 251-261.

Furtado, N.A., Fonseca, M.J. and Bastos, J.K. (2005). The Potential of an *Aspergillus fumigatus* Brazilian Strain to Produce Antimicrobial Secondary Metabolites. *Brazilian Journal of Microbiology* 36: 357-362.

Gandhimathi, R., Arunkumar, M., Selvin, J., Thangavelu, T., Sivaramakrishnan, S., Kiran, G.S. and Natarajaseenivasan, K.(2008). Antimicrobial Potential of Sponge Associated Marine Actinomycetes. *Journal of Medical Mycology* 18: 16-22.

Gebreyohannes, G., Moges, F., Sahile, S. and Raja, N. (2013). Isolation and Characterization of Potential Antibiotic Producing Actinomycetes from Water and Sediments of Lake Tana, Ethiopia. *Asian Pacific Journal of Tropical Biomedicine* 3: 426-435.

Gibbons, J. G. and Rokas, A. (2013). The Function and Evolution of the *Aspergillus* Genome. *Trends in Microbiology* 21: 14-22.

Gloer, J.B. (1995). The Chemistry of Fungal Antagonism and Defense. *Canadian Journal of Botany* 73: 1265-1274.

Gould, I.M. (2008). The Epidemiology of Antibiotic Resistance. *International Journal of Antimicrobial Agents* 32: S2–S9.

Grabley, S., Granzer, E., Hutter, K., Ludwig, D., Mayer, M., Thiericke, R., Till, G., Wink, J., Philipps, S. and Zeeck, A. (1992). Secondary Metabolites by Chemical Screening. 80 Decarestrictines, a New Family of Inhibitors of Cholesterol Biosynthesis from *Penicillium*—Strain Description, Fermentation, Isolation and Properties. *Journal of Antibiotics* 45 : 56–65.

Hu, H. Q., Li, X. S. and He, H. (2010). Characterization of an Antimicrobial Material from a Newly Isolated Bacillus Amyloliquefaciens from Mangrove for Biocontrol of Capsicum Bacterial Wilt. *Biological control* 54: 359-365.

Hwanhlem, N., Chobert, J. M., & Aran, H. (2014). Bacteriocin-producing Lactic Acid Bacteria Isolated from Mangrove Forests in Southern Thailand as Potential Bio-control Agents in Food: Isolation, Screening and Optimization. *Food Control* 41: 202-211.

Kamei, Y., Yoshimizu, M., Ezura, Y. and Kimura, T. (1988). Screening of Bacteria with Antiviral Activity from Fresh Water Salmonid Hatcheries. *Microbiology and immunology* 32: 67-73.

Kobayashi, J. I., Hosoyama, H., Wang, X. X., Shigemori, H., Sudo, Y. and Tsuruo, T. (1998). Modulation of Multidrug Resistance by Taxuspine C and Other Taxoids from Japanese yew. *Bioorganic & Medicinal Chemistry Letters* 8: 1555-1558.

Kobayashi, M., Kanasaki, R., Ezaki, M., Sakamoto, K., Takase, S., Fujie, A HINO M and Hori, Y. (2004). FR227244, a Novel Antifungal Antibiotic from *Myrothecium* cinctum No. 002: I. Taxonomy, Fermentation, Isolation and Physico-chemical Properties. *The Journal of Antibiotics*, 57(12):780-787.

Koolen, H.H.F., Soares, E.R., Araújo da Silva, F.M., Alves de Almeida, R., Afonso Leao de Souza, D., Soman de Medeiros, L., Filho, E.R. and Lima de Souza, A.Q. (2012) An Antimicrobial Alkaloid and Other Metabolites Produces by *Penicillium* sp. An Endophytic Fungus Isolated from *Mauritia flexuosa* L.f. *Quimica Nova* 35: 771-77.

Kumari, M., Myagmarjav, B. E., Prasad, B. and Choudhary, M. (2013). Identification and Characterization of Antibiotic-Producing Actinomycetes Isolates. *American Journal of Microbiology* 4: 24.

Kwon, O.E., Rho, M., Song, H.Y., Lee, S.W., Chung, M.Y., Lee, J.H., Kim, Y.H., Lee, H.S. and Kim, Y.K. (2002). Phenylpyropene A and B, New Inhibitors of acyl-CoA: Cholesterol Acyltransferase Produced by *Penicillium griseofulvum* F1959. *Journal of Antibiotics* 55: 1004–1008.

Lee, H., Churey, J. J. and Worobo, R. W. (2008). Antimicrobial Activity of Bacterial Isolates from Different Floral Sources of Honey. *International Journal of Food Microbiology* 126: 240-244.

Li, Y. L., Ma, S. C., Yang, Y. T., Ye, S. M. and But, P. P. H. (2002). Antiviral Activities of Flavonoids and Organic Acid from *Trollius chinensis Bunge*. *Journal of ethnopharmacology* 79: 365-368.

Liu, J.Y., Songa, Y.C., Zhanga, Z., Wanga, L., Guob, Z.J., Zoua, W.X. and Tana, R.X. (2004). *Aspergillus fumigatus* CY018, an Endophytic Fungus in Cynodon Dactylon as a Versatile Producer of New and Bioactive Metabolites. *Journal of Biotechnology* 114: 279–287.

Lucas, M.F., Castro, C.M. and Takahashi, J. A. (2007). Antimicrobial Properties of Sclerotiorin, Isochromophilone VI and Pencolide, Metabolites from a Brazilian cerrado Isolate of *Penicillium sclerotiorum* Van Beyma. *Brazilian Journal of Microbiology* 38: 785-789.

Meenupriya, J., & Thangaraj, M. (2011). Analytical Characterization and Structure Elucidation of Metabolites from *Aspergillus ochraceus* MP2 fungi. *Asian Pacific Journal of Tropical Biomedicine* 1: 376-380.

Mengoni, F., Lichtner, M., Battinelli, L., Marzi, M., & Mastroianni, C. M. (2002). In vitro Anti-HIV Activity of Oleanolic Acid on Infected Human Mononuclear Cells. *Pharmacological Research* 3: 8.

Mills, S.Y. and Bone, K. (2000). *Principles and Practice of Phytotherapy: Modern Herbal Medicine*. Churchill Livingstone, London.

Minotti, G., Menna, P., Salvatorelli, E., Cairo, G. and Gianni, L. (2004). Anthracyclines: Molecular Advances and Pharmacologic Developments in Antitumor Activity and Cardiotoxicity. *Pharmacological Reviews* 56: 185-229.

Mujoo, K., Haridas, V., Hoffmann, J. J., Wächter, G. A., Hutter, L. K., Lu, Y. and Gutterman, J. U. (2001). Triterpenoid saponins from *Acacia victoriae* (Bentham) Decrease Tumor Cell Proliferation and Induce Apoptosis. *Cancer Research* 61: 5486-5490.

Newman, D.J. and Cragg G.M. (2007). Natural Products as Source of New Drugs over the Last 25 Years. *Journal of Natural Products* 70: 461- 477.

Nicholls, S. J., Tuzcu, E. M., Sipahi, I., Grasso, A. W., Schoenhagen, P., Hu, T. and Nissen, S. E. (2007). Statins, High-density Lipoprotein Cholesterol, and Regression of Coronary Atherosclerosis. *Journal of American Medical Association* 297: 499-508.

Nicoletti, R., Lopez-Gresa, M.P., Manzo, E., Carella, A. and Ciavatta,M. L. (2007). Production and Fungitoxic Activity of Sch 642305, a Secondary Metabolite of *Penicillium canescens*. *Mycopathologia* 163: 295-301.

Nishihara, Y.E., Tsujii, S., Takase, Y., Tsurumi, T., Kino, M., Hino, M., Yamashita, M. and Hashimoto, S. (2000). FR191512, A Novel Anti-influenza Agent Isolated from Fungus Strain No. 17415. *Journal of Antibiotics* 53: 1333-1340.

Nithya, C. and Pandian, S. K. (2010). The *in vitro* Antibiofilm Activity of Selected Marine Bacterial Culture Supernatants against *Vibrio spp*. *Archives of Microbiology*. 192: 843-854.

Okwu, D. E. (2004). Phytochemicals and Vitamin Content of Indigenous Spices of South Eastern Nigeria. *J. Sustain. Agric. Environ.* 6: 30-37.

Omura, S., Tomoda, H., Kimura, K., Zhen, D.Z., Kumagai, H. and Igarashi, K. (1988). Atpenins, New Antifungal Antibiotics Produced by *Penicillium* sp. Production, Isolation, Physico-chemical and Biological Properties. *Journal of Antibiotics* 41: 1769-1773.

Ozcelik, B., Orhan, D. D., Özgen, S. and Ergun, F. (2008). Antimicrobial Activity of Flavonoids against Extended-spectrum β-lactamase (ESβL)-producing *Klebsiella pneumoniae*. *Tropical Journal of Pharmaceutical Research*. 7: 1151-1157.

Parra-Ruiz, J., Vidaillac, C., Rose, W. E. and Rybak, M. J. (2010). Activities of High-dose Daptomycin, Vancomycin and Moxifloxacin Alone or in Combination with Clarithromycin or Rifampin in a Novel in Vitro Model of *Staphylococcus aureus* Biofilm. *Antimicrobial Agents and Chemotherapy*. 54: 4329-4334.

Parthasarathi, S., Sathya, S., Bupesh, G., Samy, R. D., Mohan, M. R., Kumar, G. S. and Balakrishnan, K.(2012). Isolation and Characterization of Antimicrobial Compound from Marine *Streptomyces hygroscopicus* BDUS 49. *World Journal of Fish and Marine Sciences*. 4: 268-277.

Pel, H. J., De Winde, J. H., Archer, D. B., Dyer, P. S., Hofmann, G., Schaap, P. J. and Oliver, S. G. (2007). Genome Sequencing and Analysis of the Versatile Cell Factory *Aspergillus niger* CBS 513.88. Nature Biotechnology, 25: 221-231.

Petit, P., Lucas, E.M.F., Breu, L.M.A., Flenning, L.H.P. and Takahashi J.A. (2009). Novel Antimicrobial Secondary Metabolites from a *Penicillium* sp. Isolated from Brazilian cerrado soil. *Electronic Journal of Biotechnology* 12: 1-9.

Pinner, R., Teutsch, S., Simonsen, L., Klug, L., Grabers, J., Clarke, M. and Berkelman, R. (1996). Trends in Infectious Diseases Mortality in the United States. *The Journal of the American Medical Association* 275: 189-193.

Quang, D. N., Hashimoto, T., Tanaka, M., Baumgartner, M., Stadler, M., and Asakawa, Y. (2002). Chemical Constituents of the Ascomycete *Daldinia concentrica*. *Journal of Natural Products* 65: 1869-1874.

Rancic, A., Sokovic, M., Karioti, A., Vukojevic, J.and Skaltsa, H. (2006). Isolation and Structural Elucidation of Two Secondary Metabolites from the Filamentous Fungus *Penicillium ochrochloron* with Antimicrobial Activity. *Environmental Toxicology and Pharmacology* 22: 80–84.

Rojas, J. J., Ochoa, V. J., Ocampo, S. A., & Muñoz, J. F. (2006). Screening for Antimicrobial Activity of Ten Medicinal Plants Used in Colombian Folkloric Medicine: A Possible Alternative in the Treatment of Non-nosocomial Infections. *BMC Complementary and Alternative Medicine* 6: 2.

Romanenko, L. A., Uchino, M., Kalinovskaya, N. I. and Mikhailov, V. V. (2008). Isolation, Phylogenetic Analysis and Screening of Marine Mollusc-associated Bacteria for Antimicrobial, Hemolytic and Surface Activities. *Microbiological Research* **163**: 633-644.

Ryu, E. H., Yang, E. J., Woo, E. R., & Chang, H. C. (2014). Purification and Characterization of Antifungal Compounds from *Lactobacillus Plantarum* HD1 Isolated from kimchi. *Food Microbiology* 41:19-26.

Santos, O. C., Pontes, P. V., Santos, J. F., Muricy, G., Giambiagi-deMarval, M. and Laport, M. S. (2010). Isolation, Characterization and Phylogeny of Sponge-associated Bacteria with Antimicrobial Activities from Brazil. *Research in Microbiology* 161: 604-612.

Shaaban, M., Abdel-Razik, A., Abdel-Aziz, M., AbouZied, A. and Fadel, M. (2013). Bioactive Secondary Metabolites from Marine *Streptomyces albogriseolus* Isolated from Red Sea Coast. *Journal of Applied Sciences and Research* 9: 996-1003.

Sharker, S. and Shahid, I. J. (2010). Assessment of Antibacterial and Cytotoxic Activity of Some Locally used Medicinal Plants in Sundarban Mangrove Forest Region. *African Journal of Pharmacy and Pharmacology*. 4. 066- 069.

Sibanda, T., Mabinya, L. V., Mazomba, N., Akinpelu, D. A., Bernard, K., Olaniran, A. O. and Okoh, A. I. (2010). Antibiotic Producing Potentials of Three Freshwater Actinomycetes Isolated from the Eastern Cape Province of South Africa. *International Journal of Molecular Sciences* 11: 2612-2623.

Singh, S., Kumar, P., Gopalan, N., Shrivastava, B., Kuhad, R. C. and Chaudhary, H. S. (2012). Isolation and Partial Characterization of Actinomycetes with Antimicrobial Activity against Multidrug Resistant Bacteria. *Asian Pacific Journal of Tropical Biomedicine* 2: S1147-S1150.

Solomon, R. J., Kallidass, S. and Vimalan, J. (2005). Isolation, Identification and Study of Antimicrobial Property of a Bioactive Compound in an Indian Medicinal Plant *Acalypha indica* (Indian-nettle). *World Journal of Microbiology and Biotechnology* **21**: 1231-1236.

Subramani, R., Kumar, R., Prasad, P. and Aalbersberg,W. (2013). Cytotoxic and Antibacterial Substances against Multi-drug Resistant Pathogens from Marine Sponge Symbiont: Citrinin, a Secondary Metabolite of *Penicillium* sp. *Asian Pacific Journal of Tropical Biomedicine* 3: 291–296.

Takahashi, J.A., Castro,M.C., Souza,G.G., Lucas,E. and Bracarense, A. (2008). Isolation and Screening of Fungal Species Isolated from Brazilian Cerrado Soil for Antibacterial Activity against *E. coli, S. aureus, S. typhimurium, S. pyogenes* and *L. monocytogens. Journal* of *Medical Mycology* 18: 198-204.

Valli, S., Suvathi, S. S., Aysha, O. S., Nirmala, P., Vinoth, K. P. and Reena, A. (2012). Antimicrobial Potential of Actinomycetes Species Isolated from Marine Environment. *Asian Pacific Journal of Tropical Biomedicine* 2: 469-473.

Vidari, G., Finzi, P. V., Zarzuelo, A., Gαlvez, J., Zafra, C., Chiriboga, X. and Martín, M. J. (2003). Antiulcer and Antidiarrhoeic effect of *Baccharis teindalensis*. 41: 405-411.

Wallace, R. J. (2004). Antimicrobial Properties of Plant Secondary Metabolites. *Proceedings of the Nutrition Society* 63: 621-629.

Xu, H. X. and Lee, S. F. (2001). Activity of Plant Flavonoids against Antibiotic-resistant Bacteria. *Phytotherapy Research* 15: 39-43.

Yang, C. R., Zhang, Y., Jacob, M. R., Khan, S. I., Zhang, Y. J. and Li, X. C. (2006). Antifungal Activity of C-27 Steroidal Saponins. *Antimicrobial Agents and Chemotherapy* 50: 1710-1714.

Yoshikawa, M., Murakami, T., Kishi, A., Kageura, T. and Matsuda, H. (2001). Medicinal flowers. III. Marigold.(1): Hypoglycemic, Gastric Emptying Inhibitory, and Gastroprotective Principles and New Oleanane-type Triterpene Oligoglycosides, Calendasaponins A, B, C and D, from Egyptian *Calendula officinalis. Chemical and Pharmaceutical Bulletin Tokyo* 49: 863-870.

Yu, M., Wang, J., Tang, K., Shi, X., Wang, S., Zhu, W. M. and Zhang, X. H. (2012). Purification and Characterization of Antibacterial Compounds of *Pseudoalteromonas flavipulchra* JG1. *Microbiology* 158: 35-842.

Yue-Zhong, Shu. (1998). Recent Natural Products Based Drug Development: A Pharmaceutical Industry Perspective. *Journal of Natural Products* 61: 1053-1071.

Zhao, J., Guo, L., Zeng, H., Yang, X., Yuan, J., Shi, H. and Qiu, D. (2012). Purification and Characterization of a Novel Antimicrobial Peptide from *Brevibacillus laterosporus* strain A60. *Peptides* 33: 206-211.

Zhuravleva, O. I., Afiyatullov, S.S., Denisenko, V.A., Ermakova, S. P., Slinkina, N. N., Dmitrenok, P.S., and Kim, N.Y. (2012). Secondary Metabolites from a Marine-derived Fungus *Aspergillus carneus* Blochwitz. *Phytochemistry*. 80: 123-131.

Advances in Microbiology: *Applications & Significance* Pages 38-61
Edited by: Dr. Pawan Kumar 'Bharti'
ISBN: 978-93-86841-97-1
Edition: 2019
Published by: Discovery Publishing House Pvt. Ltd., New Delhi (India)

4

Optimization of Degradation Potential of Several Microorganisms against Polyethylene (PE) & Polypropylene (PP) Plastics

[1]Dr. Pawan Kumar 'Bharti'

Introduction

Plastics are synthetic or man-made organic polymers, similar in many ways to natural resins found in many trees and plants (Gorman, 1993). The versatility of these materials has led to a great increase in their use over the past three decades, and they have rapidly moved into all aspects of everyday life (Laist, 1987; Hansen, 1990). Plastics are lightweight, strong, durable, and cheap, characteristics that make them suitable for the manufacture of a very wide range of products (Laist, 1987; Pruter, 1987). Since they are also buoyant, an increasing load of plastic debris is being dispersed over long distances, and when they finally settle in sediments they may persist for centuries (Ryan, 1987; Hansen, 1990; Goldberg, 1995, 1997).

Although literally hundreds of plastic materials are commercially available, only a handful of these qualify as commodity thermoplastics in terms of their high volume and relatively low price. Low-density polyethylene (LDPE), high-density PE (HDPE), PP, PVC, PS, and PE terephthalate (PET) account for approximately 90% of the total demand.

There are currently some 20 different groups of plastics, each with numerous grades and varieties (APME, 2006). Plastics are made from hydrocarbon monomers. They are produced by chemically modifying natural substances or are synthesized from inorganic and organic raw materials. On the basis of their physical characteristics, plastics are usually divided into thermosets, elastomers, and thermoplastics. These groups differ primarily with regard to molecular structure.

Due to similar properties to conventional plastics, biodegradable plastics such as polyhydroxyalkanoates (PHAs), polylactides, polycaprolactone, aliphatic polyesters, and polysaccharides have been developed successfully over the last few years.

[1] R&D Division, Shriram Institute for Industrial Research 19, University Road, Delhi-110007, India.

Problem and Solution

During the past 3-decades, plastic materials have been increasingly used in food clothing, shelter, transportation, construction, medical and recreation industries. Plastics are advantageous as they are strong, light-weighted, and durable. However, they are disadvantageous as they are resistant to biodegradation, leading to pollution and harmful to the natural environment. Hence, it is a matter of prime concern to minimize the impacts of plastic. Degradation and bio-conversion of plastic into valuable products may be one of the biggest solutions of the problem.

Biodiversity and occurrence of polymer-degrading microorganisms vary depending on the environment, such as soil, sea, compost, activated sludge, etc. It is necessary to investigate the distribution and population of polymer-degrading microorganisms in various ecosystems. Generally, the adherence of microorganisms on the surface of plastics followed by the colonization of the exposed

surface is the major mechanisms involved in the microbial degradation of plastics. The enzymatic degradation of plastics by hydrolysis is a two-step process: first, the enzyme binds to the polymer substrate then subsequently catalyzes a hydrolytic cleavage. Polymers are degraded into low molecular weight oligomers, dimers and monomers and finally mineralized to CO_2 and H_2O.

The properties of plastics are associated with their biodegradability. Both the chemical and physical properties of plastics influence the mechanism of biodegradation. The surface conditions (surface area, hydrophilic, and hydrophobic properties), the first order structures (chemical structure, molecular weight and molecular weight distribution) and the high order structures (glass transition temperature, melting temperature, modulus of elasticity, crystallinity and crystal structure) of polymers play important roles in the biodegradation processes.

Increasing amount of synthetic polymers produced results in increasing interest in polymer biodegradation. Environmental factors such as light, heat, moisture, chemical conditions, and biological activity result in bond scission. The formation of structural homogeneities and formation of new functional groups also occurs during polymer degradation (Pospisil and Nespurek, 1997).

Depending upon the nature of the causing agents, polymer degradation has been classified as photo-oxidative degradation, thermal degradation, ozone-induced degradation, mechano-chemical degradation, catalytic degradation, and biodegradation.

The major degradation will either be photo-degradation, thermal degradation, or biological degradation. Thermo degradation means the degradation of polymer by heat energy. It generally receives support from oxygen of the atmosphere and is known as thermo-oxidative degradation. The initial stage of degradation is the process of rupture in the bonds of macromolecules resulting in radical sites. Thermal degradation generally involves changes to molecular weight of polymer.

Microbes and Plastic Degradation

Biodegradation is the ability of microorganism to influence abiotic degradation through physical, chemical, or enzymatic action (Albertsson *et al.*, 1987). Microorganisms are involved in the degradation and deterioration of both synthetic and natural polymers (Gu *et al.*, 2000). The polymers are not directly utilized by microorganisms where most of the biochemical processes takes place. The degradation of plastics is a very slow process. Initially it is initiated by environmental factors, which include temperature, pH, and UV. In order to use such materials as a carbon and energy source, microorganisms have developed a special strategy.

Microorganisms such as bacteria and fungi are involved in the degradation of plastics. The microorganisms that are responsible for biodegradation differ from each other and have their own optimal growth conditions. Biodegradation is generally considered as consisting of both enzyme-catalyzed hydrolysis and nonenzymatic hydrolysis (Wackett and Hershberger, 2001). During degradation, exoenzymes from microorganisms break down complex polymers yielding short chains or smaller molecules, for example, oligomers, dimers, and monomers, that are smaller enough (water soluble) to pass the semi-permeable outer bacterial membranes and then to be utilized as carbon and energy sources (Gu, 2003). This initial process of polymer breaking down is called depolymerization. The degradative pathways associated with polymer degradation are often determined by the environmental conditions. The complete decomposition of a polymer produces organic acids, CO_2, CH_4 and H_2O (Alexander, 1977; Narayan, 1993).

The biological degradation of polymeric substances is a complex process involving several subsequent steps induced by the action of enzymes. The most important type of enzymatic polymer cleavage reaction is hydrolysis (Schink *et al.*, 1992). The bonds such as glycosidic, ester, and peptide linkages are subjected to hydrolysis through nucleophilic attack on the carbonyl carbon atom. Generally, the biological degradation of polymeric substances is influenced by the presence of enzymes and microorganisms, biotic availability of the polymeric structure and appropriate abiotic factors.

Abiotic factors such as temperature, pH, and moisture can affect the hydrolysis reaction rates during degradation. The increased temperature and moisture leads to increase in hydrolysis reaction rates and microbial activity (Henton *et al.*, 2005). In high-moisture environmental conditions, there is an increase in hydrolysis reaction, which produces more chain scission and leads to an increase in the available sites for microorganisms to attack the polymer chains, causing faster degradation (Ho *et al.*, 1999). Among biotic factors, extracellular enzymes produced by different microorganisms may have active sites with different shapes and hence more able to biodegrade certain polymers. For example, Aspergillus niger and Aspergillus flavus fungi produce enzymes that more easily digest aliphatic polyesters derived from 6–12-carbon di-acid monomers than those produced from other monomers (Chandra and Rustgi, 1997).

Table 4.1: List of Bacteria Used for Plastic Degradation

Sl.No.	Type of Plastic	Used Microorganisms	References
1	Polyurethane	*Corynebacterium* and *Pseudomonas* sp.	Kay *et al.* (1991)
2.	Isotactic polypropylene	*Pseudomonas chlororaphis, Pseudomonas stutzeri*, and *Vibrio* sp.	Cacciari *et al.* (1993)
3.	Polyurethane	*Pseudomonas cepacia, Pseudomonas* sp., *and Arthrobacter globiformis*	El-Sayed *et al.* (1996)
4.	LDPE	*Rhodococcus ruber* C208	Chandra and Rustgi (1997)
5.	Polyurethane	*Bacillus* sp.	Blake and Howard (1998)
6.	PVC powder	*Pseudomonas aeruginosa*	Peciulyte (2002)
7.	Degradable polyethylene	*Rhodococcus rhodocorrous* ATCC 29672 and *Nocardia steroids* GK 911	Bonhomme *et al.* (2003)
8.	Polyethylene bags and plastic cups	*Streptococcus* sp., *Staphylococcus* sp., *Micrococcus* sp., *Moraxella* sp., and *Pseudomonas* sp.	Kathiresan (2003)
9.	LDPE	*Pseudomonas stutzeri*	Sharma and Sharma (2004)
10.	LDPE	*Brevibacillus borstelensis*707	Hadad *et al.* (2005)
11.	LDPE	*Rhodococcus ruber* C208	Sivan *et al.* (2006)
12.	Degradable polyethylene	*Bacillus mycoides*	Seneviratne *et al.* (2006)
13.	HDPE and LDPE	*Bacillus* sp., *Micrococcus* sp., *Listeria* sp., and *Vibrio* sp.	Kumar *et al.* (2007)
14.	Polyethylene carry bags	*Bacillius cereus, Pseudomonas* sp.	Aswale and Ade (2008)
15.	Polyethylene carry bags and cups	*Bacillus* sp., *Staphylococcus* sp., *Streptococcus* sp., *Diplococcus* sp., *Micrococcus* sp., *Pseudomonas* sp., and *Moraxella* sp.	Reddy (2008)

16.	Polyethylene carry bags	*Serratia marcescens*	Aswale and Ade (2009)
17.	HDPE, LDPE, and LLDPE	*Rhodococcus rhodochorus* ATCC 29672	Fontanella *et al.* (2009)
18.	Natural and synthetic polyethylene	*Pseudomonas* sp. (P1, P2, and P3)	Nanda *et al.* (2010)
19.	Polyethylene carry bags	*Serratia marcescens* 724, *Bacillus cereus, Pseudomonas aeruginosa, Streptococcus aureus* (B-324), and *Micrococcus lylae* (B-429)	Aswale (2010)
20.	HDPE	*Arthrobacter* sp. and *Pseudomonas* sp.	Balasubramanian *et al.* (2010)
21.	LDPE	*Staphylococcus epidermis*	Chatterjee *et al.* (2010)
22.	Polyethylene bags	*Pseudomonas aeruginosa, Pseudomonas putida,* and *Bacillus subtilis*	Nwachukwu *et al.* (2010)
23.	LDPE	*Bacillus cereus* C1	Suresh *et al.* (2011)
24.	LDPE powder	*Pseudomonas* sp., *Staphylococcus* sp., and *Bacillus* sp.	Usha *et al.* (2011)
25.	Degradable plastic	*Pseudomonas* sp., *Bacillus subtilis,staphylococcus aureus, Streptococcus lactis, Proteus vulgaris,* and *Micrococcus luteus*	Priyanka and Archana (2011)
26.	LDPE and LLDPE	*Baciilus cereus, Bacillus megaterium, Bacillus subtilis,* and *Brevibacillus borstelensis*	Abrusci *et al.* (2011)
27.	LDPE	*Pseudomonas aeruginosa* PAO1 (ATCC 15729), *Pseudomonas aeruginosa* (ATCC15692), *Pseudomonas putida* (KT2440 ATCC47054), and *Pseudomonas syringae* (DC3000 ATCC 10862)	Kyaw *et al.* (2012)

Factors Involved in Biodegradation of Plastics

Chemical and physical properties of plastics play important role in their biodegradation. Side chain possessing polymers are difficult to degrade when compared to polymers with no side chains. It should also be kept in mind that polymers with high molecular weight are difficult to degrade. Other factors involved in the biodegradation of polymers are their morphology, melting temperature, and degree of crystallinity. If the polymer is amorphous, then it will be degraded easily as compared to crystalline polymer. Polymers with high melting temperatures are difficult to biodegrade.

National and International Status

Several studies have been conducted in order to assess the ability of microbes in degrading plastics. As early as in 1998, Oda *et al.*, reported that bacterium *Alcaligenes faecalis* produces polycaprolactone depolymerase. He also isolated several polycaprolactone (PCL) degrading bacteria from soil. PCL is a biodegradable polymer, which can undergo degradation by aerobic and anaerobic microorganisms. Furthermore, PCL was also reported to be degraded by fungi *Penicillium* and *Aspergillus.* Strain ST-01 of *Aspergillus,* isolated from soil is reported to degrade PCL at incubation of 50°C for 6 days. In the case of Penicillium, strain 26-1 was studied and the results showed that PCL was degraded in 12 days by this strain. Fast enzymatic degradation of PCL by *Penicillium funiculosum* and *Aspergillus flavus* is also reported in amorphous region. Enzymes degrading PCL are lipase and esterases.

Plasticized polyvinyl chloride (pPVC) is vulnerable to microbial attack due to the presence of organic acid esters like dioctyl adipate (DOA) and dioctyl phthalate (DOP). Ester based plasticizers can be degraded by fungi and bacteria. If pPVC loses plasticizers because of microbial degradation, it leads to its failure. Owing to this, Webb and his colleagues in 2000 studied colonization of fungus and biodegradation of pPVC under in-situ and ex-situ conditions. Their study reported that *Aureobasidium pullulans* established itself on pPVC between 25 and 40 weeks of exposure. Furthermore, after 80 weeks of exposure yeast and yeast like fungi, *Rhodotorula aurantiaca* and *Kluyveromyces spp.* was found to be established on pPVC. Further studies conducted on A. pullulans demonstrated that A. pullulans can grow on undamaged pPVC as source of carbon. It degrades DOA and produces extracellular esterase. Many yeast isolated were not able to degrade DOA. Thus, this study demonstrated that fungus *A. pullulans* is important in degrading pPVC.

Polyester polyurethane (PUR) is degraded by both fungus and bacteria. In 2000, it was reported by Russell *et al.* that endophytic fungi can degrade synthetic polymer polyester polyurethane (PUR). It was reported that *Pestalotiopsis microspora* were growing on PUR and using it as sole source of carbon in aerobic as well as anaerobic conditions. Further characterization demonstrated that PUR was being degraded by serine hydrolase. Endophytes are microorganisms living in inner plant tissues and play important role in decomposition of plant after death of host tissue. Theses endophytic fungi are also able to degrade complex lignocellulose polymers suggesting that these organisms should be screened for their ability to degrade plastic which is also a complex polymer.

In another study conducted by Kathiresan in 2003, it was demonstrated that microbes from mangrove soil (bacteria as well as fungi) are able to degrade plastics but at a slower rate. These microbes comprised of gram negative and gram positive bacteria and eight species of fungi. Dominant species included *Streptococcus, Staphylococcus, Micrococcus* (Gram-positive), *Moraxella,* and *Pseudomonas* (Gram-negative) and two species of fungi (*Aspergillus glaucus* and *A. niger*). Thus, the work revealed that many plastic degrading microbes can be isolated from mangrove soil [6]. Moreover, mangrove soil from Niger delta was also studied for plastic degrading microbe population. Two *Aspergillus* species were isolated which were studied for degradation of Low-density polyethylene (LDPE) and high-density polyethylene (HDPE) films. The results obtained showed that the carbon source for the two *Aspergillus* species (*Aspergillus japonicus* and *Aspergillus terreus*) was polyethylene films. Thus, the results proved that fungi isolated form mangrove soil of Niger delta can be used for biodegradation of PE films. LDPE is the most common solid waste and accounts for 60% of total plastic production.

The garbage sites in India are filled with plastics which are still not biodegraded out of which polythene is the most common source of solid waste, more studies should done to isolate microbes which are able to biodegrade polythene and other polymers. Studies should be designed to isolate microbes on their ability to degrade plastics.

Table 4.2: Table Showing Different Microbes and their Plastic Degrading Efficiencies (Raziyafathima *et al.,* 2016)

Microorganisms	Types of plastics	Source of the microbes	Degradation Efficiency
Bacillus cereus	polyethylene	Dumpsite soil.	7.2-2.4%
Pseudomonas putida	Milk cover	Garden soil	75.3%
Streptomyces sp	LDPE	Garbage soil	46.7%
Pseudomonas sp	Natural and synthetic polythylene	Sewage sludge dumpsite	46.2% and 29.1%
Pseudomonas sp	Natural and synthetic polythylene	Household garbage dumpsite	31.4% and 16.3%
Pseudomonas sp	Natural and synthetic polythylene	Textile effluent drainage site	39.7% and 19.6%
Pseudomonas sp	Polythene and plastic	mangrove soil	20.54% and 8.16
Aspergillus glaucus	Polythene and plastic	mangrove soil	20.80% and 7.26%
Micrococcus luteus	Plastic cup	Forest soil	38%
Masoniella sp	Plastic cup	Forest soil	27.4%
Pseudomonas sp and *bacillus cereus*	Polythene carry bags	Plastic dumping sites	12.5%
Aspergillus niger and *Streptococcus lactis*	Polythene bags and plastic cups	Medicinal Garden soil, Sewage Water Soil, Energy Park soil, Sludge Area soil, Agricultural Soil	12.25% and 12.5% respectively

Rhodococcus ruber (C208)	Branched low-density (0.92 g cm”3) polyethylene	Not specified	7.5%
Phanerochaete chrysosporium and *Pseudomonas aeruginosa*	Polythene carry bags	Plastic dumping sites	50% and 35% respectively
Aspergillus niger, *Pencillium pinophilum*	Powdered LDPE	Not specified	5% and11.07% respectively
Aspergillus oryzae leads	High density polyethylene films	High density polyethylene (HDPE) film buried in soil	72%
Streptomyces KU8, *Pseudomonas sp* and *Aspergillus flavus*	Low density polyethylene powder	Garbage soil dumped site	46.16% 37.09% 20.63
Eight *Streptomyces* strains and two fungi, *M. rouxii* NRRL 1835 and Aspergillus flavus	Disposable plastic films	Nile River Delta	28.5% and 46.5% Respectively.
Pseudomonas stutzeri	Low density polythene and polythene	soil from the plastic dumping site	73.38% reduction
Arthrobacter sp. and *Pseudomonas* sp	High-density polyethylene (HDPE)	dumped sites	12% and 15%
Brevibaccillus borstelensis strain 707	Branched low-density polyethylene	Soil	11%
Psedumonas sp. *Aspergillus glaucus*	Polythene bags and plastic cups	Mangroves rhizosphere soil	20.54 ± 0.13 28.80 ± 2.40 %
Serretia marscence	Polythene carry bags	Polythene dumping site	22%
Bacillus cereus	LDPE and BPE 10	Municipal compost yard	17.036%
Aspergillus versicolor and *Aspergillus sp*	LPDE in the powdered form	Sea water	4.1594 g/L
Staphylococcal species	LDPE	Not specified	22%

Objectives

- To develop environmentally friendly method for managing the plastics waste (PE & PP) using microorganisms and associated biotechnological approaches.
- To degrading plastics (PE & PP) into more basic chemical constituents.
- To use biotechnological approach for degradation along with physico-chemical methods.

Methodology

A. Selection of target plastic

1. Polyethylene (PE)
   (*i*) LDPE
   (*ii*) HDPE
2. Polypropylene (PP)

B. Selection of target microbes

Selection of bacterial and fungal strain will be isolated from different extreme ecosystems like land fill site. A few target microbial species may be as follows:

- Penicillium sp.
- Rizopus sp.
- Aspergillus flavus
- Penicillium funiculosum
- Pseudomonas sp.
- Burkhplderia
- Flavobacterium species
- Vibrio alginolytious
- Anabena species
- Bacillus subtilis

C. Method adopted

Different types of packaging material grade plastics (PE & PP) varying in composition will be used in the present study. A commercially used biodegradable plastic was also subjected to biodegradation. The inoculums for degradation studies used include the individual isolates of the consortium and grown in nutrient broth for 72 hours and the cells were then harvested by centrifugation. The bacterial cells were then induced in aqueous media (Odusanya *et al.*, 2013).

The above said different grade plastics used for the study will be of size 15 mm × 15 mm in duplicates and were exposed to minimal (M4) medium in a shake flask containing potassium dihydrogen orthophosphate, disodium hydrogen orthophosphate and ammonium nitrate maintained at a pH of 7.5. A separate set of experiments will be done in a rotary shaker and another set in a water bath shaker at a temperature of about 26°C. The inoculums of bacterial consortium will be added to each flask and a control will also be maintained for each set of samples.

For the measurement of CO_2 in water flask, two reactors of 500 ml capacity is fabricated and the minimal medium containing best degraded plastic sample, inoculum and yeast is aerated using a diffused aerator. A solution of 0.1 N sodium hydroxide is added to absorb the carbon dioxide produced from the test material and the quantity is determined by titrating the absorbing medium with 0.1 N hydrochloric acid. The normality of the absorbing medium is found by titrating it against hydrochloric acid whose normality is determined by titrating it against 0.1 N sodium carbonate.

A High Performance Liquid Chromatography (HPLC) is used to prepare a chromatogram and the column used is RPC 18 with Eluantas Acetonitrile 40%, Water Solution 60% (Containing NaH_2PO_4 16 mM, Na_2HPO_4 4 mM) and flow rate maintained between 0.6 mL/min and 1 mL/min.

Method 2:

- Solubilization of the polyethylene/plastic material
- Isolation of microbial cultures
- Isolation of pure cultures/inoculation of plastic media
- Tests on degraded PEP by weight
- Spot tests on PE films to show indentation of plastics
- Thermal analysis
- Surface examination scanning electron microscope (SEM)

Conclusions

Based on the literature survey, it can be concluded that plastics are very useful in our day-to-day life to meet our desired needs. Due to its good quality its use is increasing day by day and its degradation is becoming a great threat. In the natural environment, different kinds of microorganisms play an important role in various steps involved in the degradation of plastics. Studying the synergism between those microorganisms will give an insight for future efforts toward the biodegradation of these materials. The plastic materials have high-molecular weight and have hydrophobic surfaces making them difficult for the microorganisms to form stable biofilms and degrade them into small molecular oligomers. The screening of soil microorganisms, isolating microorganisms from marine environment and plastic waste dump site could lead to new explored strains, with superior performance.

Various plastic-degrading methods are available but the cheapest, eco-friendly acceptable method is degradation using microbes. The microbe releases the extracellular enzymes to degrade the plastic but the detailed characterization of these enzymes is still needed to be carried out. Utilization of molecular techniques to detect specific groups of microorganisms involved in the degradation process will allow a better understanding of the organization of the microbial community involved in the attack of materials. The characterization of efficient plastic-degrading microbes at molecular level is still not available, so research should be focused in the field of genomics and proteomics, which could speed up the degradation.

REFERENCES

Albinas L. Loreta L, Dalia P. Micromycetes as Deterioration Agents of Polymeric Materials. *Int Biodeterio Biodegra* 2003; 52: 233-242.

Aswale P, Ade A. Assessment of the Biodegradation of Polythene. *Bioinfolet* 2008; 5: 239-245.

Aswale P. Studies on Bio-degradation of Polythene. PhD thesis. Aurangabad, India: Dr. Babasaheb Ambedkar Marathwada University; 2010.

Aswale PN, Ade AB. Effect of pH on Biodegradation of Polythene by Serretia marscence. *The Ecotech* 2009; 1: 152-153.

Balasubramanian V, Natarajan K, Hemambika B, Ramesh, N, Sumathi CS *et al.* High-density Polyethylene (HDPE)-Degrading Potential Bacteria from Marine Ecosystem of Gulf of Mannar, India. *Lett Appl Microbiol* 2010; 51: 205-211.

Benachour N, Aris A. Toxic Effects of Low Doses of Bisphenol-A on Human Placental Cells. *Toxicol Appl Pharmacol* 2009; 241(3): 322-328.

Benedict CV, Cook WJ, Jarrett P, Cameron JA, Huang SJ, and Bell JP. Fungal Degradation of Polycaprolactones. *J Appl Polym Sci* 1983; 28: 327–334.

Chatterjee S, Roy B, Roy D, Banerjee R. Enzyme-mediated Biodegradation of Heat Treated Commercial Polyethylene by Staphylococcal Species. *Polym Degrad Stab* 2010; 95: 195-200.

Chee JY, Yoga SS, Lau NS, Ling SC, Abed RMM and Sudesh KL. Bacterially Produced Polyhydroxyalkanoate (PHA): Converting Renewable Resources into Bioplastics, edited by Mendez Vilas A. *Applied Microbiology and Biotechnology*, 2010, p 1395.

Chomchoei A, Pathom-aree W, Yokota A, Khanongnuch C, Lumyong S. Amycolatopsis Thailandensis sp. Nov., a Poly (L-lactic Acid)-Degrading Actinomycete, Isolated from Soil. *Int J Syst Evol Microbiol* 2011; 61: 839-843.

Chua ASM, Takabatake H, Satoh H and Mino T. Production of Polyhydroxyalkanoates (PHA) by Activated Sludge Treating Municipal Waste Water: Effect of pH, Sludge Retention Time (SRT) and Acetate Concentration influent. *Water Res.* 2003; 37(15):360-361.

Chua T, Tseng M, Yang M. Degradation of Poly(γ-caprolactone) by Thermophilic Streptomyces Thermoviolaceus Subsp. Thermoviolaceus 76T-2. AMB Express. 2013; 3: 8 /"pg"14.

Deepika S, Jaya Madhuri R. Biodegradation of Low Density Polyethylene by Micro-organisms from Garbage Soil. *J Exp Bio Agri Sci* 2015; 3(1): 15-21.

El-Shafei HA, El-Nasser NHA, Kansoh AL, Ali AM. Biodegradation of Disposable Polyethylene by Fungi and Streptomyces Species. *Polym Degrad Stab* 1998; 62: 361-365.

Ghosh M, Singh SP. A Review on Phytoremediation of Heavy Metals and Utilization of Its by Products. *Appl Environ* 2005; 3: 1-18.

Gnanavel G, Mohana VP, Jeya Valli, Thirumarimurugan M, Kannadasan TA. Review of Biodegradation of Plastics Waste. *Int J Pharm Chem Sci* 2012; 1(3): 670-673.

Gray J, Evans N, Taylor B, Rizzo, JJ, Walker M. State of the Evidence: The Connection between Breast Cancer and the Environment, *Int J Occu Environ Heal* 2009; 15 (1): 43-78.

Gu JD, Ford TE, Mitton DB, Mitchell R. Microbial Corrosion of Metals. In: Review, Editor. The Uhlig Corrosion Handbook. New York: Wiley; 2000, p. 915.

Hadad D, Geresh S, Sivan A. Biodegradation of Polyethylene by the Thermophilic Bacterium Brevibacillus borstelensis. *J Appl Microbiol* 2005; 98:1093-1100.

Hao J, Wang J, Zhao W, Ding L, Gao E and Yuan W. Effect of Bisphenol a Exposure on Sex Hormone Level in Occupational Women. Wei Sheng Yan Jiu 2011; 40(3):312-214.

Hayase N, Yano H, Kudoh E, Tsutsumi C, Ushio K, Miyahara Y, Tanaka S, Nakagawa K. Isolation and Characterization of Poly (Butylene Succinate-Co-butylene adipate)-Degrading Microorganism. *J Biosci Bioeng* 2004; 97: 131-133.

Hsu L, Kjen, Tseng, Don, Tming, Yang. Biodegradation of Polyβ-hydroxybutyrate by a Novel Isolate of Streptomyces Bangladeshensis 77T-4. *Bot Stud* 2012; 53: 307-313.

Huang JC, Shetty AS, Wang MS. Biodegradable Plastics: A Review. *Adv Polym Tech* 1990; 10: 23-30.

Hugenholtz P, Goebel B, Pace N. Impact of Culture-independent Studies on the Emerging Phylogenetic View of Bacterial diversity. *J Bacteriol* 1998; 180: 4765 - 4774.

IARC (International Agency for the Research on Cancer). Agents Classified by the IARC Monographs. Lyon, France: World Health Organization; 2011; p. 321.

Ibrahim D, Bankole OC, Ma'aji SA, Ohize EJ and Abdul BK. Assessment of the Strength Properties of Polystyrene Material used in Building Construction in Mbora District of Abuja, Nigeria. *Int J Engg Res Dev* 2013; 6(12): 80-84.

Ikura Y, Kudo T. Isolation of a Microorganism Capable of Degrading Poly-(L-lactide). *J Gen Appl Microbiol* 1999; 45: 247–251.

Jarerat A, Tokiwa Y and Tanaka H. Poly (L-lactide) Degradation by Kibdelosporangium Aridum. *Biotechnol Lett* 2003; 25: 2035-2038.

Jarerat A, Tokiwa Y. Degradation of Poly (L-lactide) by a Fungus. *Macromol Biosci* 2001; 1: 136–140.

Kathiresan K. Polythene and Plastic Degrading Microbes from Mangrove soil. *Rev Biol Trop* 2003; 51: 629-640.

Kathiresan K. Polythene and Plastic Degrading Microbes from Mangrove Soil. *Rev Biol Trop* 2003; 51: 629-633.

Kim M, Park S. Degradation of poly (L-lactide) by a Mesophilicbacterium. *J Appl Polym Sci* 2010; 117: 67–74.

Konduri MKR, Anupam KS, Vivek JS, Kumar RDB, Narasu ML. Synergistic Effect of Chemical and Photo Treatment on the Rate of Biodegradation of High Density Polyethylene by Indigenous Fungal Isolates. Int J Biotech Biochem 2010; 6: 157-174.

Koutny M, Amato P., Muchova M, Ruzicka J, Delort AM. Soil Bacterial Strains Ableto Grow on the Surface of Oxidized Polyethylene Film Containing Prooxidant Additives. *Int Biodeterior Biodegrad* 2009; 63(1): 354-357.

Kumar S, Das, PM, Rebecca L J, Sharmila S. Isolation and Identification of LDPE Degrading Fungi from Municipal Solid Waste. *J Chem Pharm Res* 2013; 5(3):78-81.

Lee S, Kim M. Isolation of Bacteria Degrading Poly (butylenesuccinate-co-butylene adipate) and their Lip A Gene. *Int Biodeterior Biodegrad* 2010; 64: 184–190.

Li F, Hu X, Guo Z, Wang Z, Wang Y, Liu D, Xia H, Chen S. Purification and Characterization of a Novel Poly (Butylenes succinate)-Degrading Enzyme from Asperillus sp. *J Microbiol Biotechnol* 2011; 27:2591-2596.

Masaki K, Kamini, NR, Ikeda H, Iefuji H. Cutinase-like Enzyme from Theyeast Cryptococcus sp. Strain S-2 Hydrolyses Polylactic Acid and Other Biodegradable Plastics. *Appl Environ Microbiol* 2005; 7: 7548-7550.

Mogil'nitskii GM, Sagatelyan RT, Kutishcheva TN, Zhukova SV, Kerimov SI, Parfenova TB. Disruption of the Protective Properties of the Polyvinyl Chloride Coating under the Effect of Microorganisms. Prot Met (Engl Transl) 1987; 23: 173–175.

Muthur Noopur, Sharma Sakshi, Nupur Singh Snnuradha. Toxicity and Biodegradation of Plastics: A Review. *J Environ Dev* 2015; 9(3): 906-913.

Oda Y, Asari H, Urakami T, Tonomura K. Microbial Degradation of Poly(3-hydroxybutyrate) and Polycaprolactone by Filamentous Fungi. *J Ferment Bioeng* 1995; 80: 265–269.

Pilz H, Brandt B, Fehringer R. The Impact of Plastics on Life Cycle Energy Consumption and Greenhouse Gas Emissions in Europe, Summary Report. Vienna, Austria: Denkstatt GmbH; 2010.

Plastic Europe, An Analysis of European Plastics Production Demand and Waste Data. Belgium: EPRO; 2015.

Plastics Europe, Compelling Facts About Plastics. An Analysis of European Plastics Production, Demand and Recovery for 2008. Brussles: Plastics Europe 2009; p. 29.

Ponniah Saminathan, Anandan Sripriya, Kaliappan Nalini, Thangavelu Sivakumar, Veerapandiyan Thangapandian. Biodegradation of Plastics by Pseudomonas Putida Isolated from Garden Soil Samples. *J Adv Bot Zoo* 2014; 2348- 7313.

Pramila R, Ramesh K. Biodegradation of LDPE by Fungi Isolated from Marine Water a SEM analysis. *Afr J Microbiol Res* 2011; 5(2): 5013-5018.

Pramila R, Ramesh KV. Biodegradation of LDPE by Fungi Isolated from Municipal Landfill Area, *J. Microbiol. Biotechnol Res* 2011; 1(2): 131-136.

Pramila R, Ramesh KV. Biodegradation of Low Density Polyethylene (LDPE) by Fungi Isolated from Marine Water—A SEM Analysis. *Afr J Microbiol Res* 2011; 5: 5013-5018.

Pranamuda H, Tokiwa Y. Degradation of Poly (L-lactide) Bystrains Belonging to Genus Amycolatopsis. *Biotechnol Lett* 1999; 21: 901-905.

Premraj R, Mukesh CD. Biodegradation of Polymer. *Indian J Biotech* 2005; 4: 186-193.

Premraj R. Mukesh CD. Biodegradation of Polymer. *Indian J Biotech* 2005; 4: 186-193.

Priyanka N, Archana T. Biodegradability of Polythene and Plastic by the Help of Microorganism: A Way for Brighter Future. *J Environ Anal Toxicol* 2011; 1: 111.

Rudel Ruthann A, Attfield RK, Schifano JNand Brody JG. Chemicals Causing Mammary Gland Tumors in Animals Signal New Directions for Epidemiology, Chemicals Testing and Risk Assessment for Breast Cancer Prevention. *Cancer* 2007; 109(1): 2635-2666.

Sanchez J, Tsuchii A, Tokiwa Y. Degradation of Polycaprolactone at 50°C by a Thermotolarant Aspergillus sp. *Biotechnol Lett* 2000; 22: 849–853.

Sand W. Microbial Life in Geothermal Waters. *Geothermics* 2003; (32) 655–667.

Sekiguchi T, Sato T, Enoki M, Kanehiro H, Uematsu K, Kato C. Isolation and Characterization of Bidegradable Plastic Degrading Bacteria from Deep-sea Environments. *Rep Res Dev* 2010; 11: 33-41.

Sharma A, Sharma A. Degradation Assessment of Low Density Polythene (LDP) and Polythene (PP) by an Indigenous Isolate of Pseudomonas Stutzeri. *J Sci Ind Res* 2004; 63: 293-296.

Shimao M. Biodegradation of Plastics. *Current Opinion in Biotechnology* 2001; 12: 242-247.

Shinozaki Y, Kikkawa Y, Sato S, Fukuoka T, Watanabe T, Yoshida S, Nakajima-kambe T, Kitamoto HK. Enzymatic Degradation of Polyester Films by a Cutinase-like Enzyme from Pseudozyma Antarctica: Surface Plasmon Resonance and Atomic Force Microscopy Study. *Appl Microbiol Biotechnol* 2013; 97(19): 8591-8598.

Sivan A, Szanto M, Pavlov V. Biofilm Development of the Polyethylene-degrading Bacterium Rhodococcus ruber. *Appl Microbiol Biotechnol* 2006; 72(2): 346-352.

Sivasankari S, Vinotha T. In Vitro Degradation of Plastics (Plastic Cup) Using Micrococcus Luteus and Masoniella Sp, Sch. *Acad J Biosci* 2014; 2(2):85-89.

Smith WM. Manufacture of plastic. USA: Technology and Engineering, Reinhold Pub. Corp; 1964.

Sonil Nanda, Smiti Snigdha Sahu, Jayanthi Abraham. Studies on the Biodegradation of Natural and Synthetic Polyethylene by Pseudomonas sp. *J Appl Sci Environ Manage* 2010; 14(2): 57-60.

Sowmya HV, Ramalingappa M, Krishnappa M. Degradation of Polyethylene by Chaetomium sp. and Aspergillus flavus. *Int J Rec Sci Res* 2012; 3(1): 513-517.

Sowmya HV, Ramalingappa, Krishnappa M, Thippeswamy. Biodegradation of Polyethylene by Bacillus cereus. *Advances Polym Sci Technol: An Int J* 2014; 4(2):28-32.

Sukkhum S, Tokuyama S, Kongsaeree P, Tamura T, Ishida Y, Kitpreechavanich V. A Novel poly (L-lactide) Degrading Thermophilic Actinomycetes, Actinomadura Keratinilytica Strain T16-1 and pla Sequencing. *Afr J Microbiol Res* 2011; 5: 2575-2582.

Suman Mukherjee, Shamba Chatterjee. A Comparative Study of Commercially Available Pastic Carry Bag Biodegradation by Microorganisms Isolated from Hydrocarbon Effluent Enriched Soil. *Int J Curr Microbiol App Sci* 2014; 3(5): 318-325.

Suresh B, Maruthamuthu S, Palanisamy N, Ragunathan R, Pandiyaraj KN *et al.* Investigation on Biodegradability of Polyethylene by Bacillus Cereus Strain Ma-Su Isolated from Compost Soil. *Int Res J Microbiol* 2011; 2: 292-302.

Swapna Kumar Ghosh, Sujoy Pal, Sumanta Ray. Study of Microbes having Potentiality for Biodegradation of Plastics. *Environ Sci. Pollut Res.* 2013; 11356-013.

Swift G. Handbook of Biodegradable Polymers. CRC Press; 1998.

Swift G. Non-medical Biodegradable Polymers: Environmentally Degradable Polymers, the Lifetime of Maurtis Dekker. *J Macromol Sci Chem* 1989; 26: 1023–1032.

Szumigaj J, Zakowaka Z, Klimek L, Rosicka-Kaczmarek J, Bartkowiak A. Assessment of Polylactide Foil Degradation as a Result of Filamentous Fungi Activity. *Pol J Environ Stud* 2008; 17: 335-341.

Teeraphatpornchai T, Nakajima-Kambe T, Shigeno-Akutsu Y, Nakayama M, Nomura N, Nakahara T, Uchiyama H. Isolation and Characterization of a Bacterium that Degrades Various Polyester-based Biodegradable Plastics. *Biotechnol Lett* 2003; 25: 23–28.

The Source of this Information is a Press Release of No Plastics in the Environment (NoPE) titled 'Imports Versus Surplus: A Glut of Plastics in India Today', 10 January 2002. Courtesy Bharati Chaturvedi, Director, Chintan Environmental Organisation, New Delhi.

Tomita K, Kuroki Y, Nagai K. Isolation of thermophiles Degrading Poly (L-lactic acid). *J Biosci Bioeng* 1999; 87: 752–755.

Torres A, Li SM, Roussos S, Vert M. Screening of Microorganisms for Biodegradation of Poly (Lactic Acid) and Lactic Acid-Containing Polymers. *Appl Environ Microbiol* 1996; 62:2393–2397.

Uchida H, Nakajima-Kambe T, Shigeno-Akutsu Y, Nomura N, Tokiwa Y, Nakahara T. Properties of a Bacterium which Degrades Solid Poly (tetramethylene succinate)-Co-adipate, a Biodegradable Plastic. *FEMS Microbiol Lett* 2000; 189: 25-29.

Usha R, Sangeetha T, Palaniswamy M. Screening of Polyethylene Degrading Microorganisms from Garbage Soil. *Libyan Agric Res Cen J Intl* 2011; 2 (4): 200-204.

Usha R, Sangeetha T, Palaniswamy M. Screening of Polyethylene Degrading Microorganisms from Garbage Soil. *Libyan Agric Res Cen J Int* 2011; 2: 200-204.

Vatseldutt, Anbuselvi S. Isolation and Characterization of Polythene Degrading Bacteria from Polythene Dumped Garbage. *Int. J. Pharm.* 2014; 25(2): 205-206.

Volke-Sepulveda T, Saucedo-Castaneda G, Gutierrez-Rojas M, Manzur A, Favela-Torres E. Thermally Treated Low Density Polyethylene Biodegradation by Penicillium pinophilum and Aspergillus niger. *J Appl Polym Sci* 2002; 83: 305-314.

Vona IA, Costana JR, Cantor HA, Roberts WJ. Manufacture of Plastics. New York: Wiley; 1965; p. 141.

Watanabe T, Ohtake Y, Asabe H, Murakami N, Furukawa M. Biodegradability and Degrading Microbes of Low-densitypolyethylene. *J Appl Poly Sci* 2009; 111(1): 551-559.

BIBLIOGRAPHY

Aamer Ali Shah, Fariha Hasan, Abdul Hameed, Safia Ahmed (2008): Biological Degradation of Plastics: A Comprehensive Review. *Biotechnology Advances*, 26: 246–265

Abrusci C, Pablos JL, Corrales T, Lopez-Marín J, Marín I, and Catalina F. 2011. Biodegradation of Photo-degraded Mulching Films Based on Polyethylenes and Stearates of Calcium and Iron as Pro-oxidant Additives. *International Biodeterioration and Biodegradation* 65: 451–459.

Albertsson AC and Huang SJ. 1995. Degradable Polymers, Recycling and Plastics Waste Management. Marcel Dekker, New York, pp. 205–208.

Albertsson AC, Andersson SO, and Karlsson S. 1987. The Mechanism of Biodegradation of Polyethylene. *Polymer Degradation and Stability* 18: 73–87.

Albertsson AC, Barenstedt C, and Karlsson S. 1994. Abiotic Degradation Products from Enhanced Environmentally Degradable Polyethylene. *Acta Polymerica* 45: 97–103.

Albertsson AC. 1980. The Shape of the Biodegradation Curve for Low and High Density Polyethylenes in Prolonged Series of Experiments. *European Polymer Journal* 16: 623–630.

Albertsson AC. 1992. Biodegradation of Polymers. In: Hamid SH, Amin MB and Maadhah AG. (Eds.), Handbook of Polymer Degradation. Marcel Dekker, New York, pp. 345–363.

Alexander M. 1977. Introduction to Soil Microbiology, 2nd edn. Wiley, New York.

Ali MI. 2011. Microbial Degradation of Polyvinyl Chloride Plastics, PhD thesis. Quaid-i-Azam University, p. 122. Ali MI, Ahmed S, Robson G, Javed I, Ali N, Atiq N and Hameed A. 2013. Isolation and Molecular Characterization of Polyvinyl Chloride (PVC) Plastic Degrading Fungal Isolates. *Journal of Basic Microbiology* 54(1): 18–27.

American Chemistry Council. 2011. Life Cycle of a Plastic Product. http://www.americanchemistry.

APME. 2006. An Analysis of Plastics Production, Demand and Recovery in Europe. Association of Plastics Manufacturers, Brussels.

Artham T and Doble M. 2008. Biodegradation of Aliphatic and Aromatic Polycarbonates. *Macromolecular Bioscience* 8(1): 14–24.

Aswale P and Ade A. 2008. Assessment of the Biodegradation of Polythene. *Bioinfolet* 5: 239.

Aswale P and Ade A. 2011. Polythene Degradation Potential of Aspergillus niger. In: Sayed IU. (Ed.), Scholary Articles in Botany, Pune.

Aswale P. 2010. Studies on Bio-degradation of Polythene. PhD thesis, Dr. Babasaheb Ambedkar Marathwada University, Aurangabad, India.

Aswale PN and Ade AB. 2009. Effect of pH on Biodegradation of Polythene by Serretia marscence. *The Ecotech* 1: 152–153.

Augusta J, Müller RJ, and Widdecke H. 1992. Biologisch Abbaubare Kunststoffe: Testverfahren und Beurteilungskriterien. Chemie Ingenieur Technik 64: 410–415.

Balasubramanian V, Natarajan K, Hemambika B, Ramesh, N, Sumathi CS, Kottaimuthu R, and Rajesh Balasubramanian V, Natarajan K, Rajesh Kannan V, and Perumal P. 2014. Enhancement of in vitro high-density polyethylene (HDPE) degradation by physical, chemical and biological treatments. Environmental Science and Pollution Research 21: 12,549–12,562.

Bastioli C. 2005. Handbook of Biodegradable Polymers. Smithers Rapra Press, Billingham.
Blake RC and Howard GT. 1998. Adhesion and Growth of a Bacillus sp. on a Polyesterurethane. International Biodeterioration and Biodegradation 42: 63–73.

Bonhomme S, Cuer A, Delort AM, Lemaire J, Sancelme M, and Scott C. 2003. Environmental Biodegradation of Polythene. *Polymer Degradation and Stability* 81: 441–452.

Boubendir A. 1993. Purication and Biochemical Evaluation of Polyurethane Degrading Enzymes of Fungal Origin. Dissertation Abstract International 53: 4632.

Braun D and Bazdadea E. 1986. In: Nass LI and Heiberger CA. (Eds.), Encyclopaedia of PVC. 2nd edn, Vol. 2, Marcel Dekker, New York.

Brevibacillus borstelensis. *Journal of Applied Microbiology* 98: 1093–1100.

Cacciari I, Quatrini P, Zirletta G, Mincione E, Vinciguerra V, Lupatelli P, and Sermanni GG. 1993. Isotactic Polypropylene Biodegradation by a Microbial Community: Physicochemical Characterization of Metabolites Produced. *Applied and Environmental Microbiology* 59(11): 3695–3700.

Carpenter E.J. and K.L. Smith. 1972. Plastics on the Sargasso Sea surface. *Science,* 175: 1240-1241.

Caruso G (2015): Plastic Degrading Microorganisms as a Tool for Bioremediation of Plastic Contamination in Aquatic Environments. *J. Pollut. Eff. Cont.* 3: e112. doi:10.4172/2375-4397.1000e112

Chandra R and Rustgi R. 1997. Biodegradation of Maleated Linear Low-density Polyethylene and Starch Blends. *Polymer Degradation and Stability* 56: 185–202.

Chapelle F. 1993. Ground-Water Microbiology & Geochemistry. John Wiley & Sons, Inc., New York.

Chatterjee S, Roy B, Roy D, and Banerjee R. 2010. Enzyme-mediated Biodegradation of Heat Treated Commercial Polyethylene by Staphylococcal Species. Polymer Degradation and Stability 95: 195–200.

Chowdhury AA. 1963. Poly-β-hydroxybuttersaure abbauende Bakterien und exo-enzyme. *Archives in Microbiology* 47: 167–200.

Colton J.B., Burns B.R. and F.D. Knapp. 1974. Plastic Particles in Surface Waters of the Northwestern Atlantic. *Science,* 185: 491-497.

com/s_plastics/doc.asp?CID=1571&DID=5972 (accessed on: March 30, 2011).

Comparison of the Biodegradability of Various Polyethylene Films Containing Pro-oxidant Additives. Polymer Degradation and Stability 95: 1011–1021.

Crabbe JR, Campbell JR, Thompson L, Walz SL, and Schultz WW. 1994. Biodegradation of Colloidal Ester-based Polyurethane by Soil Fungi. *International Biodeterioration and Biodegradation* 33: 103–113.

Cruz-Pinto JJC, Carvalho MES, and Ferreira JFA. 1994. The Kinetics and Mechanism of Polyethylene Photo-oxidation. *Angewandte Makromolekulare Chemie* 216: 113–133.

Degli-Innocenti F, Tosin M, and Bastioli C. 1998. Evaluation of the Biodegradation of Starch and Cellulose under Controlled Composting Conditions. *Journal of Environmental Polymer Degradation* 6(4): 197–202.

Effects of Ester Group Chain Length and Degree of Substitution on Anaerobic Biodegradation. *Enzyme and Microbial Technology* 17: 848–852.

El-Sayed AHMM, Mahmoud WM, Davis EM, and Coughlin RW. 1996. Biodegradation of Polyurethane Coatings by Hydrocarbon- Degrading Bacteria. *International Biodeterioration and Biodegradation* 37: 69–79.

El-Shafei HA, El-Nasser NHA, Kansoh AL, and Ali AM. 1998. Biodegradation of Disposable Polyethylene by Fungi and Streptomyces Species. Polymer Degradation and Stability 62: 361–365.

Enzyme(s) by Streptomyces Species. *Applied and Environmental Microbiology* 58: 731–733.

European Bioplastics. 2011. Bioplastics at a Glance. Avaliable online: http://www.europeanbioplastics.

Fontanella S, Bonhomme S, Koutny M, Husarova L, Brusson JM, Courdavault JP, Pitteri S *et al.* 2009.

Garcia RA and Gho JG. 1998. Degradable/compostable Concentrates, Process for Making Degradable/Compostable Packaging Materials and the Products Thereof. *US Patent 5 854 304.*

Ghiglione J.F., Conan P. and M. Pujo-Pay (2009) Diversity of Total and Active Free-living vs. Particle-attached Bacteria in the Euphotic Zone of the NW Mediterranean Sea. *FEMS Microbiology Letters,* 299: 9-21.

Ghosh S.K., Pal S. and S. Ray. 2013. Study of Microbes having Potentiality for Biodegradation of Plastics. *Environmental Science and Pollution Research* 20:4339-4355.

Gilan I, Hadar Y, and Sivan A. 2004. Colonization, Biofilm Formation and Biodegradation of Polyethylene by a Strain of Rhodococcus Ruber. *Applied Microbiology and Biotechnology* 65: 97–104.

Gilmore DF, Fuller RC, and Lenz R. 1990. Biodegradation of Poly (beta-hydroxyalkanoates). In: Barenberg SA, Brash JL, Narayan R and Redpath AE. (Eds.), Degradable Materials: Perspectives, Issues and Opportunities. CRC Press, Bocan Raton, FL.

Goldberg ED. 1995. The Health of the Oceans—A 1994 Update. *Chemical Ecology* 10: 3–8.

Goldberg ED. 1997. Plasticizing the Seafloor: An Overview. *Environmental Technology* 18: 195–202.

Gopferich A. 1997. Mechanisms of Polymer Degradation and Elimination. In: Domb AJ, Kost J and Wiseman DM. (Eds.), Handbook of Biodegradable Polymers. Harwood Academic, Amsterdam, pp. 451–471.

Gorman M. 1993. Environmental Hazards—Marine Pollution. ABC-CLIO Inc., Santa Barbara.

Gu JD, Ford TE, Mitton DB, and Mitchell R. 2000. Microbial Degradation and Deterioration of Polymeric Materials. In: Review. (Ed.), The Uhlig Corrosion Handbook, 2nd edn. Wiley, New York,

Gu JD, Ford TE, Mitton DB, Mitchell R. (2000): Microbial Degradation and Deterioration of Polymeric Materials. In: Revie W, Editor. The Uhlig Corrosion Handbook. 2nd Edition. New York: Wiley; p. 439–60.

Gu JD. 2003. Microbiological Deterioration and Degradation of Synthetic Polymeric Materials: Recent Research Advances. *International Biodeterioration and Biodegradation* 52: 69–91.

Hadad D, Geresh S, and Sivan A. 2005. Biodegradation of Polyethylene by the Thermophilic Bacterium Hansen J. 1990. Draft Position Statement on Plastic Debris in Marine Environments. Fisheries 15: 16–17.

Hasan F, Shah AA, Hameed A, and Ahmed S. 2007. Synergistic Effect of Photo and Chemical Treatment on the Rate of Biodegradation of Low Density Polyethylene by Fusarium sp. AF4. *Journal of Applied Polymer Science* 105: 1466–1470.

Helbling C., Abanilla M., Lee L. and V.M. Karbhari. 2006. Issues of Variability and Durability under Synergistic Exposure Conditions Related to Advanced Polymer Composites in Civil Infrastructure. *Composites Part A: Applied Science and Manufacturing,* 37: 1102-1110.

Henton DE, Gruber P, Lunt J, and Randall J. 2005. Polylactic Acid Technology. In: Mohanty AK, Misra M and Drzal LT. (Eds.), Natural Fibers, Biopolymers, and Biocomposites. CRC Press, Boca Raton, FL, pp. 527.

Hester, RE and Harrison RM. (eds.) 2011. Marine Pollution and Human Health. Issues in Environmental Science and Technology. *Royal Society of Chemistry, Cambridge,* Vol. 33, pp. 84–85.

Higashimura T, Sawamoto M, Hiza T, Karaiwa M, Tsuchii A, and Suzuki T. 1983. Effect of Methyl Substitution on Microbial Degradation of Linear Styrene Dimers by Two Soil Bacteria. *Applied and Environmental Microbiology* 46: 386–391.

Ho KLG, Pometto AL, Gadea-Rivas A, Briceno JA, and Rojas A. 1999. Degradation of Polylactic acid (PLA) Plastic in Costa Rican Soil and Iowa University Compos Rows. *Journal of Environmental Polymer Degradation* 7(4): 173–177.

Hofrichter M, Lundell T, and Hatakka A. 2001. Conversion of Milled Pine Wood by Manganese Peroxidase from Phlebia Radiata. *Applied and Environmental Microbiology* 67: 4588–4593.

Hosler D, Burkett SL, and Tarkanian MJ. 1999. Prehistoric polymers: Rubber Processing in Ancient. *Mesoamerica Science* 284: 1988–1991.

Howard GT and Blake RC. 1999. Growth of Pseudomonas fluorescens on a Polyester-polyurethane and the Purification and Characterization of a Polyurethanase-Protease Enzyme. *International Biodeterioration and Biodegradation* 42: 213–220.

Howard GT, Norton WN, and Burks T. 2012. Growth of Acinetobacter gerneri P7 on Polyurethane and the Purification and Characterization of a Polyurethane Enzyme. *Biodegradation* 23: 561–573.

Huang SJ, Roby MS, Macri CA, and Cameron JA. 1992. The Effects of Structure and Morphology on the Degradation of Polymers with Multiple Groups. In: Vert M, Feijen J, Albertsson A, Scott G and Chiellini E. (Eds.), Biodegradable Polymers and Plastic. The Royal Society of Chemistry, Cambridge, pp. 149–157.

Hydroxybutyrate-co-3-hydroxyvalerate) Film in Soil. Applied Microbiology and Biotechnology 58: 241–247.

Iiyoshi Y, Tsutsumi Y, and Nishida T. 1998. Polyethylene Degradation by Lignin-degrading Fungi and Manganese Peroxidase. Journal of Wood Science 44: 222–229.

Indian Journal of Biotechnology 7: 235–239.

Ipekoglu B., Böke H. and O. Cizer. 2007. Assessment of Material Use in Relation to Climate in Historical Buildings. *Building and Environment,* 42: 970-978.

Jakubowicz I. 2003. Evaluation of Degradability of Biodegradable Polyethylene (PE). Polymer Degradation and Stability 80: 39–43.

Kamble Asmita, Tanwar Shubhamsingh and Shanbhag Tejashree (2015): Isolation of Plastic Degrading Micro-organisms from Soil Samples Collected at Various Locations in Mumbai, India. *International Research Journal of Environment Sciences,* 4(3):77-85.

Kannan V. 2010. High-density Polyethylene (HDPE) Degrading Potential Bacteria from Marine Ecosystem of Gulf of Mannar, India. Letters in Applied Microbiology 51: 205–211.

Kathiresan K. 2003. Diversity and Effectiveness of Tropical Mangrove Soil Microflora on the Degradation of Polythene Carry Bags. *Revista de Biologia Tropical,* 51:629-634.

Kathiresan K. 2003. Polythene and Plastic Degrading Microbes from Mangrove Soil. Revista de Biología Kay MJ, McCabe RW, and Morton LHG. 1993. Chemical and Physical

Changes Occurring in Polyester Polyurethane during Biodegradation. International Biodeterioration and Biodegradation 31: 209–225.

Kay MJ, Morton LHG, and Prince EL. 1991. Bacterial Degradation of Polyester Polyurethane. International Bio-deterioration Bulletin 27: 205–222.

Kerr RS. 1994. Handbook of Bioremediation. CRC Press, Inc. Lewis Publishers, Boca Raton, FL, pp. 85–96.

Kijchavengkul T and Auras R. 2008. Perspective: Compostability of Polymers. Polymer International 57(6): 793–804.

Kijchavengkul T. 2010. Design of Biodegradable Aliphatic Aromatic Polyester Films for Agricultural Applications Using Response Surface Methodology. School of Packaging, Doctoral Dissertation. Michigan State University, East Lansing, MI.

Kirbas Z, Keskin N, and Guner A. 1999. Biodegradation of polyvinylchloride (PVC) by White Rot Fungi. Bulletin of Environmental Contamination and Toxicology 63: 335–342.

Kister G., Cassanas G., Bergounhon M., Hoarau D. and M.Vert. 2000. Structural Characterization and Hydrolytic Degradation of Solid Copolymers of D, L-lactide-co-e-caprolactone by Raman Spectroscopy. *Polymer,* 41: 925-932.

Konduri MKR, Anupam KS, Vivek JS, Kumar RDB, and Narasu ML. 2010. Synergistic Effect of Chemical and Photo Treatment on the Rate of Biodegradation of High Density Polyethylene by Indigenous Fungal Isolates. International Journal of Biotechnology and Biochemistry 6: 157–174.

Konduri MKR, Koteswarareddy G, Kumar DBR, Reddy BV, and Narasu ML. 2011. Effect of Prooxidants on Biodegradation of Polyethylene (LDPE) by Indigenous Fungal Isolate, Aspergillus Oryzae. Journal of Applied Polymer Science 120: 3536–3545.

Korner I, Redemann K, and Stegmann R. 2005. Behavior of Biodegradable Plastics Incomposting Facilities. Waste Management 25: 409–415.

Koutny M, Sancelme M, Dabin C, Pichon N, Delort A, and Lemaire J. 2006. Acquired Biodegradability of Polyethylenes Containing Prooxidant Additives. Polymer Degradation and Stability 91: 1495–1503.

Kumar S, Hatha AAM, and Christi KS. 2007. Diversity and Effectiveness of Tropical Mangrove Soil Microflora on the Degradation of Polythene Carry Bags. Revista de Biologia Tropical 55: 777–786.

Kwpp LR and Jewell WJ. 1992. Biodegradability of Modified Plastic Films in Controlled Biological Environments. Environmental Technology 26: 193–198.

Kyaw BM, Champakalakshmi R, Sakharkar MK, Lim CS, and Sakharkar KR. 2012. Biodegradation of Low Density Polythene (LDPE) by Pseudomonas species. Indian Journal of Microbiology 52(3):411–419.

Kyrikou J and Briassoulis D. 2007. Biodegradation of Agricultural Plastic Films: A Critical Review. Journal of Polymers and the Environment 15: 125.

Laist DW. 1987. Overview of the Biological Effects of Lost and Discarded Plastic Debris in the Marine Environment. Marine Pollution Bulletin 18: 319–326.

Law K.L., Morét-Ferguson S., Maximenko N., Proskurowski G., Peacock E.E., Hafner J. and C.M. Reddy. 2010. Plastic Accumulation in the North Atlantic Subtropical gyre. *Science,* 329: 1185-1188.

Lee B, Pometto AL, Fratzke A, and Bailey TB. 1991. Biodegradation of Degradable Plastic Polyethylene by Phanerochaete and Streptomyces Species. Applied and Environmental Microbiology 57: 678–685.

Lee SY. 1996. Bacterial polyhydroxyalkanoates. Biotechnology and Bioengineering 49: 1–14.

Lucas N., Bieniame C., Belloy C., Queneudec M., Silvestre F. and J.E. Nava-Saucedo. 2008. Polymer biodegradation: Mechanisms and Estimation Techniques. *Chemosphere,* 73: 429-442.

Lugauskas A., Levinskait L. and D. Peciulyte. 2003. Micromycetes as Deterioration Agents of Polymeric Materials. *International Biodeterioration and Biodegradation,* 52: 233-242.

Luzier WD. 1992. Materials Derived from Biomass/Biodegradable Materials. Proceedings of the National Academy of Sciences of the United States of America 89: 839–842.

Maeda H and Yamagata Y. 2005. Purication and Characterization of a Biodegradable Plastic-Degrading Enzyme from Aspergillus oryzae. Applied Microbiology and Biotechnology 67: 778–788.

Maier C and Calafut T. 1998. Polypropylene: The Definitive User's Guide and Databook. William Andrew Inc., Norwich, New York, p. 14.

Mayer AM and Staples RC. 2002. Laccase New Functions for an Old Enzyme. Phytochemistry 60: 561–565.

Méndez CR, Vergaray G, Vilma R, Karina B, and Cαrdenas J. 2007. Isolation and Characterization of Polyethylene-Biodegrading Mycromycetes. Revista Peruana de Biología 13(3): 203–205.

Mergaert J. and J. Swings. 1996. Biodiversity of Microorganisms that Degrade Bacterial and Synthetic Polyesters. *Journal of Industrial Microbiology,* 17:463-469.

Milstein O, Gersonde R, Huttermann A, Chen MJ, and Meister JJ. 1992. Fungal Biodegradation of Lignopolystyrene Graft Copolymers. Applied and Environmental Microbiology 58: 3225–3232.

Molitoris HP, Moss ST, de Koning GJM, and Jendrossek D. 1996. Scanning Electron Microscopy of Polyhydroxyalkanoate Degradation by Bacteria. Applied Microbiology and Biotechnology 46: 570–579.

Morris PJT. 2005. Polymer Pioneers: A Popular History of the Science and Technology of Large Molecules. Chemical Heritage Foundation, Vol. 5, p. 88.

Nakajima-Kambe T, Onuma F, Akutsu Y, and Nakahara T. 1997. Determination of the Polyester Polyurethane Breakdown Products and Distribution of the Polyurethane Degrading Enzyme of Comamonas acidovorans strain TB-35. Journal of Fermentation Bioengineering 83: 454–458.

Nakajima-Kambe T, Shigeno-Akutsu Y, Nomura N, Onuma F, and Nakahara T. 1999. Microbial Degradation of Polyurethane, Polyester Polyurethanes and Polyether Polyurethanes. Applied Microbiology and Biotechnology 51: 134–140.

Nakajima-Kambe, T, Onuma F, Kimpara N, and Nakahara T. 1995. Isolation and Characterization of a Bacterium which Utilizes Polyester Polyurethane as a Sole Carbon and Energy Source. FEMS Microbiology Letters 129: 39–42.

Nakamiya K, Ooi S, and Kinoshita T. 1997. Non-heme Hydroquinone Peroxidase from Azotobacter beijerinckii Hm121. Journal of Fermentation and Bioengineering 84: 14–21.

Narayan R. 1993. Biodegradation of Polymeric Materials (Anthropogenic Macromolecules) during Composting. In: Hoitink HAJ, Keener HM. (Eds.), Science and Engineering of Composting: Design, Environmental, Microbiological and Utilization Aspects. Renaissance Publishers, Washington, OH, pp. 339–362.

National Research Council. 1993. In Situ Bioremediation When Does it Work? National Academy Press, Washington, DC, pp. 224.

Nwachukwu S, Obidi O, and Odocha C. 2010. Occurrence and Recalcitrance of Polyethylene Bag Waste in Nigerian Soils. African Journal of Biotechnology 9: 6096–6104.

Odusanya, S.A., Nkwogu, J.V., Alu, N., Etuk Udo, G.A., Ajao, J.A., Osinkolu, G.A. and Uzomah, A.C (2013): Preliminary Studies on Microbial Degradation of Plastics Used in Packaging Potable Water in Nigeria. *NIFOJ*. 31 (2): 63–72.

Ohtaki A, Sato N, and Nakasaki K. 1998. Biodegradation of Poly-γ-caprolactone under Controlled Composting Conditions. Polymer Degradation and Stability 61: 499–505.

Ojumu TV, Yu J, and Solomon BO. 2004. Production of Polyhydroxyalkanoates, A Bacterial Biodegradable Polymer. African Journal of Biotechnology 3: 18–24.

org/index.php?id=182 (Accessed: March 30, 2011)

Organic Compounds. ASM Press, Washington.

Osawa Z. 1992. Photoinduced Degradation of Polymers. In: Hamid SH, Amin MB, Maadhah AG (Eds.), Handbook of Polymer Degradation. Marcel Dekker, New York, pp. 169–217.

Owen ED. 1984. Degradation and Stabilisation of PVC. Elsevier Applied Science Publishers, Barking.

Pathirana RA and Seal KJ. 1985. Studies on Polyurethane Deteriorating Fungi. Part 3. Physicomechanical and Weight Changes During Fungal Deterioration. International Biodeterioration 21: 41–49.

Peciulyte D. 2002. Microbial Colonization and Biodeterioration of Plasticized Polyvinyl Chloride Plastics. Ekologija 4: 7–15.

Pettit D and Abbott SG. 1975. Biodeterioration of Footwear. In: Gilbert JR and Lovelock DW. (Eds.), Microbial Aspects of the Deterioration of Material. Academic, London, pp. 237–253.

Phua SK, Castillo E, Anderson JM, and Hiltner A. 1987. Biodegradation of Polyurethane in vitro. Journal of Biomedical Materials Research 21: 231–246.

Plastic Pollution. 2013. Encyclopædia Britannica. Online Retrieved 1 August, 2013.

Plastic Pollution. 2014. Encyclopaedia Britannica. Online Retrieved 21 May, 2014.

PlasticsEurope, 2010. Plastics—The Facts 2010. An analysis of European Plastics Production, Demand and Recovery for 2009. http://www.plasticseurope.org/documents/document/20101006091310- final_ plasticsthefacts_28092010_lr.pdf.

PlasticsEurope, 2012. Plastics—The Facts 2012. An Analysis of European Plastics Production, Demand and Waste Data for 2011. http://www.plasticseurope.org/documents/document/20121120170458-final_plasticsthefacts_nov2012_ en_web_resolution.pdf.)

Pometto AL III, Lee BT, and Johnson KE. 1992. Production of an Extracellular Polyethylene-Degrading Pospisil J and Nespurek S. 1997. Highlights in Chemistry and Physics of Polymer Stabilization. Macromolecular Symposia 115: 143–163. pp. 439–460.

Pramila R and Ramesh KV. 2011. Biodegradation of Low Density Polyethylene (LDPE) by Fungi Isolated from Marine Water—A SEM Analysis. *African Journal of Microbiological Research* 5: 5013–5018.

Priyanka N and Archana T. 2011. Biodegradability of Polythene and Plastic by the Help of Microorganism: A aay for Brighter Future. *Journal of Environmental and Analytical Toxicology* 1: 111.

Proikakis C.S., Mamouzelous N.J., Tarantili P.A. and A.G. Andreapoulos. 2006. Swelling and Hydrolytic Degradation of poly(D, L-lactic acid) in Aqueous Solution. *Polymer Degradation and Stability*,91: 614-619.

Pruter AT. 1987. Sources, Quantities and Distribution of Persistent Plastics in the Marine Environment. *Marine Pollution Bulletin* 18: 305–310.

Raaman N, Rajitha N, Jayshree A, and Jegadeesh R. 2012. Biodegradation of Plastic by Aspergillus spp. Isolated from Polythene Polluted Sites Around Chennai. Journal of Academia and Industrial Research 1(6): 313–316.

Raziyafathima M, Praseetha P K, Rimal Isaac R S. Microbial Degradation of Plastic Waste: A Review. *J Pharm Chem Biol Sci* 2016; 4(2):231-242.

Reddy RM. 2008. Impact of Soil Composting Using Municipal Solid Waste on Biodegradation of Plastics. *Research* 3: 658–663.

Rivard C, Moens L, Roberts K, Brigham J, and Kelley S. 1995. Starch Esters as Biodegradable Plastics: Russell JR. 2011. Biodegradation of Polyester Polyurethane by Endophytic Fungi. Applied and Environmental Microbiology 77: 6076–6084.

Ryan PG. 1987. The Incidence and Characteristics of Plastic Particles Ingested by Seabirds. Marine Environment Research 23: 175–206.

Sachin SS and Mishra RL. 2013. Screening and Identification of Soil Fungi with Potential of Plastic Degrading Ability. Indian Journal of Applied Research 3(11): 34–36.

Sameh AS, Alariqi Kumar AP, Rao BSM, and Singh RP. 2006. Biodegradation of γ-sterilized Biomedical Polyolefins under Composting and Fungal Culture Environments. Journal of Polmer Degradation and Stability 91: 1105–1116.

Sang BI, Hori K, Tanji Y, and Unno H. 2002. Fungal Contribution to in Situ Biodegradation of poly(3-Sangeetha Devi, Rajendran; Velu Rajesh Kannan, Krishnan Natarajan, Duraisamy Nivas, Kanthaiah Kannan, Sekar Chandru, and Arokiaswamy Robert Antony (2016): The Role of Microbes in Plastic Degradation. In: Environmental Waste Management, Taylor & Francis, pp. 341-370.

Sathya R, Ushadevi T, and Panneerselvam A. 2012. Plastic Degrading Actinomycetes Isolated from Mangrove Sediments. International Journal of Current Research 4(10): 001–003.

Sauders JH and Frisch KC. 1964. Polyurethanes: Chemistry and Technology, Part II Technology. Inter-Science Publishers, New York.

Schink B, Brune A, and Schnell S. 1992. Anaerobic Degradation of Aromatic Compounds. In: Winkelmann, G. (Ed.), Microbial Degradation of Natural Products. Verlag Chemie, Weinheim, pp. 219–242.

Schnabel W. 1992. Polymer Degradation: Principles and Practical Applications. Hanser, New York. Seneviratne G, Tennakoon NS, Weerasekara MLMAW, and Nandasena KA. 2006. Polyethylene biodegradation by a Developed Penicillium–Bacillus biofilm. Current Science 90: 20–22.

Shah AA, Hasan F, Akhter J, Hameed A, and Ahmed S. 2007. Degradation of Polyurethane by Novel Bacterial Consortium Isolated from soil. Annals of Microbiology 58: 381–386.

Shah AA, Hasan F, Akhter J, Hameed A, and Ahmed S. 2009. Isolation of Fusarium sp. AF4 from Sewage Sludge, with the Ability to Adhere the Surface of Polyethylene. African Journal of Microbiology.

Shah AA, Hasan F, Hameed A, and Ahmed S. 2007. Isolation and Characterization of Poly (3-hydroxybutyrate-co-3-hydroxyvalerate) Degrading Bacteria and Purification of PHBV Depolymerase from Newly Isolated Bacillus sp. AF3. International Biodeterioration and Biodegradation 60: 109–115.

Sharma A and Sharma A. 2004. Degradation Assessment of Low Density Polythene (LDPE) and Polythene (PP) by an Indigenous Isolate of Pseudomonas stutzeri. Journal of Science and Industrial Research 63: 293–296.

Shimao M. 2001. Biodegradation of Plastics. *Current Opinion in Biotechnology*, 12: 242–247.

Simon M., Grossart H.P., Schweitzer B., and H. Ploug. 2002. Microbial Ecology of Organic Aggregates in Aquatic Ecosystems. *Aquatic Microbial Ecology*, 28: 175-211.

Singh B. and N. Sharma. 2008. Mechanistic Implications of Plastic Degradation. *Polymer Degradation and Stability*, 93: 561-584.

Sivan A, Szanto M, and Pavlov V. 2006. Biofilm Development of the Polyethylene-degrading Bacterium Rhodococcus ruber. Applied Microbiology and Biotechnology 72: 346–352.

Sivan A. 2011. New Perspectives in Plastic Biodegradation. *Current Opinion in Biotechnology*, 22: 422-426.

Slater SC, Voige WH, and Dennis DE. 1988. Cloning and Expression in Escherichia Coli of the Alcaligenes eutrophus H16 poly-β-hydroxybutyrate biosynthesis pathway. Journal of Bacteriology 170: 4431–4436.

Stevens ES. 2003. What Makes Green Plastics Green? Biocycle 24: 24–27.

Sullivan D. 2011. Compostable Plastics and Organic Farming. BioCycle 52(3): 25.

Suresh B, Maruthamuthu S, Palanisamy N, Ragunathan R, Pandiyaraj KN, and Muralidharan VS. 2011. Investigation on Biodegradability of Polyethylene by Bacillus cereus strain Ma-Su Isolated from Compost Soil. International Research Journal of Microbiology 2: 292–302.

Suyama T., Tokiwa Y., Oichanpagdee P., Kanagawa T., Kamagata Y. 1998. Phylogenetic Affiliation of Soil Bacteria that degrade Aliphatic Polyesters Available Commercially as Biodegradable Plastics. *Applied and Environmental Microbiology*, 64: 5008-5011.

Takaku H, Kimoto A, Kodaira S, Nashimoto M, and Takagi M. 2006. Isolation of a Gram-positive poly(3-hydroxybutyrate) (PHB) Degrading Bacterium from Compost and Cloning and Characterization of a Gene Encoding PHB depolymerise of Bacillus Megaterium N-18-25-9. FEMS Microbiology Letters 264: 152–159.

Tokiwa Y and Calabia BP. 2009. Biodegradability of plastics. International Journal of Molecular Science 10: 3722–3742.

Trevino AL and Garcia G. 2011. Polyurethane foam as Substrate for Fungal Strains. Advances in Bioscience and Biotechnology 2: 52–58.

Trivedi Priya, Adria Hasan, Salman Akhtar, M. Haris Siddiqui, Usman Sayeed and M. Kalim A. Khan (2016): Role of Microbes in Degradation of Synthetic Plastics and Manufacture of bioplastics. *Journal of Chemical and Pharmaceutical Research*, 8(3):211-216 Tropical 51: 629–633.

Tsuchii A, Suzuki T, and Takahara Y. 1977. Microbial Degradation of Styrene Oligomer. Agricultural and Biological Chemistry 41: 2417–2421.

Underkoer LA. 1958. Production of Microbial Enzymes and their Applications. Applied Microbiology 6: 212–221.

USEPA. 1987. Ground water: Office of Research and Development, Center for Environmental Research Information, Robert S. Kerr Environmental Research Laboratory, EPA/625/6-87/016.

Usha R, Sangeetha T, and Palaniswamy M. 2011. Screening of Polyethylene Degrading Microorganisms from Garbage Soil. Libyan Agricultural Research Center Journal International 2: 200–204.

Veethahavya K.S., Rajath B.S., Sabike Noobia, Manoj Kumar B. (2016): Biodegradation of Low Density Polyethylene in Aqueous Media. *Procedia Environmental Sciences*, 35: 709 – 713

Volke-Sepulveda T, Saucedo-Castaneda G, Gutierrez-Rojas M, Manzur A, and Favela-Torres E. 2002. Thermally Treated Low Density Polyethylene Biodegradation by Penicillium Pinophilum and Aspergillus niger. Journal of Applied Polymer Science 83: 305–314.

Wackett LP and Hershberger CD. 2001. Biocatalysis and Biodegradation; Microbial Transformation of Webb JS, Nixon M, Eastwood IM, Greenhalgh M, Robson GD, and Handley PS. 2000. Fungal Colonization and Biodeterioration of Plasticized Polyvinyl Chloride. Applied and Environmental Microbiology 66(8): 3194–3200.

Williams SF and Peoples OP. 1996. Biodegradable Plastics from Plants. Chemtech 38: 38–44.

Witt U, Muller RJ, and Deckwer WD. 1997. Biodegradation Behavior and Material Properties of Aliphatic/Aromatic Polyesters of Commercial Importance. Journal of Environmental Polymer Degradation l5: 81–89.

Yamada-Onodera K, Mukumoto H, Katsuyaya Y, Saiganji A, and Tani Y. 2001. Degradation of Polyethylene by a Fungus Penicillium Simplicissimum YK. Polymer Degradation and Stability 72: 323–327.

Yayasekara R, Harding I, Bowater I, and Lonergan G. 2005. Biodegradability of Selected Range of Polymers and Polymer Blends and Standard Methods for Assessment of Biodegradation. Journal of Polymer Environment 13: 231.

Yutaka Tokiwa, Buenaventurada P. Calabia, Charles U. Ugwu and Seiichi Aiba (2009): Biodegradability of Plastics. *Int. J. Mol. Sci.*, 10, 3722-3742; doi:10.3390/ijms10093722

Zettler E.R., Mincer T.J. and L.A. Amaral-Zettler. 2013. Life in the ''Plastisphere'': Microbial Communities on Plastic Marine debris. *Environmental Science and Technology*, 47: 7137-7146.

Web help:

http://www.thehindu.com/sci-tech/science/plastic-degrading-bacteria-isolated/article8337703.ece

https://www.newscientist.com/article/dn14764-plastic-munching-bugs-turn-waste-bottles-into-cash/

https://pubs.acs.org/doi/full/10.1021/es801010e

http://science.sciencemag.org/content/351/6278/1196

Advances in Microbiology: *Applications & Significance* Pages 62-85
Edited by: Dr. Pawan Kumar 'Bharti'
ISBN: 978-93-86841-97-1
Edition: 2019
Published by: Discovery Publishing House Pvt. Ltd., New Delhi (India)

5

Antibiotics and their Mechanism of Action

[1]Harpreet Kaur, [2]Priyanka Chandra,
[1]Gurinderjeet Kaur and [1]Daljit Singh Arora

ABSTRACT

The chemotherapy of infectious diseases has proved to be a continuous struggle and for many years, the control of various diseases was confined to symptomatic cure which included personal hygiene, isolation of patient and good health. Chemotherapy started with the vaccination discovered by Edward Jenner but the term 'chemotherapy' was originally coined by Paul Ehrlich who discovered the first effective chemotherapeutic agent-arsphenamine/salvarsan, which opened the door to future developments in chemotherapy and antibiotics. The 20th century has witnessed a complete transformation in treatment of infectious diseases. The antibiotic era began with therapeutic applications of sulfonamides in 1930s, followed by a "golden" period (1935-1970) with a flurry of discoveries of effective antibiotics. Success story of antimicrobial drugs decreased the mortality rate and generated a misconception in the late 1960s and early 1970s that infectious diseases had been conquered. However, 1980s saw a decline in the discovery of new agents for clinical use. This period with a reduced rate of introduction of new agents has been accompanied by an alarming increase in drug-resistant microorganisms. Antimicrobial drug resistance may occur due to a pre-existing factor in the microorganisms or it may be due to some acquired factors by genetic changes or non-genetic mechanisms. Antimicrobial resistance can be categorized as microbial, clinical, cross and parallel or co-resistance. The most common mechanisms underlying bacterial resistance are: production of enzymes capable of inactivating the antimicrobials, altered binding sites, altered membrane permeability and enhanced efflux of antimicrobials. Enzyme production (β-lactamase) is the major mechanism of resistance to β-lactam antibiotics in many organisms while alterations in penicillin-binding proteins and decreased permeability of the bacterial outer membrane to β-lactams are the other rare mechanisms of resistance. Multiple drug-resistant microorganisms have increased around the world and pathogens such as methicillin-

1 Department of Microbiology, Guru Nanak Dev University, Amritsar-143005, India
2 ICAR-Central Soil Salinity Research Institute, Karnal, Haryana -132001, India

resistant *Staphylococcus aureus* (MRSA); vancomycin-resistant *Staphylococcus aureus* (VRSA); vancomycin-resistant Enterococci (VRE); extended spectrum β-lactamases (ESBLs) producing- *Escherichia coli* and *Klebsiella pneumoniae*; penicillin resistant *Streptococcus pneumoniae*; and *Pseudomonas aeruginosa*, are becoming resistant to almost every available antibiotic drug. The emergence and spread of antimicrobial resistance is an array of problems caused by various interconnected factors, many of which are related to over and misuse of antibiotics. Thus, antimicrobial resistance in addition to cost, toxicity and various side effects related to antibiotic consumption remains one of the biggest challenges all over the globe. Hence, this book chapter presents the description and the mechanism of the antibiotics.

Introduction

Ecosystem consists of a myriad of microorganisms belonging to diverse groups including actinomycetes, bacteria, viruses and fungi. Microorganisms are ubiquitous in nature and they are found in soil, mud, water, air, dead wood, clothes, food products, plants, animals. Many kinds of microorganisms colonize our body surface, alimentary tract and orifices. Our health and well being are influenced by the presence or absence of microorganisms in the environment. Their diverse activities vary from recovery of metals, increasing soil fertility, production of various useful compounds, to causing diseases in humans, animals and plants.

Humanity has been suffering from pandemics of cholera, plague, influenza, typhoid, tuberculosis and other infectious diseases. For centuries, man has been struggling to find cure against infections and diseases caused by microorganisms. A disease may be defined as any departure from normal state of health. Although chemotherapy started with the vaccination discovered by Edward Jenner in 1798 for small pox using cow pox vaccine against vaccinia virus but the term 'chemotherapy' was originally coined by German chemist-Paul Ehrlich, father of chemotherapy and immunology, whose contributions opened the door to future development in chemotherapy and antibiotics. Chemotherapy referred to the use of chemical substances to kill pathogenic microorganisms without injuring the host while modern definition of chemotherapy refers to the use of chemical substances to treat various aspects of a disease. The term generally implies to a chemical that has been synthesized by chemists or produced by the modification of a preexisting chemical. By contrast, antibiotics are the metabolic products of microorganisms. In general, naturally occurring substances are distinguished from the synthetic compounds by the name 'antibiotics' (French, 2006; Frere, 1995).

The word antibiotic is derived from the Greek term "antibiosis" which literally means 'against life'. The term antibiotic was originally coined by Paul Vuillemin but the present day use of the term was proposed by Waksman in 1945 as applying to those chemical substances of microbial origin which in small amount exert their antimicrobial effect (Alcamo, 2001). Although the majority of antibacterial and antifungal agents in clinical use are derived from natural products of microbial fermentations (e.g. aminoglycosides); most are semisynthetic *i.e.* chemically modified by the addition of extra chemical groups to improve their antibacterial or pharmacological properties (e.g. methicillin, ampicillin, cephalosporins and carbapenems). However, many more agents are purely synthetic e.g. sulphonamides, quinolones etc (Gould, 2007; 2009).

Microbes have made a phenomenal contribution to the health and well-being of people throughout the world. They produce a number of secondary metabolites which are an integral part of the pharmaceuticals currently available in the market (Demain and Sanchez, 2009).

It was the discovery of one of the most beneficial secondary metabolites *i.e.* penicillin from *Penicillium notatum* by Alexander Fleming in 1929, which revolutionized the field of modern medicine. The antibiotic era began in 1930s with the therapeutic applications of sulfonamides, (also termed as prontosil), the first commercially available antibacterial antibiotic, developed by a research team led by Gerhard Domagk. Discovery and development of sulfonamides was followed by a "golden" period (1935-1970) with a flurry of discoveries of antibiotics leading to more than a dozen classes of antibiotics including sulphonamides, β-lactams, aminoglycosides, chloramphenicol, tetracycline, macrolides, trimethoprim, rifamycins, quinolones, and glycopeptides (Golemi-Kotra *et al.*, 2003).

The emergence and spread of antimicrobial resistance is an array of problems caused by various interconnected factors, many of which are related to over and misuse of antibiotics (Overbye and Barrett, 2005). Thus, antimicrobial resistance in addition to cost, toxicity and various side effects related to antibiotic consumption remains one of the biggest challenges all over the globe (DiazGranados *et al.*, 2008; Hooper, 2001).

This demands the development of new antimicrobial compounds to answer the problem posed by resistant and other microorganisms (Chopra *et al.*, 1997). The answer lies in the modification of existing antibiotics, development of vaccines, or to develop some novel antimicrobial agents to which microorganisms have not yet been exposed. Natural resources especially actinomycetes, fungi and plants have been a rich repository for producing various antimicrobial agents. Recent years have witnessed a renewed interest towards exploring plants for developing potent antimicrobial agents with better efficacy and minimal side effects to fight microbial diseases (Girish and Satish, 2008).

Antibiotics and their Mode of Action

Most antibiotics used for the treatment of bacterial infections may be categorized either according to their principal mechanism of action or on the basis of their chemical structure. The main mechanism of action of antibiotics includes (Table 5.1).

- "Inhibition of cell-wall synthesis."
- "Disruption of cell membrane."
- "Inhibition of protein synthesis."
- Inhibition of DNA synthesis.
- "Interference with the synthesis of essential metabolites."

Table 5.1: Group of Antibiotics with their Mode of Action

Inhibits Cell Wall Synthesis			
Penicillins			
(bactericidal in nature: acts by blocking the cross linking catalysed by the enzyme transpeptidase)			
Group of antibiotics	Drugs	Antibacterial spectrum	Possible side effects
Penicillins **β- lactams**	Aqueous penicillin G Penicillin G Benzathine penicillin G Procaine penicillin G Penicillin V	*Streptococcus. pyogenes* *Streptococcus. agalactiae* *C. perfringens*	Hypersensitivity reaction Hemolytic anemia
Aminopeniclins	Ampicillin Amoxicillin	*Streptococcus. pyogenes* *Streptococcus. agalactiae* *C. perfringens* Gram-negative: *E. coli*	Hypersensitivity reaction Hemolytic anemia
Penicillinase-resistant-penicillins	Methicillin Nafcillin Oxacillin	*Streptococcus. pyogenes* *Streptococcus. agalactiae* *C. perfringens*	Hypersensitivity reaction Hemolytic anemia Interstitial nephritis
Penicillinase – susceptible penicillins	Cloxacillin, Dicloxacillin, Amoxicillin, Ampicillin, Flucloxacillin	*E. coli and* Penicillinase – producing *Staph. aureus*	
Antipseudomonal penicillins	Carbenicillin		Hypersensitivity reaction
	Ticarcillin	*Pseudomonas aeruginosa*	Hemolytic anemia
	Piperacillin		Interstitial nephritis

Cephalosporins			
First generation	Cefazolin Cephalexin	*S. aureus* *S. epidermidis* Some Gram-negatives: *E. coli* *Klebsiella*	Allergic reaction Coombs-positive anemia (3%)
Second generation	Cefoxitin	*Staph. Aureus*	Allergic Reaction
	Cefaclor	*Staph . epidermidis*	ETOH Disulfiram reaction
	Cefuroxime	Some Gram-negatives:	
	Cefamandole	*E. coli*	
	Cefprozil	*Klebsiella*	
Third generation	Cefixime, Ceftriaxone	*S. aureus*	Allergy, hypopro-thrombinemia
	Cefotaxime	*S. epidermidis*	ethanol Disulfiram reaction
	Ceftazidime	Gram-negative bacteria:	
	Cefoperazone	*Escherichia coli*	
	Cefpodoxime	*Klebsiella* spp.	
		Pseudomonas	Hypersensitivity,
Fourth generation	Cefepime	*Staph. aureus*, *Strep. pneumoniae*, *P. aeruginosa*, and *Enterococci*	Gastroin-testinal upset and nausea
Fifth generation	Ceftobiprole	methicillin-resistant *Staphy aureus*, penicillin-resistant *Strep pneumoniae*, *P. aeruginosa*, and *Enterococci*	
Other Cell Wall Inhibitors			
Glycopeptide	Vancomycin, Teicoplanin, Decaplanin	MRSA	Red man syndrome
(bactericidal: disrupts peptioglycan cross-linkage)		*Staph. Aureus*	Nephrotoxicity
		Staph. Epidermidis	"Ototoxicity"

b-**lactam antibiotic-Inhibitors**	Ampicillin-Sulbactam, Amoxicillin-Clavulanic Acid	*S . aureus*	Hypersensitivity Reaction
		S. epidermidis	Hemolytic anemia
		Escherichia coli	
		Klebsiella spp.	
Carbapenems	Imipenem (+ cilastatin)	*Enterococci, Staphylococccal* spp. *Listeria, Streptococci Enterobacteriaceae,* bacteroides *Acinetobacter* species	diarrhea, nausea, vomiting, skin rash and pruritus.
	Meropenem		
	Doripenem		
	Ertapenem		
Aztreonam	Aztreonam	*E. coli P. mirabilis Acinetobacter anitratus*	Chest discomfort cough difficulty with breathing or troubled breathing fever
Polymyxins	Polymyxin B	Topical Gram-negative infections	May cause redness, pain and edema at the injection site. If used as eye drops, may cause burning sensation, itching or temporary blindness .
	Polymyxin E		
			Nephrotoxicity
Bacitracin	Bacitracin	skin infection- associated bacteria.	Nephrotoxicity (albuminuria, cylindruria, azotemia, rising blood concentrations of the drug); GI effects (nausea, vomiting); pain at injection site; hypersensitivity reactions (rash)

Protein Synthesis Inhibition			
Are bactericidal in nature and cause damage by binding irreversibly to 30S ribosomal subunit.			
Aminoglycosides	Gentamicin Neomycin Amikacin Tobramycin Streptomycin	*Enterobacteriaceae* *Pseudomonas*	Nephrotoxic in nature. Ototoxic in nature
Tetra-cyclines (bacteriostatic: blocks tRNA)	Tetracycline Doxycycline Minocycline Demeclocycline	*Rickettsia* *Mycoplasma* *Spirochetes* (Lyme's disease)	Hepatotoxicity Tooth discoloration Impaired growth
Are bactericidal in nature and cause damage by binding irreversibly to 50S ribosomal subunit			
Macrolides	Erythromycin Azithromycin Clarithromycin	Some Species of *Streptococcus* *Haemophilus. Influenzae* *Mycoplamsa pneumonia*	Coumadin Interaction (cytochrome P450)
Chloram phenicol(broad spectrum)	Chloramphenicol	*Staphylococcus aureus, E. coli and Streptococcus pneumoniae,, Neisseria meningitidis, Strep pneumoniae* and *Haemophilus influenza*	Aplastic Anemia
Lincosamides	Clindamycin	Treatment of *Staphylococcal* and *Streptococcal infections. Bacteroides fragilis* some anaerobic strains	*Clostridium difficile*–associated diarrhea (pseudo-membranous colitis) clindamycin may cause esophagitis
Linezolid(variable)	Linezolid	VRE*Streptococcal* spp. MRSA	Side effects such as vomiting, Nausea, and Vaginal candidiasis

Strepto gramins	Quinupristin Dalfopristin Pristinamycin Virginamycin	VRE, VRSA	local irritation at peripheral administration sites, centrally mediated myalgia and arthralgia, nausea, and reversible rise in conjugated bilirubin -.
Inhibition of DNA Synthesis			
Fluoroquinolones			
(bactericidal by nature :mode is by inhibiting DNA gyrase)			
First generation	Nalidixic acid	Crucial for treatment of nosocomial infections	Adverse reactions are nausea, vomiting, and diarrhea, insomnia and serious neurological disorder myasthenia gravis. Overdose may also cause tendon rupture.

(http://www.orthobullets.com/basic-science/9059/antibiotic-classification-and-mechanism)

Inhibition of Cell Wall Synthesis

β-Lactam antibiotics such as cephalosporins (cephems), derivatives of penicillin (penams), carbapenems and monobactams are bactericidal and inhibit the peptidoglycan layer synthesis. Penicillin binding proteins (PBPs) promote the final step of peptidoglycan synthesis. The binding site of PBPs differs for β-Lactam antibiotics .

β-Lactam antibiotics have a structure analogous to the D-alanyl-D-alanine terminal portion of the NAM/NAG subunits in the cell wall. This structural similarity allows the nucleus of the antibiotics to bind to PBPs, which are essential for cross linking of the nascent peptidoglycan layer. "This irreversible inhibition of the PBPs prevents the final crosslinking (transpeptidation) of the nascent peptidoglycan layer, disrupting cell wall synthesis". Teichoplanin and vancomycin are the examples of such antibiotics which exert this mode of action. Vancomycin acts by interfering "with the formation of the glycosidic bonds between the sugars of the peptidoglycan monomers and those in the existing cell wall" (Bambeke *et al.*, 2004). **D-cycloserine** inhibits two enzymes involved in the precursor synthesis, preventing both conversion of L-alanine to D-alanine by racemase, and the construction of D-alanyl-D-alanine by D-Ala-D-Ala ligase. In the cytoplasm, muramyl pentapeptide is anchored via a water-soluble UDP-glucosamine moiety. Bacitracin binds to bactoprenol, a transporter protein which resulted in dephoshorylation of the molecule. Bactoprenol could not collect new monomers, so they are not inserted into nascent cell wall. "As the autolysins continue to break the peptide cross-links and new cross-links fail to form, the bacterium bursts from osmotic lysis" (Stone and Strominger, 1971). Several transpeptidases and transglycosylases connect the newly formed peptidoglycan structures to the cell wall peptidoglycan matrix.

Beta-lactams and glycopeptides are the two important classes of antibiotics which are involved in inhibition of cell wall synthesis. Planosporicin is one such lentibiotic with peptide origin, isolated from the *Planomonospora alba. This antibiotic* acts by binding to "lipid II, the immediate precursor for cell wall biosynthesis" resulting in inhibition of cell wall synthesis.

Disruption of Cell Membrane

The plasma membrane is a bilayered structure that separates the intracellular organelles from the exterior micro environment. Plasma membrane plays a crucial role in a number of cell functions by aiding in attachment to solid surfaces,functioning of ion conducting channels and promoting cell signal process. It also tethers together : the cell wall and the cytoskeleton. Rapid depolarization may occur due to plasma membrane disruption, which compromises membrane potential and subsequent inhibition of protein and nucleic acid synthesis may result in cell death.

Antibiotics like Colistin and Polymyxin B are produced from *Bacillus* spp. These antimicrobials have a general structure consisting of a cyclic peptide head attached to a long hydrophobic tail, which interacts with the gram negative outer membrane and cytoplamic membrane displacing bacterial counterions, causing outer membrane destabilization. They exert their antimicrobial activity in a detergent like manner, where the amino group (positive charged) of the peptide head electrostatically interacts with a portion of LPS layer carrying the negative charge. This interaction results in the outer membrane destabilization causing disruption of both outer and inner membranes (Newton, 1956; Chen and Fenigold, 1973; Imai *et al.*, 1975; Silverman *et al.*, 2003; Falagas and Kasiakou, 2005; Steenbergen *et al.*, 2005). Similarly, daptomycin has a distinct mechanism of action, disrupting multiple aspects of bacterial cell membrane function. It inserts into the cell membrane in a phosphatidyl glycerol dependent fashion, where it then aggregates. The aggregation of daptomycin alters the curvature of the membrane, which creates holes that leak ions. This causes rapid depolarization, resulting in a loss of membrane potential leading to inhibition of protein, DNA and RNA synthesis, which results in bacterial cell death (Pogliano *et al.*, 2012).

Protein Synthesis Inhibition

Translation is a fundamental process involving the mRNA template, larger 50S and smaller 30S ribosomal subunit, aminoacyl tRNA, GTP and some factors required for assemblage of the initiation complex. Within the ribosome, three sites, i.e., A, P and E are involve in translation process. The aminoacyl tRNA enters at tha A site; formation of peptidyl tRNA occurs at P site and finally the uncharged tRNA exists the ribosome through E site by contributing its amino acid to the peptide sequence.

Protein synthesis is an intricate process which involves several enzymes. However, the majority of antibiotics which inhibit protein synthesis act by interfering the translational steps involving either the 30S or 50S subunit of the bacterial ribosome. The antibiotics act by inhibiting 30S initiation complex consisting of an mRNA template, 30S subunit and f-met-tRNA, complexation of 30S initiation complex and the 50S ribosome to form 70S subunit and the elongation process of the polypeptide chain. Tetracyclines e.g. **Doxycycline** is a group of antibiotics which blocks the A site of the ribosome, thus preventing the aminoacyl-tRNA binding.

"Aminoglycoside antibiotics have an affinity for the 30S ribosome subunit. **Streptomycin**, one of the most commonly used aminoglycosides, interferes with the creation of the 30S initiation complex. **Kanamycin** and **tobramycin** also bind to the 30S ribosome and block the formation of the larger 70S initiation complex" (Kestell *et al.*, 2002).

Erythromycin is one such representative of macrolides, forms a complex with50S ribosome through its 23S rRNA component, by virtue of which the 50S subunit fails to assemble. Also, roxithromycin, clarithromycin, Erythromycin exhibit their mode of action by preventing the occurrence of the final transpeptidation step due to blockage polypeptide exporting tunnel (Menninger and Otto, 1982; Usary and Champney, 2001; Oyama *et al.*, 2007).

Peptidyl transferase is an important enzyme required in the final step, i.e., protein elongation. Antibiotics such as clindamycin and lincomycin inhibits peptidyl transferases whereas macrolides are not the inhibitors for this enzyme (Chang *et al.*, 1966). **Puromycin acts by causing termination in chain elongation process where it acts on 3′ terminus of aminocyl tRNA** (Nathans, 1964; Azzam and Algranati, 1973).

An aminoglycoside, **hygromycin B, bins to the 30S subunit of tRNA. It has been reported that binding of hygromycin B deforms the A sit of ribosome which further resulted in translocation of protein elongation** (McGaha and Champney, 2007).

Inhibition of DNA Synthesis

Interference with DNA synthesis requires several steps. These antimicrobial agents hamper the synthesis of nucleotides or their inter conversion, preventing

DNA from acting as a template and by interfering with the polymerization step of DNA synthesis thereby inhibiting the replication and transcription step. Antimicrobial drugs have been developed to target each of these steps. For example, the antimicrobial rifampin binds to DNA-dependent RNA polymerase, thereby inhibiting the initiation of RNA transcription. Quinolones are one such group of antibiotics which readily inhibits topoisomerase II (DNA gyrase), a key enzyme required for DNA replication (Nakamura and Yura, 1976; Schulz and Zillig, 1981; Campbell *et al.*, 2001). DNA gyrase causes uncoiling of the superhelical DNA strand by transient breakabe and joining of its phosphodiester backbone. This opens up the DNA strand for subsequent action by DNA/ RNA polymerases. **Norfloxacin, levofloxacin** and ciprofloxacin are some of the antibiotics which exhibit this mode of action (Hooper, 2001).

Interference with the Synthesis of Essential Metabolites

Sulfonamides or sulfa drugs represent a category of compounds whose mechanism is directed towards specific enzyme system. Sulfonamides are known to competitively inhibit para-aminobenzoic acid (PABA) due to their structural similarity with PABA. Many bacteria require para-aminobenzoic acid as a precursor to their synthesis of the essential coenzyme tetrahydrofolic acid (THFA). PABA is a structural part of the THFA acid molecule. In bacteria, dihydropteroate synthetase (DHPS) is an important enzyme needed for synthesis of folic acid from PABA, as it is essential for DNA synthesis. Sulfonamides act by competitively inhibiting DHPS, due to which PABA is not converted into folic acid. Sulfonamides are usually bacteriostatic in nature. The selective action of sulfonamides is explained by the fact that the PABA molecule and the sulfonamide molecule are so similar that the sulfonamide may enter the reaction in place of the PABA and block the synthesis of an essential cellular constituent (Henry, 1943; Smith *et al.*, 2000).

Antimicrobial Resistance

Antimicrobial resistance is one of the biggest challenges all over the globe specially in the treatment of nosocomial infections. Ernest Duchesne and Alexander Fleming originally discovered the antibacterial potential of *Penicillium* spp. in 1928 by isolation of penicillin (Cantas, 2013). Success stories of natural antibiotic penicillin, has revolutionized the world. Since then, a number of compounds with antimicrobial properties have been found. So these metabolites play a vital role in the development of modern medicine. Since their discovery, antibiotics have saved millions of people from life-threatening diseases. As bacterial resistance is increasing now a days, its treatment with ongoing antibiotics is a big question worldwide (Pouillard, 2002; Levy and Marshall, 2004; Alanis, 2005; Pallett and Hand, 2010). Supporting the foreseen development of antimicrobial resistance, Alexander Fleming, the discoverer of penicillin, once gave a statement in the New York Times that "the microbes are educated to resist penicillin and a host of penicillin fast organisms is bred out which can be passed to other individuals and from them to others until they reach someone who gets a septicemia or pneumonia which penicillin cannot save" (Levy, 2002). Active resistance is caused by selective environmental pressure which is linked to a class of antibiotic whereas passive resistance is a result of non-antibiotic linked processes. Antimicrobial resistance is attributed to various factors which mainly include human practices. Resistance to antibiotics is either natural or intrinsic and mutational or acquired. Thus, normally susceptible populations of bacteria may become resistant to antimicrobial agents through pre-existing factor in the microorganisms or it may be due to some factors acquired by genetic changes or non genetic mechanisms. Genetic resistance may be chromosomal (due to mutations in chromosomal DNA) and/or extra chromosomal resistance (due to resistant plasmids occurring via transduction and conjugation). Misuse of antibiotics by prescribing the antibiotics in a wrong manner by physicians leading to a development of antimicrobial resistance (Arnold and Straus, 2005). The past few decades have seen an alarming increase in the prevalence of antibiotic resistance microorganisms (Livermore, 2009). Over the last few decades multidrug resistant organisms are becoming difficult to treat thus causing number of diseases worldwide. These includes VRE (Vancomycin Resistant *Enterococci*), MRSA (methicillin/oxacillin-resistant *Staphylococcus aureus),* PRSP - penicillin-resistant *Streptococcus pneumonia,* ESBLs - Extended-spectrum beta-lactamases (which are resistant to cephalosporins and monobactams). MRSA and VRE and PRSP are the leading cause of diseases in non- hospital associated settings.whereas ESBL result in various nosocomial infections all over the globe (Toadar, 2009). MRSA are resistant not only to methicillin's action as well as Beta-lactams such as cephalosporin and penicillin. But to several classes of antibiotics. Several troublesome reports on MRSA, VRSA (Vancomycin-resistant *S. aureus*), Hospital-Associated MRSA (HA-MRSA) or Community-Associated MRSA (CA-MRSA) are the major contributors to the struggling medical history against the *Staphylococcal* infections. HA-MRSA occurs most frequently in patients with weak immunity. Life threatening infections, such as blood and surgical infections is commonly associated with MRSA. "More people in the U.S. die from MRSA infection than AIDS. Methicilin resistant *S. aureus* was responsible for an estimated 94,000 life threatening infections, as reported by US Centers for Disease Control and prevention (CDC). That same year, roughly 16,000 people in the U.S. died from AIDS, according to CDC" (Klevens *et al.*, 2007). "Each year in the United States, at least 2 million people acquiring serious infections with bacteria that are resistant to one or more of the commercially available antibiotics, as reported by US department of Health and Human Services, (2013)". It has been observed that Gram negative bacteria are now a days the major contributors in developing resistance The most serious gram negative infections are health care associated including pathogens like *Enterobacteriaceae, Pseudomonas aeruginosa* etc.

Extended-Spectrum Beta-Lactamase (ESBL) - Producing Gram-Negative Bacteria

"Extended-spectrum β-lactamases (ESBLs) are a group of plasmid-mediated, diverse, complex and rapidly evolving enzymes that are posing a major therapeutic challenge today in the treatment of hospitalized and community-based patients" (Rawat and Nair, 2010) and are commonly found in *Enterobacteriaceae.* ESBLs hydrolyse penicillins, oxyimino-cephalosporins (cefotaxime, ceftazidime), cephalosporins (extended- and narrow-spectrum), monobactams such as Aztreonam. Most common ESBL producers are *E. coli* and *Klebsiella pneumoniae,* and, but also include *Enterobacteriaeae.* The ESBL encoding genes can be easily transferred to various bacteria by means of plasmids, which may also carry genes for some other non- beta Lactams such as chloramphenicol,tetracyclines and sulfamethoxazole-trimethoprim, in addition to ESBL thus proving their treatment to be a biggest challenge. ESBL producers are mostly found in catheter tips, blood, sputum, peritoneal fluid etc. ESBLs owe their emergence to overuse and misuse of antibiotics which are mostly having extended spectrum as well as transmission from patient to patient or health care workers; where the lower portion of GI tract mainly harbours these organisms. Thus we can say that the resistance problem is widespread and continuously bothering the world. So to overcome the problem, researchers need to know the mechanism of antibiotic resistance.

Mechanism of Bacterial Resistance

There are different mechanisms by which bacteria offer resistance depending upon the species: (*i*) Antibiotic inactivation–antibiotic molecule is inactivated directly. (Wright, 2005) (*ii*) Target modification leading to alteration in antibiotic sensitivity (*iii*) "Efflux pumps and outer membrane (OM) permeability changes" leading to reduction in intracellular drug concentration or (*iv*) Target bypass, a mechanism, by virtue of which " some bacteria become refractory to specific antibiotics by bypassing the inactivation of a given enzyme" (Fig. 5.1)

This mechanism of resistance has been found in many sulfonamide- and trimethoprim- resistant bacteria. Antibiotics such as trimethoprim and sulfonamides have been found to inhibit dihydrofolate reductase (DHFR) and dihydropteroate synthase (DHPS) enzymes respectively, which play a key role in tetrahydrofolate biosynthesis. Thus, the resistance mechanism adopted by an organism depends upon the nature and target site of the antibiotic within the cell and involvement of either the chromosomal mutation or resistance plasmid.

Mechanism of Drug Resistance

Inactivation of Antibiotic
- Group transfer
- Hydrolysis
- Redox process

Genetic approach

Biochemical approach

Mutations
- Hypermutators
- Spontaneous mutations
- Adaptive mutagenesis

Modification of Efflux pumps and Outer Membrane Permeability

Target bypass

Horizontal gene transfer
- Plasmids
- (conjugative) transponsons
- Integrons

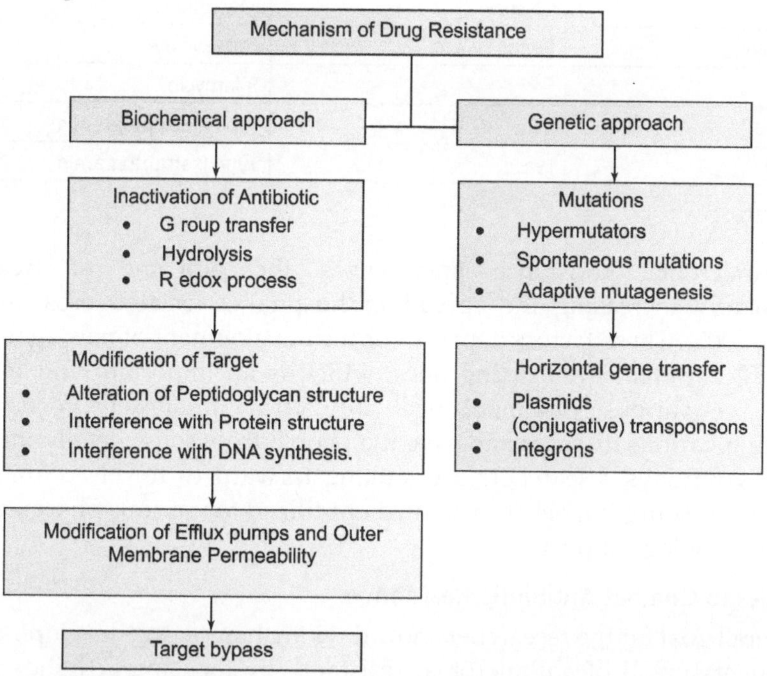

Fig. 5.1: Diagrammatic Representation of Drug Resistance mechanism

Modification of Target

- Alteration of Peptidoglycan structure.
- Interference with Protein structure.
- Interference with DNA synthesis.

Table 5.2: Enzymatic approach for inactivation of antibiotics

Method	Enzyme/ groups involved	Target Antibiotics
Hydrolysis	β-lactams	Macrolides
		Aminoglycosides
		Chloramohenicol
Group transfer	Acyl	Type A streptogramin
	Phorphoryl	Aminoglycosides
		Macrolides
		Rifamycin
		Peptide
	Thiol	Fosfomycin
	Nucleotidyl	Aminoglycoside
		Lincosamide
	ADP-ribosyl	Rifamycin
	Glycosyl	Macrolide
Other	Redox	Tetracycline
		Rifamycin
		Type A streptogramin
	Lyase	Type B streptogramin

(Wright, 2005)

Antimicrobial resistance antagonizes the outcome of treatment, subsequently increasing the spread of hospital associated cross-infection (French, 2005). These factors demand for the development of new agents with better efficacy than the existing ones; which is an important and foremost priority of various pharmaceutical industries immensely focusing on combating various diseases and save the people from these deadly infectious agents. Nowadays researchers are looking forward to novel antimicrobials from various sources which can be further utilized for various pharmaceutical and biotechnological purposes.

Strategies to Combat Antibiotic Resistance

The overall goal for the researchers now days are hampering development and subsequent spread of antimicrobial resistance by focusing activities around the following aims.

1. Thorough knowledge of antimicrobial resistance.
2. "Conserve and steward the effectiveness of existing treatments".
3. Promote the development of novel antimicrobials which could be of use for diagnostics and novel therapies.

Description of Some of the Pathogenic Bacteria

Gram-positive Bacteria

Enterobacter faecalis: Gram-positive cocci, catalase negative and occur in chains. It mainly inhabitates human colon, however, urethra and female genital tract can also be colonized. The bacterium causes urinary and biliary tract infections most frequently while it may also enter bloodstream during gastrointestinal (GI) or genitourinary tract infections.

Staphylococcus aureus: Staphylococci are Gram-positive, facultatively anaerobic, non-motile, non-sporulating cocci and occur in irregular clusters. They give coagulase and catalase positive; oxidase, indole and H_2S negative reactions. *S. aureus*, a common human pathogen and is mainly a nasal resident but also found on human skin and its transmission occurs via hands. *S. aureus* is responsible for a number of hospital-acquired infections. It is often responsible for abscesses of many organs, endocarditis, gastroenteritis (food poisoning), toxic shock syndrome, hospital acquired pneumonia, surgical wound infection and sepsis.

Staphylococcus epidermidis: Gram-positive cocci occur in clusters, catalase positive and coagulase negative. *S. epidermidis* occurs as normal flora of human skin and mucous membranes. It is a major cause of hospital acquired infections and is mainly responsible for endocarditis on prosthetic heart valves, prosthetics hip infection, intravascular catheter infection, cerebrospinal fluid shunt infection and neonatal sepsis

Streptococcus pneumoniae: Gram-positive "lancet shaped" cocci occur in pairs (diplococci) or short chains. They are catalase negative and possess prominent polysaccharide capsule. *S. pnemoniae* inhabitates upper respiratory tract and the transmission occurs via respiratory droplets. The most common diseases caused by the organism are pneumonia and meningitis in adults; and otitis media and sinusitis in children.

Gram-negative Bacteria

Escherichia coli: Gram-negative motile rods, catalase positive, oxidase negative, facultatively anaerobic and ferment lactose. *E. coli* mainly inhabits human colon but can also colonizes vagina and urethra. It is mainly acquired during birth in neonatal meningitis and by the faecal-oral route in diarrhea. Urinary tract infections (UTI), sepsis, neonatal meningitis and traveller's diarrhea are the most common diseases caused by *E. coli*.

Klebsiella pneumoniae: Facultative, short, plump, non-motile, Gram-negative rods with large polysaccharide capsule. It gives urease, nitrate and Voges-prausker positive reactions. However, it does not produce indole and are methyl red negative. Colonies are large, round and typically mucoid. *K. pneumoniae* is often present in human upper respiratory tract and enteric tracts. It causes pneumonia, may also be responsible for urinary tract and wound infections, septicemia and meningitis.

Pseudomonas aeruginosa: Pseudomonads are aerobic Gram-negative and non-lactose fermenting rods producing a blue pigment (pyocyanin), and are oxidase-positive which distinguishes it from members of family Enterobacteriaceae. Environmental water sources are their main habitat e.g. hospital respirators and humidifiers. Pseudomonads also inhabit the skin, upper respiratory tract and colon (10%) of people. It causes wound infections, urinary tract infections, pneumonia and sepsis.

Salmonella species: Facultative, Gram-negative, non-lactose fermenting rods and produces H_2S. Mainly human colon is the only habitat while some *Salmonella* spp. are also found in the colon of animals. Three kinds of clinical diseases are associated with *Salmonella* infections- enteric fever (typhoid), food poisoning and septicaemia.

Shigella flexneri: Facultative, non-motile, non-lactose fermenting, Gram-negative rods. It inhabits human colon only, unlike *Salmonella,* there are no animal carriers for *Shigella.* It causes a severe diarrhea called bacillary dysentery (enterocolitis).

Methodology for the Biochemical Characterization of Pathogenic Bacteria

Gram Staining

A bacterial smear prepared in a drop of water on a glass slide should be air dried and heat fixed. The smear should be covered with crystal violet for 1 min and washed off with tap water. After washing, the smear should be flooded with Gram's iodine solution for 1 min. Iodine should be drained off and the smear should be decolourized with 95% ethyl alcohol till purple colour of crystal violet failed to wash out from smear. Again after washing under tap water and draining completely, the smear should be counterstained with safranin for 45 seconds. Then it should be washed off with tap water and after air drying, and then first observed under low power objective of microscope, then under high power objective and finally under oil immersion. Gram-positive bacteria stained dark violet in colour whereas the Gram-negative bacteria should be stained pink with counterstain.

Catalase Test

This test is used to differentiate catalase producing bacteria such as staphylococci from non-catalase producing bacteria such as streptococci.

Catalase enzyme produced by the test organism act on hydrogen peroxide to produce hydrogen and oxygen which is indicated by the production of gas bubbles. A small amount of the culture to be tested should be picked up with a sterile glass rod and immersed in 3 ml of 3% (v/v) hydrogen peroxide (H_2O_2) solution. Appearance of bubbles is indicative of the catalase production.

Coagulase Test

This test is performed to differentiate *S. aureus* from *S. epidermidis*. *S. aureus* produces an enzyme coagulase which causes plasma to clot by converting soluble fibrinogen to insoluble fibrin. A uniform suspension of the bacterial isolate should be made in a drop of normal saline on a slide and should be mixed with a drop of plasma. A positive reaction indicated by visible clumping of the suspension with plasma within a minute.

Nitrate Reduction Test

This test is used to differentiate nitrate reductase producing members of Enterobacteriaceae from Gram-negative bacteria that do not produce the enzyme. Sterilized nitrate broth is inoculated with the organisms to be tested and incubated for 4 h at 37°C. Nitrate reductase producing organisms reduce nitrate to nitrite, which is tested by adding one drop each of sulphanilic acid and α-naphthylamine reagents. The broth should be mixed well and the formation of pink-red colour indicated the positive reaction.

Oxidase Test

Oxidases producing bacterial cultures such as *P. aeruginosa* are differentiated using oxidase test depending upon their ability to oxidize a redox dye tetramethyl-p-phenylenediamine dihydrochloride to a deep purple colour. Two ml (2 ml) of freshly prepared oxidase reagent should be added to a piece of filter paper. Then a colony of the culture to be tested should be smeared onto it using a sterilized glass rod. A positive reaction indicated by an intense deep purple colour appearing within 5-10 sec.

Urease Test

This test is helpful in differentiating enterobacteria as urease enzyme produced by cultured bacteria act on urea and ammonium carbonate is formed with the release of ammonia. The medium becomes alkaline and a change in its colour is observed due to change in the phenol red indicator. Motility indole urea (MIU) agar slants should be inoculated with bacteria to be tested and incubated overnight at 37°C. A red-pink colour of the slant is indicative of the positive test.

Indole Test

This is an important test for the identification of Enterobacteriaceae such as *E. coli*. It demonstrates the ability of certain bacteria to break down the amino acid tryptophan to indole which is then tested by a colorimetric reaction using p-dimethylaminobenzaldehyde.

Peptone water (5 ml) should be inoculated with the organisms to be tested and incubated at 37°C for 24 h. After incubation, 0.5 ml of Kovac's reagent should be added and mixed thoroughly. After mixing, the alcoholic layer separated from aqueous layer and reddening of alcoholic layer within few minutes is indicative of the positive reaction.

Methyl Red Test

This test is employed to detect enterobacteria which ferment glucose to produce sufficient acidity by causing pH to drop below 4.4 and is detected with methyl red as an indicator. The organisms to be tested should be inoculated into 5 ml of sterile glucose phosphate broth and incubated overnight at 37°C. Then five drops of methyl red should be added and mixed thoroughly. Bright red colour is indicative of positive test while yellow colour suggested a negative test.

Voges-Proskauer Test

This test is helpful to further differentiate enteric organisms such as *E. coli, K. pneumoniae* and some strains of *Enterobacter*. Voges-Proskauer (VP) test determines the capability of these organisms to ferment sugars and produce nonacidic or neutral end products such as acetylmethylcarbinol (or acetoin) which is converted to diacetyl. It is then converted to a pink coloured compound by the action of reagents.

The test organisms should be inoculated into 2 ml of glucose phosphate peptone water and incubated at 37°C for 24 h. Then 0.6 ml of Barritt's A and 0.2 ml of Barritt's B reagents should be added to the test tube, mixed thoroughly and then kept at room temperature for 1 h. Pink red colour formation demonstrate a positive reaction.

Citrate Utilization Test

This test is performed for identification of enterobacteria and based on the ability of an organism to utilize citrate (the only source of carbon) and ammonia (the only source of nitrogen). The citrate utilization followed by an alkaline reaction (change of the colour from light green to blue) in the medium is taken as positive reaction.

Sterile Simmon's citrate medium should be inoculated with the cultures to be tested and incubated at 35°C up to 4 days. Blue colour and streak of growth indicate positive result while persistence of original green colour and no growth indicate negative result.

Gelatin Liquefaction Test

This test is performed for the identification of pseudomonads. Gelatinase enzyme secreted by organisms, act on gelatin which is then liquefied. Nutrient gelatin medium should be inoculated with the test organism and incubated at 37°C for 72 h. Then the tubes should be chilled at 4°C for 30 min and results were recorded. Medium in fluid state shows a positive test while medium in solid state indicates negative test.

Hydrogen Sulphide Production

This test is performed mainly for the identification of hydrogen sulphide producing enteric bacteria and also helpful in differentiating *Salmonella* spp. from the coliforms. Decomposition of sulphur containing amino acids by enterobacteria produces hydrogen sulphide which reacts with ferrous ions and formation of ferric sulphide imparts black colour to the medium. Triple sugar iron (TSI) agar slants should be streaked with inoculum, incubated at 37°C for 7 days and observed for the blackening caused by H_2S production.

Biochemical Reactions on Triple Sugar Iron (TSI) Agar Slants

TSI agar slant identification is helpful in differentiating members of Enterobacteriaceae by their specific reactions, such as, alkaline reaction (red colour) is shown by the organisms which do not ferment any of the sugars; fermentation of sugars is indicated by yellow colour of the indicator phenol red; gas production ($CO_{2)}$ is indicated by splitting of the agar; and H_2S production which reacts with ferrous ions and imparts black colour to the medium. TSI slants should be streaked with the culture to be tested and after inoculation, the slants should be incubated at 37°C for 18-24 h and should be observed for the various reactions.

Description of Antibiotic Assays

The following methods describe the methodology to carries out antibiotic assay:

Disc Diffusion Method

Sensitivity of different bacterial strains to antibiotics can be measured in terms of zone of inhibition using agar well diffusion assay (Bauer *et al.*, 1966). This is the modified version of the Kirby-Bauer method. The plates containing Mueller-Hinton/Nutrient agar media should be spread with 0.2 ml of the inoculums of the pathogens. Disc of 8mm diameter should be placed on the agar plates using a sterilized forceps. The plates inoculated with different bacteria were incubated at 37ºC upto 48 h and diameter of any resultant zone of inhibition was measured. For each combination of antibiotics and the bacterial strain, the experiment should be performed in duplicate and repeated thrice.

Viable Cell Count Method

Bactericidal activity of antibiotics can be measured by viable cell count method (Toda *et al.*, 1989). Five ml of 4 h grown inoculum was diluted serially to 10^{-3} with double strength nutrient broth. Equal volumes of the diluted inoculum and the antibiotics to be tested should be mixed and incubated at 37ºC. At different time intervals *viz.* 0, 1, 2, 3..., 24 h, 0.1 ml of the mixed suspension should be spread on two separate nutrient agar plates which should be incubated for 24 h at 37ºC. The mean number of colonies were obtained and compared with that of control in which the sample was replaced with sterilized distilled water/acetone. Each experiment should be repeated thrice and the results can be expressed as number of viable cells as a percentage of control.

Minimum Inhibitory Concentration (MIC)

Minimum inhibitory concentration of the antibiotics can be worked out by agar dilution method. A stock solution of antibiotics at the concentration of 200 mg/ml should be prepared and incorporated into nutrient agar medium. The final concentrations of the antibiotics in the medium containing plates ranged from 1-10% (w/v). These plates should be inoculated with 0.1 ml of the activated bacterial strain/s. The plates should be incubated at 37ºC for 24 h and the lowest concentration of the extract causing complete inhibition of the bacterial growth was taken as MIC. The results should be compared with that of control in which the sample was replaced with sterilized distilled water. The experiment should be performed in duplicate and repeated three times.

REFERENCES

Alanis, A.J. (2005). Resistance to Antibiotics: Are We in the Post-antibiotic Era? *Archives of Medical Research* 36: 697–705.

Alcamo, E. (2001) *Fundamentals of Microbiology* 6th Edition. Jones and Bartlett Publishers, Sudbury, Massachusetts.

Arnold, S. and Straus, S. (2005) Interventions to Improve Antibiotic Prescribing Practices in Ambulatory Care. *Cochrane Database of Systematic Reviews* 4: CD003539.

Azzam, M.E. and Algranati, I.D. (1973) Mechanism of Puromycin Action: Fate of Ribosomes After Release of Nascent Protein Chains from Polysomes. *Proceedings of the National Academy of Sciences* USA 70: 3866–3869.

Bambeke, V.F., Van Laethem, Y., Courvalin, P., and Tulkens, P. M. (2004). Glycopeptide Antibiotics. *Drugs* 64: 913-936.

Bauer, A.W., Kirby, W.M.M., Sherris, J.C. and Turck, M. (1966). Antibiotic Susceptibility Testing by a Standardized Single Disk Method. *American Journal of Clinical Pathology* 43: 493-496.

Campbell, E.A., Korzheva, N., Mustaev, A., Murakami, K., Nair, S., Goldfarb, A. and Darst, S.A. (2001). Structural Mechanism for Rifampicin Inhibition of Bacterial RNA Polymerase *Cell* 104: 901–912.

Cantas, L., Shah, S.Q.A., Cavaco, L.M., Manaia, C.M., Walsh, F., Popowska, M., Garelick, H., Bürgmann, H. and H. Sorum, H. (2013). A Brief Multi-disciplinary Review on Antimicrobial Resistance in Medicine and Its Linkage to the Global Environmental Microbiota. *Frontiers in Microbiology* 4: 96.

Chang, F. N., Sih, C. J. and Weisblum, B. (1966). Lincomycin, An Inhibitor of Aminoacyl sRNA Binding to Ribosomes. *Proceedings of the National Academy of Sciences of the United States of America* 55: 431.

Chen, C.H. and Feingold, D.S. (1973). The Mechanism of Polymyxin B Action and Selectivity Toward Biologic Membranes. *Biochemistry* 12: 2105–2111.

Chopra, I., Hodgson, J., Metcalf, B. and Poste, G. (1997). The Search for Antibacterial Agents Effective Against Bacteria Resistant to Multiple Antibiotics. *Antimicrobial Agents and Chemotherapy* 41: 497-503.

Demain, A. L. and Sanchez, S. (2009). Microbial Drug Discovery: 80 Years of Progress. *The Journal of Antibiotics* 62: 5-16.

DiazGranados, C.A., Cardo, D.M. and McGowan Jr., J.E. (2008). Antimicrobial Resistance: International Control Strategies, with a Focus on Limited-resource Settings. *International Journal of Antimicrobial Agents* 32: 1-9.

Falagas, M.E. and Kasiakou, S.K. (2005). Colistin: the Revival of Polymyxins for the Management of Multi-drug Resistant Gram-negative Bacterial Infections. *Clinical Infectious Diseases* 40: 1333–1341.

French, G. L. (2005). Clinical Impact and Relevance of Antibiotic Resistance. *Advanced Drug Delivery Reviews* 57: 1514-1527.

French, G. L. (2006). Bactericidal Agents in the Treatment of MRSA Infections- The Potential Role of Daptomycin. *Journal of Antimicrobial Chemotherapy* 58: 1107-1117.

Frere, J.M. (1995). Beta-lactamases and Bacterial Resistance to Antibiotics. *Molecular Microbiology* 16: 385-395.

Girish, H.V. and Satish, S. (2008). Antibacterial Activity of Important Medicinal Plants on Human Pathogenic Bacteria—A Comparative Analysis. *World Applied Sciences Journal* 5: 267-271.

Gould, I.M. (2007). Antimicrobials: An Endangered Species? *International Journal of Antimicrobial Agents* 30: 383-384.

Gould, I.M. (2009). Antibiotic Resistance: The Perfect Storm. *International Journal of Antimicrobial Agents* 34: S2-5.

Golemi-Kotra, D., Cha, J.Y., Meroueh, S.O., Vakulenko, S.B. and Mobashery, S. (2003). Resistance to β-lactam Antibiotics and its Mediation by the Sensor Domain of the Transmembrane Blar Signaling Pathway in *Staphylococcus aureus*. *Journal of Biological Chemistry* 278: 18419-18425.

Henry, R. J. (1943). The Mode of Action of Sulfonamides. *Bacteriological Reviews* 7: 175-262.

Hooper, D.C. (2001). Emerging Mechanisms of Fluoroquinolone Resistance. *Emerging Infectious Diseases* 7: 337-341.

Hooper, D.C. (2001). Mechanisms of Action of Antimicrobials: Focus on Fluoroquinolones. *Clinical Infectious Diseases* 15: 9-15.

Imai, M., Inoue, K. and Nozima, S. (1975). Effect of Polymyxin B on Liposomal Membrane Derived from *Escherichia coli* Lipids. *Biochimica et Biophysica acta* 375: 130-137.

Kestell, D., Lai, S., Liang, G., Waters, S. and Wladichuk, A. (2002). Effects of Kanamycin and Streptomycin on the Macromolecular Composition of Streptomycin-Sensitive and Resistant *Escherichia coli* Strains. *The Journal of Experimental Microbiology and Immunology* 2: 103-108.

Klevens, R.M., Morrison, M.A., Nadle, J., Petit, S., Ken Gershman, K., Ray, S., Harrison, L.H., Lynfield, R., Dumyati, G., Townes, J.M., Craig,A.S., Zell, E.R., Fosheim, G.E., McDougal,

L.K., Carey, R.B. and Fridkin, S.K. (2007). Invasive Methicillin-Resistant *Staphylococcus aureus* Infections in the United States. *The Journal of the American Medical Association* 298: 1763-1771.

Levy, S. B. and Marshall, B. (2004). Antibacterial Resistance Worldwide: Causes, Challenges and Responses. *Nature Medicine* 10: 122–129.

Levy, S.B. (2002). Factors Impacting on the Problem of Antibiotic Resistance. *Journal of Antimicrobial Chemotherapy* 49: 25-30.

Livermore, D.M. (2009). Has the Era of Untreatable Infections Arrived? *Journal of Antimicrobial Chemotherapy* 64: i29–i36.

McGaha, S.M. and Champney, W.S. (2007). Hygromycin B Inhibition of Protein Synthesis and Ribosome Biogenesis in *Escherichia coli*. *Antimicrobial Agents and Chemotherapy* 51: 591–596.

Menninger, J.R., and Otto, D.P. (1982). Erythromycin, Carbomycin and Spiramycin Inhibit Protein Synthesis by Stimulating the Dissociation of Peptidyl-tRNA from Ribosomes. *Antimicrobial Agents and Chemotherapy* 21: 810–818.

Nakamura, Y. and Yura, T. (1976). Effects of Rifampicin on Synthesis and Functional Activity of DNA-Dependent RNA Polymerase in *Escherichia coli*. *Molecular Genetics and Genomics* 145: 227–237.

Nathans, D. (1964). Puromycin Inhibition of Protein Synthesis: Incorporation of Puromycin Into Peptide Chains. *Biochemistry* 51: 581-592.

Newton, B.A. (1956). Properties and Mode of Action of the Polymyxins. *Bacteriological Reviews* 20: 14- 27.

Overbye, K.M. and Barrett, J.F. (2005). Antibiotics: Where Did We Go Wrong? *Drug Discovery Today* 10: 45-52.

Oyama, T., Matsushita, K., Sakuta, T., Tokuda, M., Tatsuyama, S., Nagaoka, S. and Torii, M. (2007). Roxithromycin Inhibits Tumor Necrosis Factorαinduced Matrix Metalloproteinase1 Expression through Regulating Mitogenactivated Protein Kinase Phosphorylation and Ets1 Expression. *Journal of Periodontal Research*. 42: 53-61.

Pallett, A. and Hand, K. (2010). Complicated Urinary Tract Infections: Practical Solutions for the Treatment of Multiresistant Gram-negative Bacteria. *Journal of Antimicrobial Chemotherapy* 65: 25–33.

Pogliano, J., Pogliano, N. and Silverman, J.A. (2012). Daptomycin-mediated Reorganization of Membrane Architecture Causes Mislocalization of Essential Cell Division Proteins. *Journal of Bacteriology* 194: 4494–4504.

Pouillard, J. (2002). A Forgotten Discovery: Doctor of Medicine Ernest Duchesne, thesis (1874-1912). *Journal of the History of Medicine and Allied Sciences* 36: 11–20.

Rawat, D. and Nair, D. (2010). Extended-spectrum β-lactamases in Gram Negative Bacteria. *Journal of Global Infectious Diseases* 2: 263-274.

Schulz, W. and Zillig, W. (1981). Rifampicin Inhibition of RNA Synthesis by Destabilization of DNA-RNA Polymerase-oligonucleotide Complexes. *Nucleic Acids Research* 9: 6889–6906.

Silverman, J.A., Perlmutter, N.G. and Shapiro, H.M. (2003). Correlation of Daptomycin Bactericidal Activity and Membrane Depolarization in *Staphylococcus aureus*. *Antimicrobial Agents and Chemotherapy* 47: 2538–2544.

Smith, W.L., DeWitt, D.L. and Garavito, R.M. (2000). Cyclooxygenases: Structural, Cellular, and Molecular Biology. *Annual Review of Biochemistry* 69: 145–182

Steenbergen, J. N., Alder, J., Thorne, G. M. and Tally, F. P. (2005). Daptomycin: A Lipopeptide Antibiotic for the Treatment of Serious Gram-positive Infections. *Journal of antimicrobial Chemotherapy* 55: 283-288.

Stone, K.J. and Strominger, J.L. (1971). Mechanism of Action of Bacitracin: Complexation with Metal Ion and C&&-Isoprenyl Pyrophosphate. *Proceedings of the National Academy of Sciences* USA 68: 3223–3227.

Toda, M., Okubo, S., Hiyoshi, R. and Shimamura, T. (1989). The Bactericidal Activity of Tea and Coffee. *Letters in Applied Microbiology* 8: 123-125.

Todar, K. (2009). Online Textbook of Bacteriology. http://textbookof bacteriology.net/

Usary, J. and Champney, W.S. (2001) Erythromycin Inhibition of 50S Ribosomal Subunit Formation in *Escherichia coli* Cells. *Molecular Microbiology* 40: 951–962.

Wright, G. D. (2005). Bacterial Resistance to Antibiotics: Enzymatic Degradation and Modification. *Advanced Drug Delivery Reviews* 57: 1451-1470.

Advances in Microbiology: *Applications & Significance* Pages 86-122
Edited by: Dr. Pawan Kumar 'Bharti'
ISBN: 978-93-86841-97-1
Edition: 2019
Published by: Discovery Publishing House Pvt. Ltd., New Delhi (India)

6

Interactions of Fungal Entomopathogens with their Insect Hosts

[1]D. Sudha Rani, [2]Ch. Chiranjeevi, [3]T. Madhumathi and [4]S. Krishnam Raju

Fungi are grouped as a separate kingdom in taxonomy which posses a wide variety of organisms that reproduce by spores including the mushrooms, molds, yeasts and mildews. A group of fungi that kill an insect by attacking and infecting its insect host is called entomopathogenic fungi (Singkaravanit *et al.*, 2010). These Entomopathogenic fungi (EPF) act as a parasite of insects either by killing or seriously disabling them. EPFs are considered to be common natural enemies of arthropods worldwide as they cause lethal infections and regulate insect and mite population in nature by epizootic and hence regarded as potential biological control agents (Burges, 1981). These fungi usually attach to the external body surface of insects in the form of microscopic spores.

History

- Aristole was the first person to mention in his book "*Historia Animalium*"- about the disease of honey bee.
- Disease of insects as included in the book "An Introduction of Entomology" by Kirby and Spence (1826).
- An Italian scientist Agostiono Bassi showed that a microorganism *Beauveria bassiana* white muscardine fungus of silkworm.
- Later, Louis Pasteur studied the disease of silkwork (1865-70).
- Concept of utilizing disease to control insect was used by Russian Scientist, Elia Metchnikoff in 1879 by infecting the beetle grubs of *Anisoplia austriaca* with *Metarizhium anisophliae* the green muscardine fungus.
- First laboratory for Insect pathology was established in the year 1943 at the University of California.

[1] Scientist (Entomology) & Head, Agricultural Research Station, Garikapadu, Krishna District-521175, Andhra Pradesh, India

[2,3] Professor (Entomology), Agricultural College, Bapatla, Andhra Pradesh 522101, India

[4] Principal Scientist (Plant Pathology), APPRI & RARS, Maruteru, Andhra Pradesh 534122, India

Coevolution of Fungi and Host

The pathogen and host adapt to maximize their reproductive output and ultimate fitness by adopting physiological, ecological and behavioral adaptations that are as diverse as the organisms themselves.

Coevolution is a process in which each interacting species changes its genetic structure in response to a genetic change in its partner. Pathogens and hosts provide excellent models for studies on co-evolution

It has traditionally been accepted that a co-evolutionary arms race between a pathogen and its host would inevitably result in commensalism

Interaction of Entomopathogenic Fungi with Insect Hosts

The interaction is antagonistic in nature *i.e.,* Parasitism Interaction of two organisms belonging to different species, in which one organism (parasite) lives permanently or temporarily at the expense of the other one (host). Fungal entomopathogens occur in all habitats in which insects are present. Parasitism of fungi on insects is an extreme example of lethal parasitism.

Classification of Entomopathogenic Fungi (EPF)

Current Classification of the Genera of EPF

(Roy *et al.,* 2006)

Division	Class	Order	Family	Genus
Ascomycota	Sordario-mycetes	Hypocreales	Clavicipi-taceae	*Beauveriaa Cordyceps Cordycepioideus Lecanicilliuma Metarhiziuma Nomuraea*
Zygomycota	Zygomycetes	Entomo-phthorales	Entomoph-thoraceae	*Entomophaga Entomophthora Erynia Eryniopsis Furia Massospora Strongwellsea Pandora Tarichium Zoophthora*
			Neozygi-taceae	*Neozygites*

Classification of Entomopathogenic Fungi

(Gul *et al.,* 2014)

Phylum Oomycota

The fungi that have cellulose in their coenocytic hyphae, without chitin and biflagellate zoospores are considered as oomycetes. Sexual reproduction can occur either on the same hyphae or on different hyphae between archegonia and antheridia (collectively called as gametangia). Numerous species are parasites and saprophytes of plants and animals while species of two genera are infecting to mosquito larvae. A mosquito larvae pathogen, *Lagenidium giganteum* is studied best (Glare, 2010). Some other *Lagenidium* species are pathogenic to crabs and other aquatic crustaceans. The other species pathogenic to mosquito larvae, other Diptera and Chironomids are *Leptolegnia* spp. (Saprolegniales).

Phylum Chytridiomycota

The fungal groups that are without cellulose and contain chitin walls are included in this phylum. Single flagellum zoospores and gametes are settled and a thallus is grown which then converts into a coenocytic hyphae or a resting spore. When the comparisons are based on SSU rRNA phylogenetic, then this fungal group is considered as basal. Most of the usual insect infecting Chytridiomycetes is contained in Blastocladiales genus Coelomomyces. In Coelomomyces, above 70 insect pathogenic species are described (Barr, 2001).

Mostly the Hemipterans and Dipteranas were recognized as the source of these fungi. Sporangia of these fungi like copepods, is thick walled and resistant and the zoospores are flagellated. Insect pathogenic *Myriophagus* (Chytridiales) are found on pupae of Diptera and Coelomycidium (Blastocladiales) found on mosquitos and blackflies contain some other species.

Phylum Zygomycota

Hyphae that are multicellular, non-septate, and zygospores by the joining of gametangia, are considered as of phylum Zygomycota conventionally. But, Zygomycota has not been found as monophyletic on the basis of molecular analyses (Tanabe *et al.,* 2000). The class Trichomycetes, within the phylum Zygomycota, consists of species that are mostly related with insects. The species *Smittium morbosum* (Trichomycetes) was reported by Cooper and Sweeney (1986), as mosquito pathogen. Trichomycetes has mostly weak or symbiotic associations unlike true infectious agents (Beard and Adler, 2002). Insect death is mostly related to some species of *Mucor* (Mucorales). The order Entomophthorales, contain above 200 insect infecting species within phylum Zygomycota. Some species are capable of producing secondary spores from primary spores and some produce long lasting resting spores.

Ascomycota and Deuteromycota

Ascomycota includes the fungi with haploid and septate mycelia and the ascospores (sexual spores), are produced in a sac called ascus on the ascomata, the fruiting body. Normally, in every ascus, the number of ascospores produced is eight. Zoospores are not produced in ascomycetes (Shah and Pell, 2003). The taxonomy of sexual (teleomorphic) and asexual (anamorphic) conidial stages always remained in confused classification when their production is not on single occurrence. More than 300 insect infecting species are present in Cordyceps that is best known ascomycete. Chalkbrood disease in bees occurs by the genus *Ascosphaera,* which has dimorphism in sexuality. Klich, (2007) described that the spores of Ascosphaera, in an unusual manner of insect infecting species are ingested by the bee larvae that germinate in gut causing infection.

The most important insect infecting species occur in *Aspergillus, Metarhizium, Hirsutella, Beauveria, Aschersonia, Culicinomyces, Lecanicillium, Paecilomyces, Tolypocladium* and *Sorosporella*. Mostly, these genera have a linkage with one or many genera that can be verified with biological studies or by the molecular studies presenting the genetic relationship between telemorphs and anamorphs.

Basidiomycota

A very few Basidiomycetes have been noticed that act as insect pathogenic. It has been described by some researchers that *Uredinella* and *Septobasidiales* genera *Septobasidium* are considered infection causing agents in insects but most of them have a symbiotic relationship with insects like scales.

Life Cycle and Infection Process of EPF

- The life cycle of entomopathogenic fungus consists of a **parasitic phase** (from host infection to its death) and a **saprophytic phase** (after host death) (Fig. 6.1).
- Infection of host is usually caused by direct contact with spores that may be present on the plant surface, in- sect cadavers or in soil.
- The development of fungal infection is closely dependent on climatic conditions, particularly temperature and humidity.
- Entomopathogens present in the soil are also affected by its physical and chemical properties. After host death, the fungus colonizes the cadaver and during 2-3 days overgrows its cuticle and then sporulates.

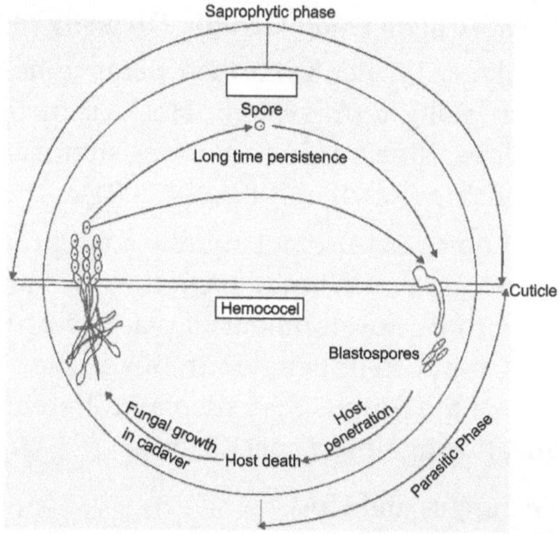

Fig. 6.1: The life cycle of entomopathogenic fungi from the order Hypocreates.

Mutual Adaptations

Parasite-host system is a very dynamic system linking many various adaptations and relationships that arose in the process of co-evolution. This is unquestionably the result of natural selection, which operates simultaneously on both sides of the system. Each parasite species had to evolve special adaptations that enable infection of a host and survival in it.

The spores of entomopathogenic fungi are usually covered with a layer of mucus composed of proteins and glucans, which facilitates their attachment to the insect cuticle.

Germinating spores of several entomopathogenic fungi produce specialized structures called appressoria. The appressorium is responsible for attachment of germinating spore to the epicuticular surface. The process of penetration of the insect cuticle is a result of mechanical pressure and enzymatic activity of the germ tube.

The major role in the penetration plays the secretion of sequential lipases, proteases and chitinases. Inside the insect body most entomopathogenic fungi grow as yeast- like propagules (blastospores), hyphal bodies or protoplasts lacking a cell wall. These structures are spread through the haemocoel.

Death of an insect is usually a result of mechanical damage caused by growing mycelia inside the insect (mummification), or toxins produced and released by the pathogen (Baazy 2000).

Host defenses also evolve in response to attacks by parasites. In defence against infection, insect may produce on the surface of its body fungistatic compounds that inhibit spore germination and growth. It was found that certain fatty acids on the surface

Parasitic Specialization, Virulence and Genetic Diversity of the Pathogen

The parasite may be highly virulent in a new parasite-host system, but may become less virulent in along-term system. Host, in turn, also may become more or less resistant, depending on the costs of resistance and the phylogenetic longevity of the relationship (Restif and Koella, 2004).

Different species of hosts are also not equally susceptible to infection from a particular species or strain of the fungus. On the one hand, susceptibility of the host may change with its development (larvae are usually more sensitive than adults) and may depend on its behaviour. But on the other hand, different species or even strains of the fungus may display different levels of virulence and parasitic specialization against a specific host.

Relationship between Fungus and Host

Entomopathogenic fungi infect their insect hosts by penetrating through the cuticle or through body openings. They have evolved specialized mechanisms for the enzymatic degradation of the integument and for overcoming insect defense compounds

The relationships by which different fungal species obtain energy from their insect hosts (econutritional mode) include:

- Biotrophy (nutrition derived only from living cells, which ceases once the cell has died)
- Necrotrophy (utilization of dead tissues), and
- Hemibiotrophy (initially biotrophic and then becoming necrotrophic).
- Recent phylogenetic studies indicate that the ability to utilize insects as a source of nutrition has arisen more than once among fungi (Spatafora *et al.*, 2007).
- Scale insects, particularly Coccidae and Aleyrodidae possess greatest diversity of fungal pathogens (Humber, 2008).

Infection Process or Virulence of EPF

The virulence of EPF involves certain activities which are influenced by a range of integrated intrinsic and external factors, which ultimately determine the pathogenicity. The activities includes:

- Adhesion
- Germination
- Differentiation
- Penetration

Adhesion

A successful infection is achieved through adhesion (attachment) of pathogen propagules to the host which is necessary and achieved through the secretion of mucilage. However, lectin enzymes, hydrophobic and electrostatic forces also play a role. The virulence is recognized first by adhesion to an insect body. The failure of a pathogen to adhere with the epidermis is considered a feature of virulent strains in insects. Entomopathogenic fungi secrete lipases, proteases and chitinases which aid in hydrolysis of epidermis.

Germination

Spore germination is influenced by a wide range of factors such as water, ions, fatty acids and nutrients on the cuticle surface and the physiological state of the host. Successful germination requires assimilation of utilizable nutrients and a tolerance to any toxic compound present on the surface.

Differentiation

After germination, appresoria appear at the end of short germ tubes, subterminally or on the side branches. Appressorium morphology is reported to be found either in swollen clavate or spherical structures to slightly swollen terminal hyphae.

Penetration

Penetration of the cuticle is accomplished by the germ tube itself or by the formation of an appressorium that attaches to the cuticle and gives rise to a narrow penetration peg. Penetration is both a mechanical and an enzymatic process.

Most terrestrial pathogens are known to penetrate directly, rarely through wounds, sense organs or spiracles.The penetration process is considered to be a combination of enzymatic and mechanical forces.

The exact mechanism for entry is usually peculiar to the species. A range of cuticle degrading enzymes is produced during penetration into the host colonization of the haemocoel by fungal hyphae (Castrillo *et al.*, 2005).

Interactions of Fungal Entomopathogens with Insect Hosts

Each interacting fungi and insect undergoes changes in its genetic structure in response to a change in its partner. They adapt to maximize their reproductive output and ultimate tness that are as diverse as the organisms themselves.

The adaptations include

- Behavioural
- Immunological
- Ecological
- Physiological
- Genetical

Behavioural Interactions

The behavior adaptations of both pathogen and the host interactions are complex in nature which led to their fitness.

Behavioural Fever

Insect species that naturally thermo regulate can maintain body temperatures that restrict pathogen growth without changing their normal behavior. Increased body temperature in infested insects result in suppression of pathogen activities or death or delay in time until death.

Behavioural fever in house flies *Musca domestica* with *Entomophthora schizophorae* or *E.muscae* (Olesen, 1984).

Fungus infected grasshoppers and caterpillars there is raise in body temperature of grasshopper (Carruthers, 1992).

The effect of behavioural fever of the desert locust, *Schistocerca gregaria* (host) on interaction between the host and the pathogen, *Metarhizium anisopliae* var. *acridum* resulted in delay of death time. All infected locusts ultimately succumbed to disease, with median survival times of 8, 15 and 21 days post-infection at below (poor), normally preferred temperature (Sub Optimal) and unrestricted (Optimal respectively). The pathogen is observed to be virulent at 27-30 °C (Fig. 6.2). (Elliot *et al.*, 2002)

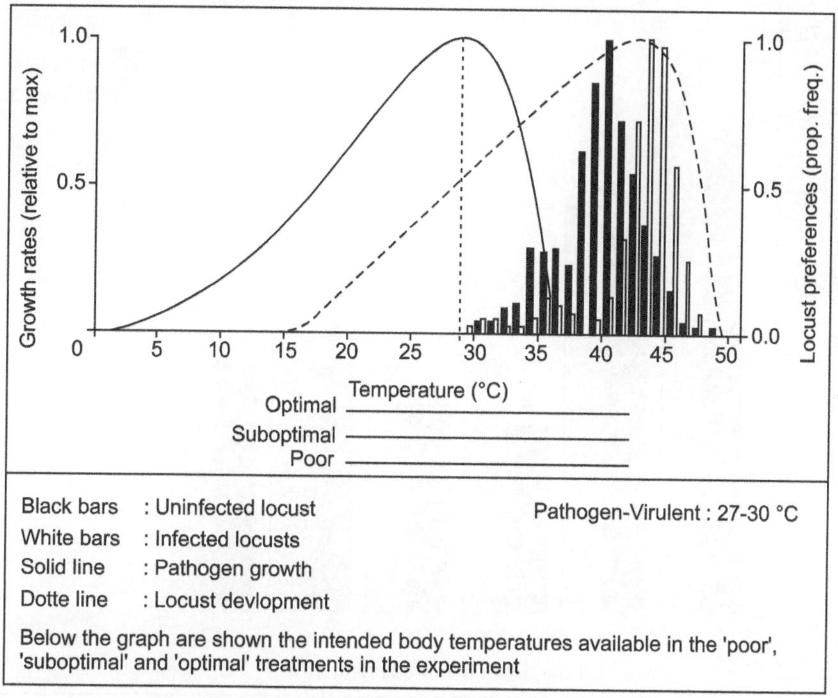

Fig. 6.2: The effect of behavioural fever of the desert locust

Feeding Behavioural

(*a*) Changes in Food consumption: Infected insects eat less than healthy ones and damage to crops is decreased during the disease incubation period. There is a significant decrease in feeding as early as 1 to 4 days after incubation in infected insect species with the hypocrealean fungi, *Metarhizium* spp or *Beauveria* spp (Blanford and Thomas, 2001).

Larvae of Gypsy moth, *Lymantria dispar* infected with *E.maimaiga* reduced feeding two days before death (Hajek, 1987).

Larvae of Spruce budworm, *Choristoneura fumiferana* infected with *E.aulicae* and Diamond back moth *Plutella xylostella* infected with *Zoophthora radicans* assimilate food same as healthy one until 24h before death (Furlong and Pell, 1997).

The long horned grasshopper (*Uvarovistia zebra)* infected with *Beauveria bassiana and Metarhizium anisopliae (5 × 10^6 spores/ml)* showed 60 and 63%

reduction in mean food consumption/insect, respectively. Reduction in feeding of the infected insects started 2DAT, but a significant reduction in feeding was not observed until 3–4DAS treatment (Fig. 6.3).

(Mohammadbeigi and Port, 2015)

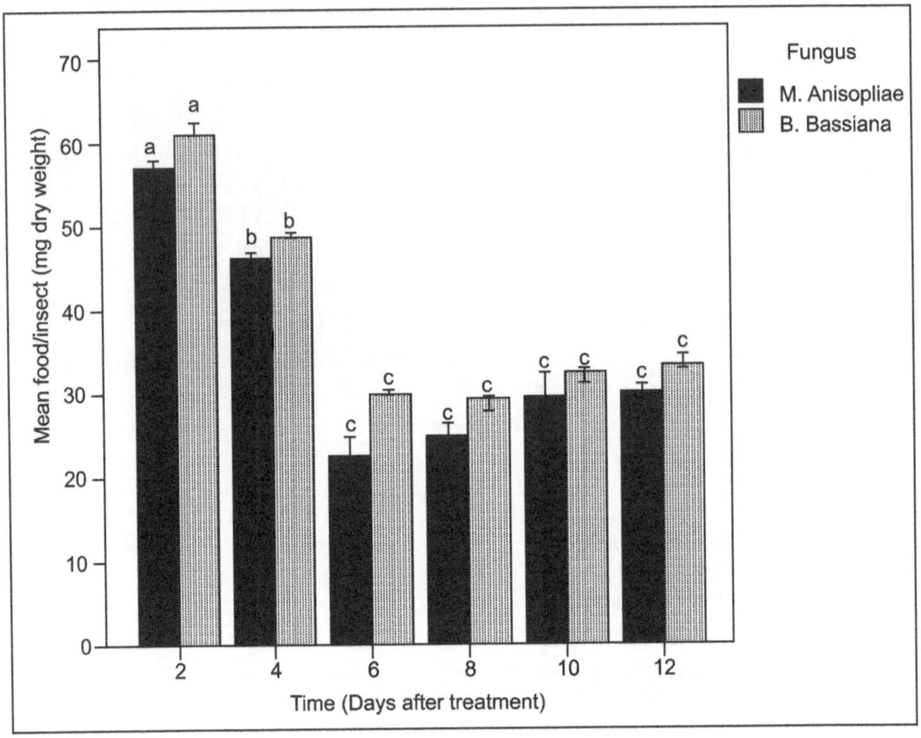

Fig. 6.3. Mean (± SE) food consumption/insect (*n*=45 nymphs within three replicates) by insects treated with 5 × 10^6 spores/ml of *Beauveria bassiana* and *Metarhizium anisopliae*

(*b*) **Changes in feeding location:** Infected hosts exhibit shift in feeding location during disease incubation. Pea aphids, *Aphis pisum* infected with *Pandora neoaphids* were found on underside of the leaves had left alfalfa plants and were found in surrounding habitat more frequently than were healthy aphids (Jensen *et al.*, 2001). Aphids attempting Kin selection and suicide (Roit berg, 1987)

Reproductive Behavior

(*a*) **Effect on fecundity:** Infected host produce less progeny especially with hypocrealean and entomophthoraean fungi. Desert locust, *S.gregaria* infected with *M.anisopliae* var. *acridium* exhibited low reproductive output than uninfected individuals (Blanford and Thomas, 2001)

Adult carrot flies, *Chamaepsila rosae* infected *with E.schizophorae* deposit their eggs on the ground near base of the food plants and after hatching the larvae move into the soil and feed on roots. But infected flies seek elevated positions such as top of the trees and shrubs and sporulated cadavers are found several meters above groundlevel. (Eilenberg, 1987) *(Plate 1)*.

Pea aphids, *A. pisum* infected with *Beauveria bassiana* and *P. neoaphidis* exhibited reduction in reproductive output (nymphs produced/female) within 24h of infection (Baverstock *et al.*, 2004).

(*b*) Sexual attractiveness: EPF infected or killed female insect adults possess exposed abdomen which is apparently highly attractive males of that population seeking a mate for copulation. Male house ies, *M. domestica,* are signicantly more attracted to fungus killed females than to uninfected females (Ludek *et al.*, 2002).

It is assumed that this increased attractiveness is a result of

- Swollen abdomen of the infected females.
- Smaller infected females are more attractive to males than.
- Reduction in production of sex pheromone infected female house ies
- Other visual or chemical cues of host
- Production of semiochemicals by fungus that attracts males.

Increased sex attractiveness is advantageous to the fungus

- Males may themselves receive infection during physical contact with sporulating cadavers.
- Males trying to copulate with the cadavers may transmit conidia to uninfected females that they subsequently copulate with

Disadvantages to Hosts (flies)

- Mortality increases
- Decrease in fecundity by females after mating with infected males

(Watson and Peterson, 1993). (Plate 2).

(*c*) Effect on Production of Sex Pheromones: There is a drastic reduction in production of sex pheromone by Females of *Plutella xylostella* moths infected by *Z. radicans* (Reddy *et al.*, 1998).

Besides swollen abdomen, visual and chemical cues the effect of sex pheromone component (Z)-9-tricosene and other cuticular hydrocarbons including n-tricosane, n-pentacosane, (Z)-9-heptacosene on sexual attractiveness of male houseflies to the infected female cadavars were evaluated young (7 days old) and old (18 days old) unmated females. Young ones accumulated significantly less sex pheromone and other hydrocarbons on their cuticular surface than uninfected females (Ludek *et al.*, 2002)

Pre-mortality Effects

Side effect of fungal tissue invasion where in the interaction of EPF with insects led to disruption in normal host behavior prior to host death. As the normal life span of moths in the eld is only about 5 days it is to the benet of the fungus to keep the insect alive as long as possible because it cannot develop saprophytically on a cadaver and needs 3 to 4 days to kill.

(Furlong *et al.*,1997)

Social Behavior

Many reports empahiszed that host mediated behavior reduces pathogen transmission within colonies. Host behaviors include

- Increased grooming
- Increased nest cleaning
- Secretion of antibiotics,
- Pathogen avoidance,
- Dispersal of infected individuals
- Relocation of the entire colony.

(Siebeneicher *et al.*, 1992)

The number of *B. bassiana* conidia on the integument of both larval and adult red imported re ants, *Solenopsis invicta,* was signicantly reduced by grooming (Pereira, 1993).

Although an increase in grooming behavior would appear benecial to the host in terms of reducing infection, inoculum could be incidentally disseminated within the nest (Kramm, 1982).

Infective propagules that are removed by grooming with mouthparts are not ingested but are stored in an infrabuccal cavity within the buccal chamber, where they are discharged as a pellet. Infection can occur if inocula germinate and penetrate through the buccal chamber, but it has been hypothesized that the labial gland, which produces secretions rich in chitinases has a fungistatic function (Febvay, 1984).

Imported red re ants, *S. invicta,* have also been observed to bury nest mates infected with *B. bassiana,* and this reduces transmission. Ants also use antimicrobial secretions that are sprayed from the gaster over the brood (Pereira and Stimac, 1992).

The presence of *B. bassiana* within the nest correlates with an increase in the concentration of these antimicrobial substances, and so it can be inferred that release of these secretions is induced by the pathogen.

Grooming in social insects are integral in reducing horizontal transmission of disease. In non groomed pathogenic conidia completely cover the bases of sensilla and in groomed insects abdomen have no conidium on their surface. (Plate 3) (Zhukovskaya *et al.*, 2013)

The presence of fungus with in nest colonies leads to increase of antimicrobial substances which interrupt the pathogenicity. These secretions are sprayed from gaster over the brood. Propagules removed in grooming with mouthparts are not ingested by the insect but stored in infrabuccal cavity and discharged as pellet (Pereira, 1993).

Dispersal of Infected Individuals

A behavioral alteration of social insects infected with fungal pathogens is dispersal from the colony. This has been termed "adaptive suicide" (Plate 4).

Immunological Interactions

Insects employ various defensive strategies ranging from crypsis to dramatic escape behaviors. Defensive reactions of hosts to pathogens are considered from an immunological perspective.

Termites (*Reticulitermes avipes* and*Zootermopsis angusticollis*) detect the presence of conidia of the fungal pathogen *M. anisopliae* and exhibit a striking vibratory display (Rosengaus *et al.*, 1999).

S. gregaria locusts infected with *M. anisopliae* increased locomotion within 3 days of infection (11 days to kill). Later in infection they became sluggish and less able to escape predation. (Arthurs and Thomas, 2001)

Pea aphids infected with *P. neoaphidis* become less responsive to alarm pheromone produced by conspecics. As a result, infected aphids could be more susceptible to attack by predators and this would reduce the pathogen density. Infected aphids continue to produce alarm pheromone and elicit a response in neighboring aphids which is advantageous to pathogen transmission because host movement enhances transmission

Predator avoidance is another classic defensive behavior and could explain why termite (*Macrotermes* sp.) alates infected with the ascomycete fungus *Cordycepi- oideus bisporus* have rarely been observed in the eld. Infected cadavers can only be found at the time of alate swarming (the rainy season), and the pathogen appears to induce behavioral modication in the host, resulting in alates moving under stones, where they die alone or in small groups (Roy *et al.*, 2006) (Plate 5).

Ecological Interactions

Ecological interactions include phototropic and geotropic responses. The normal behavior of avoiding light by hosts is completely changed when infected with EPF.

Common armyworm larvae, *Pseudaletia separata*, normally spend the day in the soil, where it is dark, and they leave the soil to feed at night. However, when infected with the entomophthoralean fungus *E. aulicae*, many larvae spend the day in the light instead and even move vertically upward on plants. Therefore Such a change in behavior that exposes larvae to visual predators could be risky, but it could also benet the fungus because larvae die in exposed locations. (Ohbayashi and Iwabuchi, 1991)

Larvae of sciarid ies normally live in the upper soil layers but infected by *Erynia sciariae* is the larvae move to the top of the soil or growth medium to die after which the fungus sporulates. This behavior appears to benet the fungus because infective conidia are dispersed on the soil surface, where they infect small larvae moving into the soil (Plate 6).

In General Entomophthoralean Fungi Kill Insect Hosts during the Late Afternoon or Evening

Entomophthora planchoniana and *P. neoaphidis* each caused death within 4-h intervals, with peaks at 8 to 9 and 14 h after dawn, respectively.

Zoophthora radicans caused some deaths throughout the 24-h light cycle but with a peak at 12 hours after dawn, and for the remaining three species peak mortality was less distinct.

Studies on house ies, *M. domestica*, infected with *E. muscae* have documented death 0 to 5 h before the onset of darkness, but deaths of ies held in constant dark after infection did not follow this rhythm. However, ies exposed to 12:12 (light:dark) for 3 days after infection and then maintained in the dark displayed periodicity in death. (Kramer, 1981)

Endgames (Final interactions)

At the end of an infection cycle Entomopathogens usually causes death of the host. Pathogens employ or adopt certain strategies to maximize their dispersal for fitness.

Pathogen infections result in the host dying in situ, where it normally exists.

Eg: Pupae of Beetles infected by hypocrealean fungi (*M. anisopliae, B. bassiana)* dying in soil. In Entomophthorales, the host apparently does not alter its behavior but become sluggish immediately before death).

Cabbage ies infected by *E. muscae* become sluggish and move to the soil surface, where they produce resting spores for winter survival. Resting spores are only produced after midsummer in the eld, suggesting a strong inuence of declining day length. Such a death may thus indicate a high degree of adaptation or co-evolution of the pathogen to its host, because the host may be in the optimal site and at the optimal time for the pathogen to survive and infect future hosts.

In many cases the nal interactions, or endgames, between a host and pathogen involve complex behavioral modications such as the infected insect seeking an elevated position where wind currents can effectively disseminate conidia. Eg: Larva of *Lymantria monacha* (the nun moth) infected with baculoviruses migrated to the tops of trees where they died (Steinhaus, 1949).

This host-altered behavior was named "Wipfelkrankheit" or "Wipfelsucht" (meaning tree top disease in German) for viral diseases (Hoffman, 1981) and "summit disease" for fungal diseases (Evans,1989 and Yamazaki *et al.*, 2004).

Classic Summit Disease

Insect hosts infected with Entomophthorales climb to an elevated position to die (Plate 7).

Insect host	EPF
Grasshoppers	*Entomophaga grylli*
True armyworm larvae, *Pseudaletia unipuncta*	*Furia virescens*
sugarbeet root aphids, *Pemphigus betae*	*P. neoaphidis*. move up to the foliage of plants just prior to death and die and sporulate in a position that ensures horizontal transmission

Summit Disease Benefits Either the Host or the Pathogen

Benets the fungal pathogen by placing the host in sites conducive to widespread dispersal usually by wind. Increase in the host's inclusivetness because the host moves away from clonal or closely related individuals. It can result in greater predation or scavenging on infected hosts, thereby reducing the dissemination of the pathogen.

Hypothetical Reasons for Occurrence of Summit Disease

Fungus affects the host's nervous system and releases compounds that induce the behavior or impair the respiratory system.

Summit Disease of Aquatic Hosts: Flotation

Flotation is a rare type of interaction in which an aquatic host infected with the conidial stage oats on the water surface.

Eg: Mosquito larvae and pupae killed by infections with *Erynia aquatica* are buoyant and the conidiophores grow out into the air from the cadaver and discharge conidia on to nearby mosquito pupae and emerging adults (Plate. 8)

Host Attachment to Substrate by Fungal Holdfasts

Behavioral alterations leading to summit disease are always accompanied by other adaptations such as attachment of the host to the substrate by production of specialized fungal structures formed from hyphae, rhizoids, or glue like materials secreted by hyphae. However, the formation of fungal holdfasts may exist in conjunction with modications in host behavior such as elevation seeking.

In either case, hosts attached by fungal structures may persist on substrates such as leaves, twigs, or even window glass for days or even weeks. This appears to benet the pathogen because the host remains rmly xed in a position that increases the chances of new hosts encountering the pathogen through feeding, resting, or mating. The fungal holdfasts also ensure the pathogen persists in the infected host, often surviving adverse environmental conditions (such as sunlight) and resulting in wide distribution of conidia.

Fungal holdfasts are employed by many groups of fungi and take various forms depending on the particular fungal species.

(a) Subcategories of the Fungal Holdfast Type

Basic Fungal Holdfasts

Fungal holdfasts are not highly differentiated from conidiophores. The interaction between the true armyworm, *P. unipuncta,* and the conidial form of *F. virescens*. The larvae are weakly held to grass stems by the growth of apparently undifferentiated conidiophores and the larval prologs.

The larvae usually rest on the ground beneath grasses during the day but infected larvae that produce conidia exhibit summit behavior. Interestingly, larvae that produce pathogen resting spores do the exact opposite and are attached to the soil by rhizoids (Plate 9) (Steinkraus *et al.*, 1993).

Rhizoidal Holdfasts

These are structurally more complex fungal structures which are differentiated from conidiophores. Aphids infected with *P. neoaphidis* or *E. planchoniana* are strongly attached by rhizoids to leaves. Infected aphids die in situ at their feeding sites, still in their aphid colonies, beneting transmission of the fungus when conidia are explosively discharged around each host cadaver (Elkassabany *et al.*, 1992).

Fungal rhizoids also rmly attach various rhagionid ies infected with *Erynia ithacensis* to the undersides of leaves of woody plants (Kramer and Steinkrau, 1981) (Plate. 10).

Adult Trichoptera held rmly beneath logs and stones around rivers by rhizoids of *Erynia rhizospora* Adult Culicidae infected with the resting spore stage of *E. aquatica* held to moist logs near snowpools.

Homopterans such as *Spissistilus festinus* held rmly to soybean plants by rhizoids of *Erynia delphacis*.

Dipterans infected with *E. muscae* or *E. schizophorae* whereby rhizoids are restricted to the host's proboscis, growing out of the labellae and attaching the host to smooth surfaces such as leaves, wood, and even window glass. Along with the rhizoids, glue like material strongly xes the host to the substrate hyphal differentiation occurs and whether it is driven by the other hyphal bodies or by cues from the proboscis.

***(b)* Host Attachment to Substrate by Host Structures:** Some fungi do not produce rhizoids, but the host is held in situ by host structures alone, namely the legs or mouthparts (mandibles or stylets). The pose of the dead insect is generally characteristic of the pathogen species involved. (Plate 11)

Legs: *E. grylli* infected grasshoppers and *E. scatophagae* infected yellow dung ies seek elevated positions on grasses or other vegetation and cling tightly (death grip) with their legs. Tipulids infected with fungal species from the genera *Eryniopsis* and *Entomophaga* also attach to grasses with their long legs, often overhanging water.

Mandibles: Eg: Coleoptera (Cantharidae) infected with Entomophthorales. Adult beetles infected with *Eryniopsis lampyridarum* or *Entomophthora* sp. grip plants, particularly the owers, by biting the plant with their mandibles. Fungal holdfasts are not involved. This attachment method is long lasting and this benets the fungus because many living hosts are present on the owers, feeding and mating (and so readily contact conidia.

Stylet: Attachment of the host through the stylet is typied by aphids infected with the conidial stage of *Neozygites fresenii*. Infected aphids generally die attached to the undersides of leaves or at the base of pine needles held only by their stylets embedded within the leaf tissue. The aphid's body becomes a source of explosively discharged conidia, which disperse rapidly over a wide area including the leaf surface, infecting other aphids in the colony. The fungus benets from the higher humidity of the lower leaf surface or pine needle base (Steinkraus and Kramer, 1988).

Alternative Mechanisms

In some insects Hypocrealean fungi do not produce specialized holdfasts but have evolved alternative mechanisms of ensuring the cadaver is held in position for optimal transmission (Plate. 12).

Grasshoppers dying from infection by *Sorosporella* sp. become attached to foliage at both ends of their bodies by fungus induced vomiting and defecating (Shah and Evans, 1997).

Cordyceps spp usually kill their hosts belowground but then produce a large and highly visible fruiting structure above ground to aid dispersal. Some hypocrealean species that infect scarabaeid larvae produce exudates from their fruiting bodies that attract surrounding insect fauna that vector the fungus to other hosts (Evans, 1989).

Host Liquefaction

Transmission of EPF conidia often relies on the host attached to the substrate or at elevated position within the environment. But in some insects, infected with the resting spore stage of the fungus liquefy and thus released from the host into the environment. Liquefaction ensures resting structures enter the soil from which they can germinate and infect hosts in subsequent seasons.

Aphids infected with the resting spore stage of several *Neozygites* species. Lepidopteran larvae infected with the resting spore stage of *Erynia gammae* exhibit host liquefaction.

Utilizing an Active Host for Transmission

The conidial formation and resting spores occurs in or on the still living host serves to disperse the inoculum to new hosts and in the environment. Adult Diptera infected by *Strongwellsea,* the fungus growth is largely conned to the abdomen. Open wounds develop on the abdomen and conidia are discharged through the holes.

Infected ies remain active and seem to continue behaving normally In *Cicads* infected with *Massospora* spp. the hosts become living disseminators of both the conidia and resting spores, though both spore forms do not occur in the same host.

In both the conidial and resting-spore states living cicadas continue to y and interact with other cicadas while their abdomens are lled with fungal material. The caudal segments of the abdomen are sloughed off and conidia or resting spores are dispersed.

Physiological Interactions (Enzymatic interactions)

The interactions between entomopathogenic fungi and insect cuticle surface can elicit specific behavioral responses to limit the ability of the pathogen to parasitize the host.

Simple moulting provides a means for avoiding infection. Protease inhibitors highly inhibitory towards *M. anisopliae*

Pr1 protease has been detected in the molting fluid of the tobacco hornworm, *Manduca sexta* (Milner and Prior, 1994).

Rapid ecdyces in aphids and molting in the diamondback moth (*Plutella xylostella*) aid in minimizing the ability of fungal pathogens to fully infect the host (Vandenberg, *et al.*, 1998)

On the other hand the entomopathogenic fungi inhibit moulting of their hosts through oxidative inactivation of host ecdysteroid.

Injection of the fungal-conditioned medium of *Nomuraea rileyi* into *Bombyx mori* larvae in the mid-4th instar inhibited larval molt but induced precocious pupal metamorphosis, and its injection into 5th instar larvae blocked pupal metamorphosis. *N. rileyi* secretes a specific enzyme that oxidizes the hydroxyl group at position C22 of hemolymph ecdysteroids and prevents molting in silkworm larvae. (Kiuchi *et al.*, 2003)

EPF exhibit various adaptations to overcome the immune system (defense) of insects during their interactions. Pathogenicity depends on enzymatic ability of the fungus. Cuticle Penetration is the result of combined action of mechanical force and enzymatic acti.

EPF Secrete Enzymes that Aid in Breakdown of Insect Integument Include

Lipases, Proteases, Chitinases

Lipases

Aids in cuticle penetration and initial nutrients release and improves the adhesion of spores to the epicuticle.

In *Spodoptera litura* larval mortality increases due to significant improvement in Conidial germination of *N. rileyi* fungus (combined with 8.13 kDa lipase produce *N.rileyi* (Supakdamrongkul *et al.*, 2010).

CYP52 (Cytochrome P450 monooxygenase) increases the enzymatic activity in breaking down of insect epicuticle (Silva *et al.*, 2010).

In *B. Bassiana* the gene encodes the lipase activity is Bbcyp52x1 corresponding to the enzymatic complex CYP52X1 which involves degradation of hydrocarbons (Zhang *et al.*, 2012).

In *M. robertsii,* Mr CYP52 gene from Cytochrome P450 was identified (Lin *et al.*, 2011).

Insect cuticular lipids are comprised of a diverse array of compounds with much variation in content and composition which extends to the different life stages. Genomic, genetic, and biochemical data indicate that the fungus contains a repertoire of cytochrome P450enzymes with overlapping speciûcities that act to assimilate insect hydrocarbons (Pedrini *et al.*, 2013).

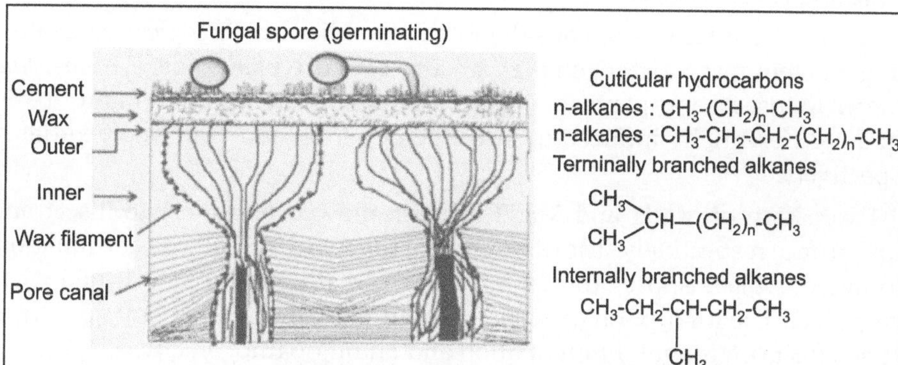

Fig. 6.4: Composition of insect cuticle

Proteases

Degrades the proteinaceous material in procuticle. Plays important role in pathogenicity and also virulence (Mustafa and Kaur, 2009). protease Pr1 is a virulence indicator for the entomopathogenic fungi (Moguel *et al.*, 2007).

Proteolytic Enzymes : subtilisin-like serine-protease Pr1 and trypsin-like protease Pr2 (Leger *et al.*, 1994).

The activities of Pr1 and Pr2 have been determined in *B. bassiana, M. anisopliae, Lecanicillium lecanni, Nomuraea rileyi and M. flavoviride* (Bidochka and Meltzer, 2010) protease Pr1 is the key extracellular involved in the cuticle penetration and that, without this enzyme the infection process cannot be achieved (Sun and Liu, 2006).

M. anisopliae was transformed with the introduction of gene *aaIT,* which encodes a neurotoxin of the *Androctonus australis (*scorpion), regulated by the gene *mcl*1 promoter. (Wang and Leger, (2007).

Chitinases

Act synergically with proteases in order to degrade insect cuticle and are associated with germination, hypal growth, morphogenesis, nutrition and defense against competitors (Adams, 2004).

Chitinases have been recognized as powerful biological control agents due to antifungal activity in *Fusarium equiseti* and as bioinsecticides in the diamond-back moth reducing the time of death. (Prasanna *et al.,* 2013).

The first molecular characterization of a chitinase was for the chit1 gene in *M. anisopliae,* CHIT1 protein present a molecular weight of 42 kDa and it is homologue to the *Aspergillus* album and *Trichoderma harzianum* chitinases (Bogo *et al.,* 1998).

The Molecular and Genomics of *M. anisopliae and B.bassiana* at Enzyme Level (Wang and Leger, 2007)

M. anisopliae is a fungus of considerable metabolic and ecological versatility, being a potent insect pathogen that can also colonize plant roots. *M. anisopliae* adheres to insects and plants using two different proteins, MAD1 and MAD2 that are differentially induced in insect hemolymph and plant root exudates, respectively.

Expression of Mad1 and Mad2 in *yeast* allowed to adhere to insect and plant surface respectively. The disruption of Mad1 in EPF delayed germination, suppressed blastospore formation, and greatly reduced virulence to caterpillars. The disruption of Mad2 blocked the adhesion to plant epidermis but no effects on fungal differentiation and entomopathogenicity.

Thus it is inferred that regulation, localization, and specicity controls the functional distinction between Mad1 and Mad2 and enable *M. anisopliae* cells to adapt their adhesive properties to different habitats. Mad 1 is involved in cytoskeleton organization and cell division. Thus the disruption of *Mad1* in *M. anisopliae* delayed germination, suppressed blastospore formation, and greatly reduced virulence to caterpillars. (Fig. 6.4a, 6.5).

Adhesion Assays

90% of the parental Wild Type conidia adhered to either locust cuticle or onion epidermis and could not be washed off with 0.05% Tween 20 Only 5.3% ± 1.2% of the " Mad1 conidia adhered to locust cuticle, "Mad2 conidia were as adherent as the Wild type

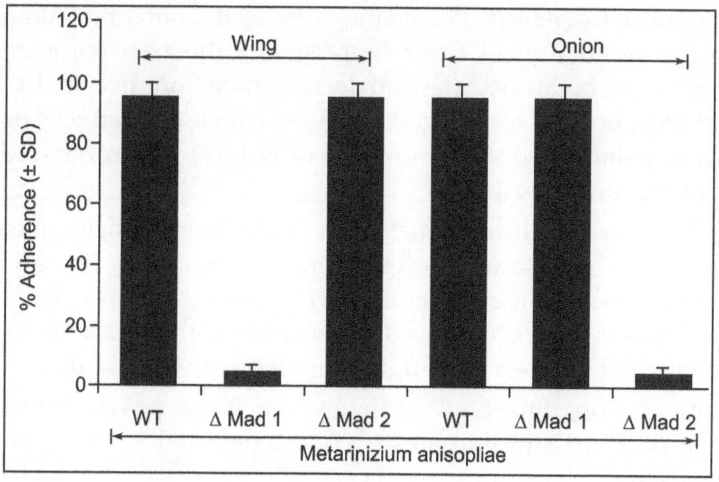

Fig. 6.4a: Disruption of *Mad1 and Mad2* blocks adhesion of *M. anisopliae* to insect and plant surfaces

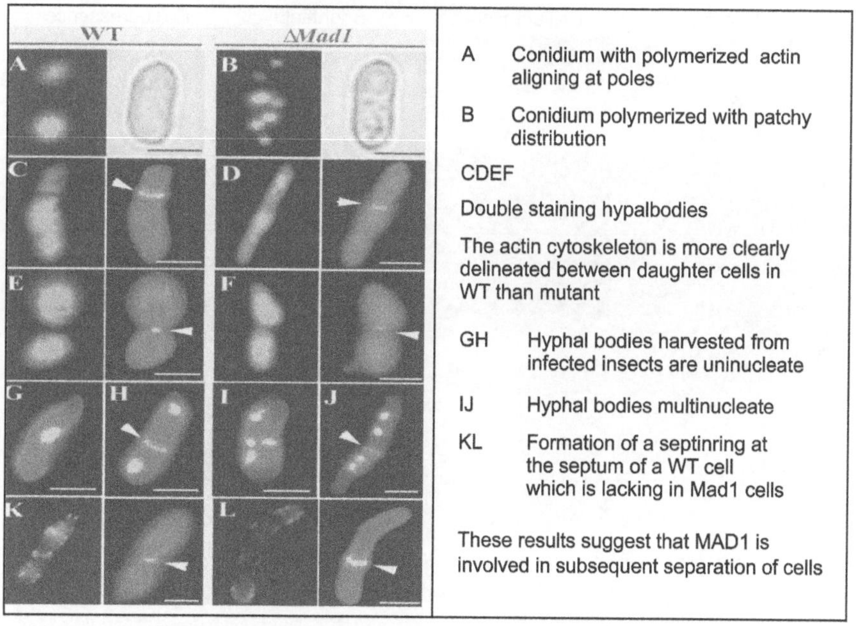

Fig. 6.5: Mad1 involved in cytoskeleton organization and cell division

Carboxylate Transporter Gene *JEN1* from the Entomopathogenic Fungus, *Beauveria bassiana* is Involved in Conidiation and Virulence (Jin *et al.,* 2010)

The alkalinization of the cuticle is a physiological signal triggering the production of pathogenicity. A gene (*B. bassiana* JEN1 [BbJEN1]) homologous to JEN1 encoding a carboxylate transporter in yeast was identied in a *B. bassiana* transfer DNA (T-DNA) insertional mutant.

Disruption of the gene decreased the carboxylate contents in hyphae, while increasing the conidial yield. Over expression of this transporter resulted in signicant increases in carboxylates and decreased the conidial yield. Compared to the wild type, BbJEN1 alkalinized the insect cuticle to a reduced extent. The bioassay results indicated that disruption of BbJEN1 signicantly reduced the virulence of the fungus to aphids.

BbJEN1 expressed during penetration of the insect cuticles. Green peach aphids (*Myzus persicae*) and cabbage worms (*Pieres rapae*) were inoculated with the wild-type strain and the BbJEN1p:: egfp transformant. After 48 h, the infected insects were sliced into 15-m sections with a Leica microtome and observed with epiuorescence or bright-eld microscopy (Fig. 6.6).

During infection, uorescence in the hyphae in the penetrated cuticle was observed in *BbJENIP* and no uorescence was detected in the hyphae of the wild-type strain.

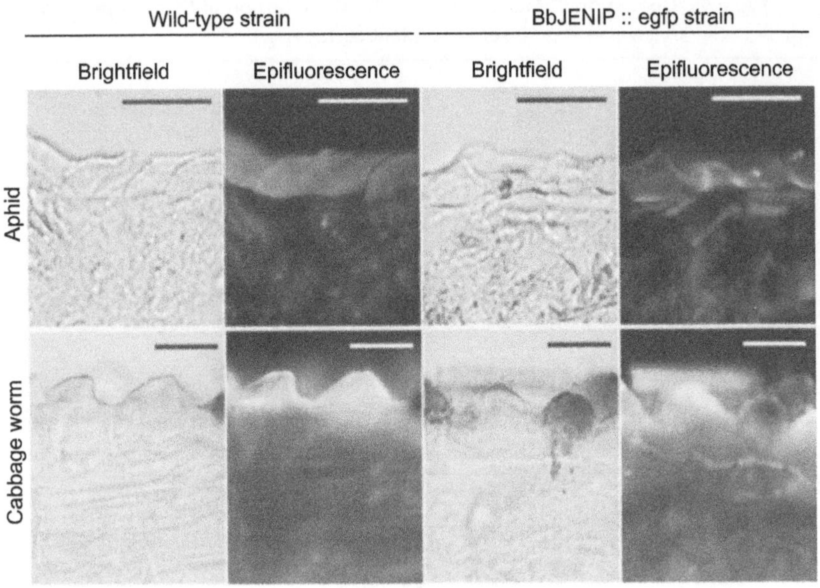

Fig. 6.6: *BbJEN1* expressed during penetration of the insect cuticles Bars=25µm

Genome Sequencing and Comparative Transcriptomics of the Model Entomopathogenic Fungi *Metarhizium anisopliae* and *M. acridum* (Gao *et al.,* 2011)

The studies stated that differentially regulated signaling pathways were employed by *M. anisopliae* and *M. acridum* infecting cockroach and locust cuticles. Both the MAP kinase and cAMP dependent protein kinase A (PKA) pathways were activated by *M. anisopliae* and *M. acridum* infecting cockroach and locust cuticles. PLC, phosphatidyl inositol-specific phospholipase C; PIP2, phosphatidylinositol 4,5-bisphosphate; IP3, inositol 1,4,5-triphosphate; DAG, diacylglycerol; PKC, protein kinase C; CaMK, calcium/calmodulin regulated kinase; ERK, extracellular signal-regulated protein kinase; CREB, a basic leucine zipper transcription factor that is a potential cAMP response element-binding protein (Fig. 6.7).

Transcriptional analysis of both fungi during early infection processes provided further insights into the genes and pathways involved in infectivity and specificity. Of particular note, *M. acridum* transcribed distinct G-protein coupled receptors on cuticles from locusts (the natural hosts) and cockroaches, whereas *M. anisopliae* transcribed the same receptor on both hosts.

The information on signaling pathway and transcription facilitates the identification of virulence genes and the development of improved biocontrol strains with customized properties.

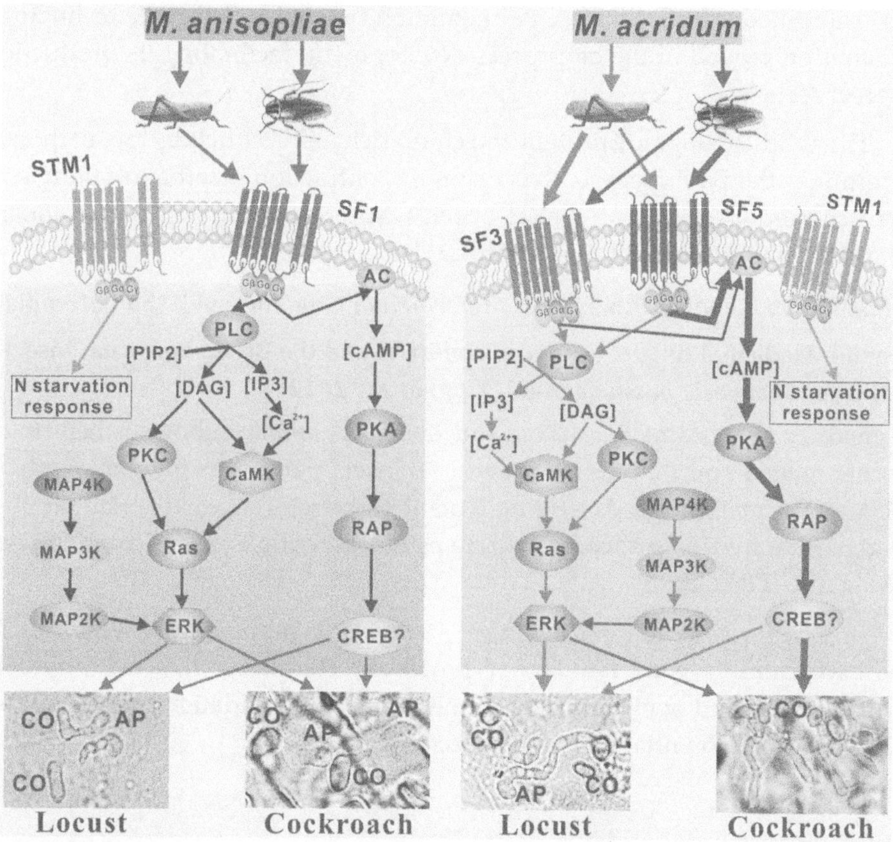

Fig. 6.7: Signaling pathways by *M. anisopliae* and *M. acridum* infecting cockroach and locust cuticles CO, conidium; AP, appressorium.Thicker arrows indicate pathways that are more highly expressed by *M. acridum* **on either locust or cockroach cuticles**

Genetic Diversity of EPF

The parasite may be highly virulent in a new parasite host system, but may become less virulent in a long term system.

Depending on the costs of resistance and the phylogenetic longevity of the relationship, host may also become more or less resistant (Restif and Koella, 2004).

EPF with a wide range of hosts such as *Beauveria* spp. The isolates of diverse geographical origin obtained from the same host species show a greater similarity in the genetic structure than the isolates from the same site but isolated from different host species (Castrillo and Brooks 1998, Glare and In wood 1998).

Due to this fact, the entomopathogenic fungi enzymes production systems are established. The Solid State Fermentation (SSF) is an adequate technology which is employed in the bioprocess development, facilitating its production at great scale.

The ability to degrade protein and chitin rich insect cuticle by any pathogen determines the pathogenesis Expansion or contraction of protein family size has occurred in different fungal species in association with evolutionary adaptations for different hosts and lifestyles.

Comparative Genomic Analysis of *Metarhizium* Genomes with the Caterpillar Specific Medicinal fungus *Cordyceps militaris* and the Broad-Spectrum Insect Pathogen *Beauveria bassiana* (Xiao, Ying, *et al.*, 2012)

A genomic analysis of *B. bassiana* and *Cordyceps militaris* showed them to be closely related and that they evolved into insect pathogens independently of the *Metarhizium* lineage. Accordingly plant pathogens have expanded families of glycoside hydrolases, carbohydrate esterases, cutinases, and pectin lyases to degrade (Fig. 6.8).

B. bassiana genome resembles *Metarhizium* spp. and *C. militaris* in the expansion of gene families of proteases, chitinases, lipases, fatty acid hydroxylases, and acyl-CoA dehydrogenases (for β-oxidation of fatty acids), which all have potential targets in insect hosts (Fig. 6.9).

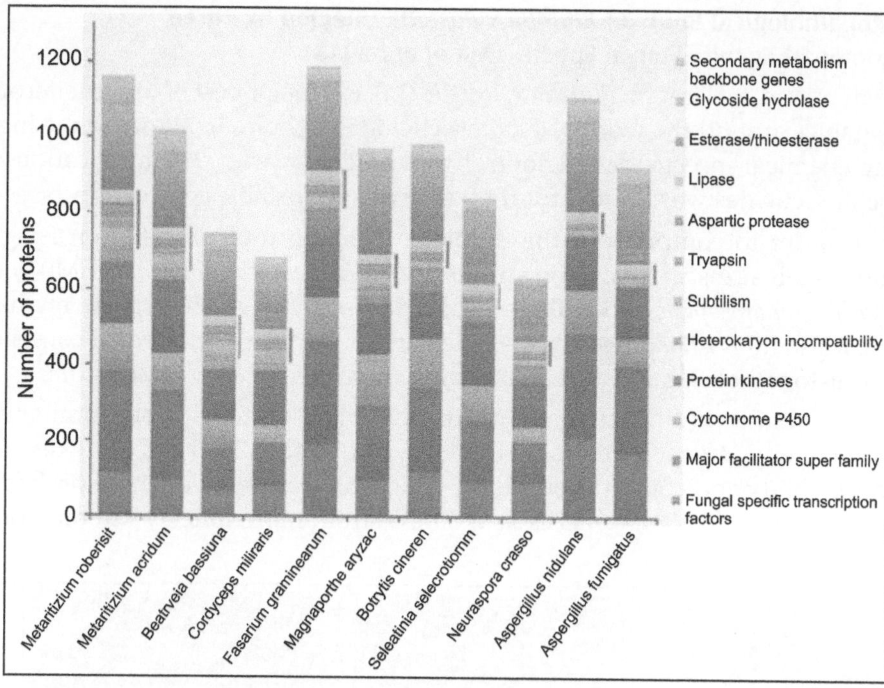

Fig. 6.8: The protein family size of insect pathogens relates to their insect killing strategies. The protein families of proteases and lipases involved in degrading insect cuticles are expanded and highlighted in red scale bar.

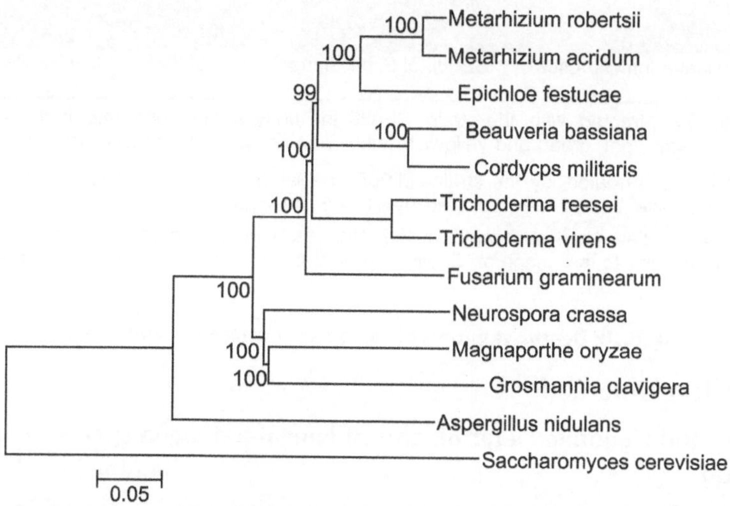

Fig. 6.9: Phylogenomic relationships of insect pathogenic fungi (branches highlighted in thicker lines) with other fungi . *B. bassiana* and *C. militaris* are closely related and evolved into insect pathogens independently of the *Metarhizium* lineage.

Histopathological Study of *Plutella xylostella* Infected by Three Entomopathogenic Fungal Species (Xia *et al.*, 2013)

The diamond back moth, *Plutella xylostella* (L.), is a major pest of the cruciferous vegetables around the world. Mycoinsecticide is a choice to alternate the high toxic chemical insecticides to control this pest. However, the application of mycoinsecticides was limited for their slower and instable control effects.

In order to comprehend the different infection rates of different fungal strains against insect hosts, the strains SB005 of *Beauveria bassiana,* SM016 of *Metarhizium anisopliae* and SP020 of Isaria *fumosorosea,* which respectively had the LT90s (1.0 × 107 sporces/mL) 4.5, 6.3 and 6.1 d, were selected to compare their histopathological feature in infecting the larvae of *Plutella xylostella.*

The results indicated that SM016 and SP020 strains were similar in symptons and infection process. Differently, the strain SB005 had more disease spots on body and could penetrate the cuticle of headcapsule. These probably are the reasons for *Beauveria bassiana* SB005 strain more quickly kill diamond moth (Fig. 6.10).

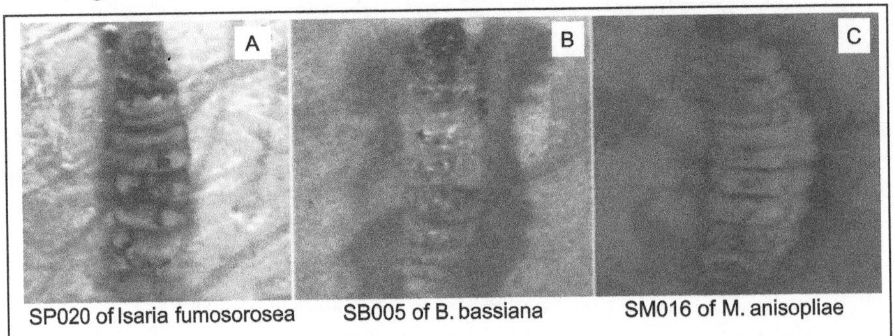

A After 72 h treated with the strain SP020, the body shrank and deformed to a shape as "C" with light green and yellowish color and occasionally moved when touched

B At the 56 h treated by the strain SB005, the larvae were closed to die, the inactive and red-like bodies were covered by a few white hyphae

C Larval bodies were spasticity at the mid-term of the infection and then shrank deformation to the shape of "C" with green thoracic feet and abdomen and yellowish back

Fig. 6.10: Death Symptoms of Larvae after treatment with fungus

Genomic level interactions

Trajectory and Genomic Determinants of Fungal-pathogen Speciation and Host Adaptation (Jinming Xia *et al.*, 2013)

Host pathogen interactions are a major driving force for diversification, but the genomic basis for speciation and host shifting remains unclear. The fungal genus *Metarhizium* contains species ranging from specialists with very narrow host ranges to generalists that attack a wide range of insects.

By genomic analyses of seven species, the generalists evolved from specialists via transitional species with intermediate host ranges and that this shift paralleled insect evolution. Studies on specialization of fungus associated with retention of sexuality and rapid evolution of existing protein sequences was made. Generalization was associated with protein-family expansion, loss of genome-defense mechanisms, genome restructuring, horizontal gene transfer, and positive selection that accelerated after reinforcement of reproductive isolation.

Metarhizium species differ from each other in spore size and shape. Formation of appresorial infection structures is the hallmark of host recognition and specificity. Monophyletic *Metarhizium* lineage diverged from clavicipitacean plant pathogens and endophytes about 231 million years ago (MYA), and MAM diverged from other *Metarhizium* species about 117 MYA (Fig. 6.11).

Reconstruction of the evolutionary trajectories of *Metarhizium* and insect-host species.

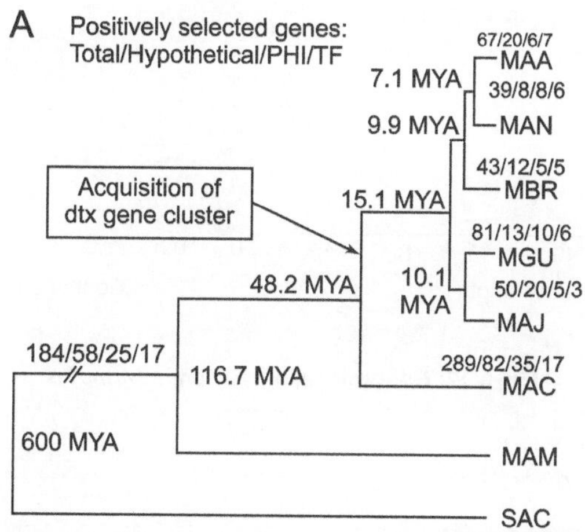

Fig. 6.11. (A)Maximum-likelihood phylogeny analysis of *Metarhizium* species rooted by the yeast *S. cerevisiae* (SAC). The estimated divergence times million years ago (MYA)] for each lineage are labeled above each branch. The number of positively selected genes (PSGs) is provided for each examined branch or clade. On the right are shown the spores of each species, showing their size and shape differences. PHI, pathogen–host interaction genes; TF, transcription factor genes.

Transposable Elements and Genome-Structure Diversification

Consistent with RIP operating exclusively in specialist species, MAM and MAC have fewer transposable elements (TEs) encoding both DNA-type transposases (averages 39 vs. 57) and RNA-type retro transposases (averages 9 vs. 57) than other *Metarhizium* species.

TEs cause gene mutation, gene duplication, or genome-structure reorganization (31) so, not surprisingly, specialists have fewer pseudo genes than other species (average 219 vs. 351) and the non specialists exhibit numerous genome-structure re arrangements.

In particular, k-mer and contig length distribution analyses identified two peaks in the MAJ genome (Fig. 12 A and B). One possibility is that MAJ is a heterozygote because fungal asexual sporulation is a process of haploidization (32). The mating-type (MAT) locus represents the sex mini chromosome in fungi (33).

Analysis of the MAT loci showed that MAJ is unique among *Metarhizium* species in having both MAT1-1 and MAT1-2 loci (Fig. 6.13A), which was confirmed by PCR (Fig. 6.13 B). The spores of each *Metarhizium* species are uninucleate (Fig. 6.12C), precluding MAJ being a heterokaryon (*i.e.*, two nuclei in one spore). Synteny analysis of MAJ and the closely related MGU confirmed the presence of duplicated segments in the MAJ genome.

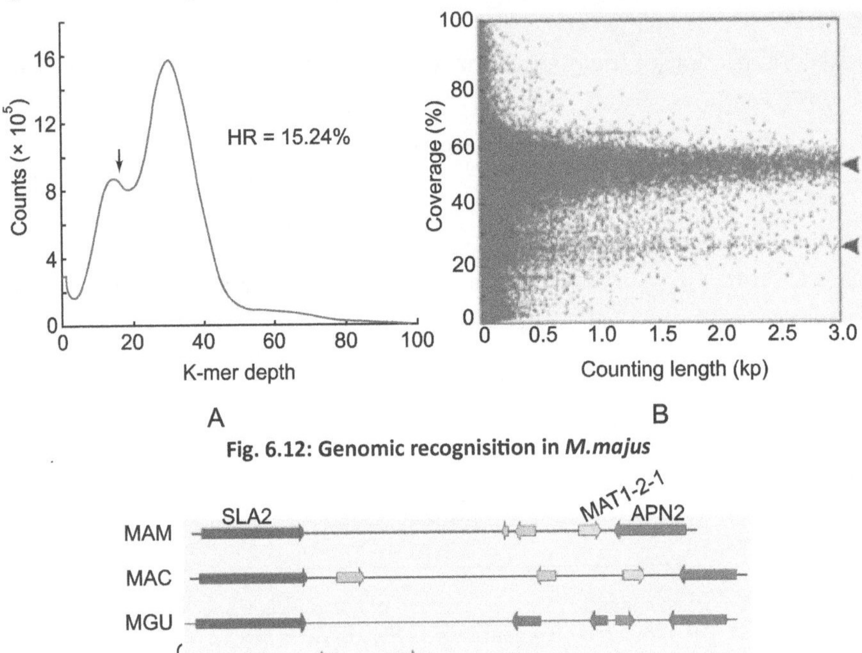

Fig. 6.12: Genomic recognisition in *M.majus*

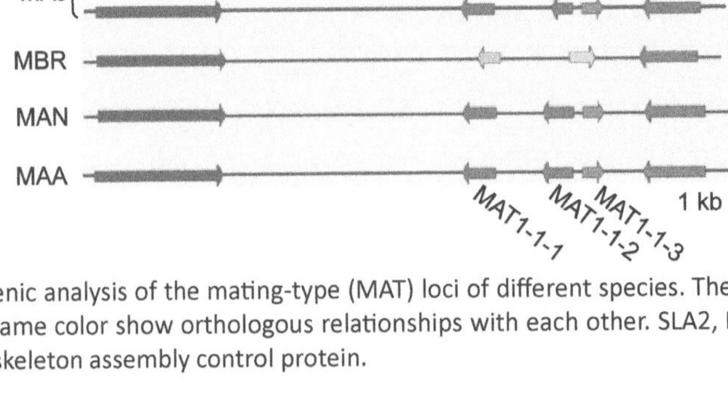

A. Syntenic analysis of the mating-type (MAT) loci of different species. The genes labeled in the same color show orthologous relationships with each other. SLA2, DNA lyase; APN2, cytoskeleton assembly control protein.

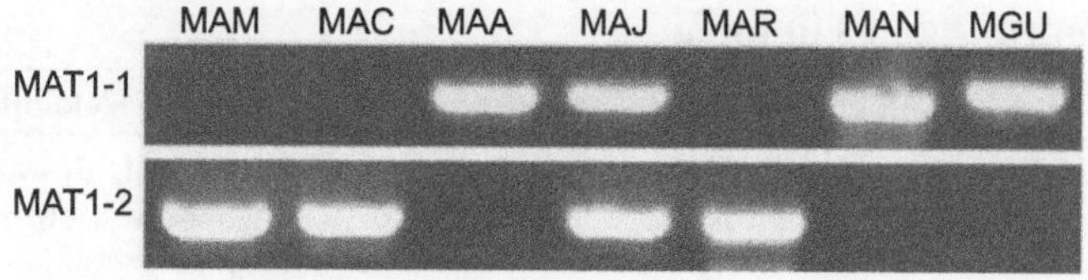

B. PCR verification of the presence of MAT1-1-1 or MAT1-2-1 in the genomes of different spp.

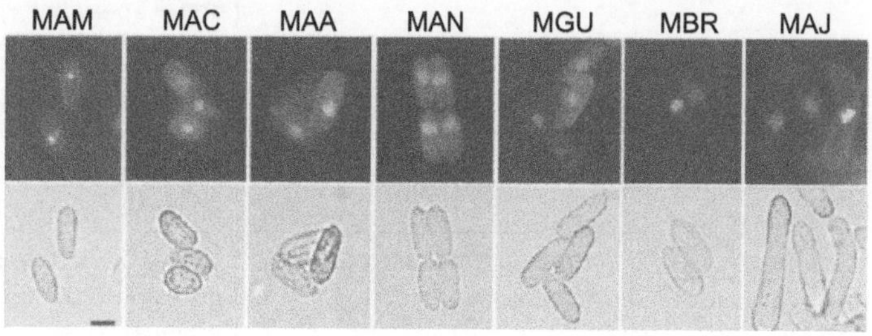

C. Nucleic staining showing the presence of a single nucleus per spore in different Metarhizium spp. (Scale bar: 5 ìm.)

Fig. 6.13: Karyotype characterization of different *Metarhizium* species.

These results advance understanding of speciation and genomic signatures that underlie pathogen adaptation to hosts. The results provided clear connections between phenotype, genotype, and pathogen fitness that underlie the evolutionary trajectory of speciation and host adaptation

Entomopathogenic Fungi as Mycoinsecticides

EPFs are regarded as effective mycoinsecticides in various fields of agriculture, horticulture and forestry (Inglis *et al.*, 2000; Carruthers *et al.*, 1997) because:

- The mass production of EPF is not very expensive.
- Its storage is very easy.
- Act efficiently on a wide range of humidity and temperature.
- Host specific.
- Low risk to non target organisms (Beneficial insects).
- Can infest wide range of insects in field and stored products.
- Most bio-pesticides can be used in conjunction with synthetic chemical insecticides because in most cases the microbial product is not deactivated or damaged by residues of conventional insecticides.

EPF as Biocontrol Agents in India

Fungus	Pest & Crop	Field efficacy
Beauveria bassiana	Rice Hispa, *Dicladispa armigera*	Spray of *B. bassiana* spore suspension 10 million spores/ml
	Coffee berry borer, *Hypothenemus hampei*	Spray of *B. bassiana* spore suspension (1X10^7 spores/ml) containing 0.1% sunflower oil and 0.1per cent wetting agent during monsoon
	Tea looper, *Buzura suppressaria*	Spray of *B. bassiana* spore suspension (2.5 g/l) gave 88 per cent reduction in West Bengal
	Sunflower: *Helicoverpa armigera*	Spray of oil suspension of *B. bassiana* (200mg/l) in Andhra Pradesh
	Green gram	Soil application @5X10^{13} conidia/ha
	White grubs	Effective control achieved in Assam
B.Brongniarti	Sugarcane: white grub, *Holotrichia serrata*	Soil application @ 1kg /acre. Highest yield recorded
Metarhizium anisopliae	Coconut: Rhinoceros beetle, *Oryctes rhinoceros*	Spraying of Spores in its breeding sites @ 5X10^{11} spores/m3 to the compost pits and manure heaps
	Sugarcane: White grub	*M. anisopliae* at 1x10^{13}/ha gave yield of 91.18 q/ha as compared with chlorpyrifos (93.29 q/ha) in Karnataka
	Pigeon pea: Pod borer, *Helicoverpa armigera*	*M. anisopliae* conidia in an oil formulation was effective in reducing 66.74% *H. armigera* as compared to 62.58% with endosulfan in Maharastra
	Potato White grub, *Brahmina* sp.	Soil application @ 5x10^{13} conidia/ha along with chlorpyrifos 20 EC at 200 g a.i./ha resulted in the highest tuber yield (155 q/ha) in HP.
	Soyabean: white grub *Holotrichia longipennis*	Soil application formulation applied @ 5x10^{13} conidia/ha, 61.50 per cent reduction in grubs

L.lecanii	Coffee green scale, *Coccus viridis*	Spraying spores@ 16 X 10^6 spores/ml along with Tween-80 twice at 2 weeks interval caused 97.6 per cent mortality of the pest
		Spraying of spore ($2x10^6$spores/ml) along with 0.005 per cent quinalphos and 0.05per cent Teepol was found highly effective killing 95.58per cent and 97.55 per cent scales in coffee and citrus respectively
	Indian mustard and Rapeseed: Mustard aphid, *Lipaphis erysimi*	Spray @ (10^6 spores/ml) resulted in significant reduction in aphid infestation at 10 DAS
Nomuraea rileyi	Castor: *Spodoptera litura*	Spraying of spore ($10x10^{10}$spores/ml) along with 0.02per cent Tween-80.
	Soybean: *S.litura Helicoverpa armigera Thysonoplusia orichalcea*	*N. rileyi* spores spraying @ $2X10^8$/ml twice at 10 days interval during Kharif in North Karnataka was cheaper than insecticidal treatment and cost effective

(Ramanujam *et al.,* 2014)

EPF Enzymes as Biocontrol Agents

There is a correlation between pathogenicity and enzymes production in interactions of hosts and EPF. Hence a new potentiality in relation to enzymes as biocontrol agents in insects is being used.

The enzymes efficacy has been proved against cotton aphid (*Aphis gossypi*). The insecticide action is mainly caused by chitinases.

In larvae of Diamond back moth enzymes application significantly affects its growth and metamorphosis.

Due to this fact, the entomopathogenic fungi enzymes production systems are established. The Solid State Fermentation (SSF) is an adequate technology which is employed in the bioprocess development, facilitating its production at great scale (Perez *et al.,* 2014).

Multitrophic Interactions

EPF and arthropod natural enemies may contribute to the suppression of insect pest populations either as individual species or as species complexes.

Natural enemies can interact either synergistically or antagonistically in the interaction.

Synergist : Enhanced transmission /dispersal of insect pathogens.

Antagonist : Parasitism or infection or predation or competition.

Both components of the parasite host interactions are affected, either directly or indirectly.

Directly by mortality, changes in growth and development and indirectly through modifications of other biocoenosis elements. Also influenced by abiotic and biotic factors. The most important biotic factor affecting herbivore insect entomopathogenic fungus interactions are often parasitoids. Their direct impact on its host population is mainly based on limiting its abundance, as well as changing distribution and behaviour of host individuals.

Role of Exo or Endo-genous Microbes in Hosts

Drosophila bearing the endosymbiotic bacterium *Wolbachia* appear to display a generalized resistance to insect pathogens including *B. bassiana* [Panteleev *et al.,* 2007]

Symbiotic bacteria from antibiotic producing *Streptomyces* species have been implicated in protecting larvae of a solitary hunting wasp from fungal infection [Kaltenpoth *et al.,* 2004]

The Southern chinch bug, *Blissus insularis* have midgut crypts that contain high densities of *Burkholderia* bacterial species produce potent antifungal compounds and account for enhanced resistance against entomopathogenic fungi [Boucias *et al.,* 2012]

Tritrophic interactions

A parasitoid and entomopathogenic fungus developing at the same time inside a host insect interact with each other by competing for resources, and the faster-growing fungus usually wins the slower developing parasitoid (Brooks 1993).

Santiago-Alvarez *et al.* (2006) found that mortality of sweet potato whitefly, *Bemisia tabaci* (Hemiptera: Aleyrodidae), caused by *B. bassiana* was significantly affected by the host plant on which the nymphs were reared. In that study, the host plant also had a significant effect on the sporulation of the pathogen.

An aleyrodid, *Trialeurodes vaporariorum* (greenhouse whitefly), was more susceptible to infection caused by Paecilomyces fumosoroseus when fed on cucumber than on tomato (Bolckmans *et al.* 1995).

Depending on the host plant, Colorado potato beetle, *Leptinotarsa decemlineata* (Coleoptera: Chrysomelidae), showed different susceptibility to infection by *B. bassiana* (Hare and Andreadis 1983).

However, there is no effect of host plant on herbivore susceptibility to infection by entomopathogenic fungi (Costa and Gaugler 1989, Vidal *et al.*, 1998, Ugine *et al.*, 2007).

Various mechanisms may be involved in the interactions that occur in tritrophic system (pathogen-insect-host plant). In defence against herbivores, plants may produce different types of chemicals and volatile substances. These substances often can affect a pathogen directly by inhibiting its growth and germination of spores, which reduce an ability of the pathogen to infect insect (Poprawski and Jones 2000, Klingen *et al.*, 2002).

Conclusion

Interactions of EPF with their insect hosts depend on behavioural, immunological and physiological adaptations which reflect on diversity of pathogens and hosts. Alterations of host behaviour during interactions are diverse, intricate and of great scientific interest. Passive or active behavioral changes in insects are reminiscent of evolutionary adaptations that either promotes cross kingdom control by fungi or altruistic behavior by the hosts.

It is difficult to predict whether the adaptations are beneficial to the host or pathogen. The host specific fungi modify the behaviour of hosts which affects its virulence or transmission to increase their fitness. EPF assigns an adoptive function to all the host altered behaviours.

There are still significant gaps in our understanding of the molecular mechanisms underlying behavioral alterations in insects during their interactions with fungi. Due to the taxonomic diversity of both insects and fungi, the molecular machinery involved in insect behavior changes could vary among the interacting species pairs or function on a case-by-case basis.

The establishment of an ideal model system, the acquisition of genomic information, and the deployment of the knowledge and techniques of the sciences of fungal genetics, secondary metabolism, chemistry, and insect physiology and neurology would help uncover the biological secrets behind changes in insect behavior. Studies at molecular and genomic level will facilitate the identification of virulence genes and the development of improved biocontrol strains with customized properties, for synergistic combinations with other technologies (in combination with semiochemicals, other natural enemies, resistant plants, chemigation, remote sensing, etc.) that will enhance the effectiveness and sustainability of integrated control strategies.

REFERENCES

Adams, D.J. 2004. Fungal Cell Wall Chitinases and Glucanases. *Microbiology*, **150**, 2029-2035.

Arthurs S, Thomas MB. 2001. Behavioural Changes in *Schistocerca gregaria* Following Infection with a Fungalpathogen: Implications for Susceptibility to Predation. *Ecological Entomology*, 26:227–34.

Baazy S., 2000. Zró¿nicowanie Grup funkcyjnych grzybów owadobójczych, Biotechnologia, 3:11-32.

Barr, D. J. S. 2001. Chytridiomycota. In *Systematics and Evolution* (pp. 93-112). Springer Berlin Heidelberg.

Baverstock J. 2004. *Interactions Between Aphids, their Insect and Fungal Natural Enemies and the Host Plant*. PhDthesis. Univ. Nottingham. 167 pp.

Beard, C. E., & Adler, P. H. 2002. Seasonality of Trichomycetes in Larval Black Flies from South Carolina, USA. *Mycologia*, 94(2), 200-209.

Bidochka M J and Meltzer M J. 2000. Genetic Polymorphisms in Three Subtilisin-Like Protease Isoforms (Pr1A, Pr1B, and Pr1C) from *Metarhizium* Strains. *Canadian Journal Microbiology*, 46: 1138-1144.

Blanford S, Thomas M B. 2001. Adult Survival, Maturation and Reproduction of the Desert Locust *Schistocerca gregaria* Infected with the Fungus *Metarhizium anisopliae* var. *acridum*. *Journal of Invertebrate Pathology*, 78: 1–8.

Blanford S, Thomas MB, Langewald J.1998. Behavioural Fever in the Senegalese Grasshopper *Oedaleus senegalensis*, and Its Implications for Biological Control Using Pathogens. *Ecological Entomology*, 23:9–14.

Bogo, M.R., Rota, C.A., Rota, H., Pinto Jr, H., Ocampos, M., Correa, C.T., *et al.* 1998. A Chitinase Encoding Gene (*chit*1 Gene) from the Entomopathogen *Metarhizium anisopliae*: Isolation and Characterization of Genomic and Full-Length cDNA. *Current Microbiology*, 37: 221-225.

Bolckmans K., Sterk G., Eyal J., Sels B., Stepman W. 1995, PreFeRal (*Paecilomyces fumosoroseus* (Wise) Brown and Smith, strain Apopka 97), a New Microbiological Insecticide for the Biological Control of Whiteflies in Greenhouses, Med. Fac. Landbouww. Univ. Gent., 60:719–724.

Boucias, D.G, Garcia-Maruniak, A, Cherry, R., Lu, H.J., Maruniak, J.E., Lietze, V.U. 2012. Detection and Characterization of Bacterial Symbionts in the Heteropteran, Blissus Insularis. *FEMS Microbial Ecology*, 82: 629- 641.

Brooks W.M. 1993. Host-parasitoid-pathogen Interactions, in: Beckage N.E., Thompson S.N., and Federici B.A. (eds) "Parasites and Pathogens of Insects" Vol. 2 Pathogens, *Academic Press, San Diego*, 231-272.

Burges, H. D. 1981. Safety, Safety Testing and Quality Control of Microbial Pesticides. In: Burges HD, Editor. *Microbial control of Pests and Plant Diseases* 1970-1980. London: Academic Press, pp. 737-767.

Carruthers RI, Larkin TS, Firstencel H. 1992. Influence of Thermal Ecology on the Mycosis of a Rangeland Grasshopper. *Ecology*, 73:190–204.

Carruthers, R. I., Ramos, M. E., Larkin, T. S., Hostetter, D. L., & Soper, R. S. 1997. The *Entomophaga grylli* (Fresenius) Batko Species Complex: Its Biology, Ecology and Use for Biological Control of Pest Grasshoppers. *Memoirs of the Entomological Society of Canada*, *129*(S171), 329-353.

Castrillo L A, Roberts D W and Vandenberg J D. 2005. The Fungal Past, Present and Future: Germination, Ramification and Reproduction. *Journal of Invertebrate Pathology*, 89: 46–56.

Castrillo L.A., Brooks W.M., 1998, Differentiation of *Beauveria bassiana* Isolates from the Darkling Beetle, *Alphitobius diaperinus*, Using Isozyme and RAPD Analyses, *Journal of Invertebrate Pathology*, 72: 190-196.

Costa S.D., Gaugler R. 1989. Influence of *Solanum* Host Plants on Colorado Potato Beetle (Coleoptera: Chrysomelidae) Susceptibility to the Entomopathogen *Beauveria bassiana, Environmental Entomology,* 18: 531–536.

Eilenberg J. 1987. Abnormal Egg-laying Behaviour of Female Carrot Flies (*Psila rosae*) Induced by the Fungus *Entomophthora Muscae. Entomologia Experimentalis et Applicata,* 52:17–24.

Elkassabany NM, Steinkraus DC, McLeod PJ, Correll JC, Morelock TE. 1992. *Pandora neoaphidis* (Entomophthorales: Entomophthoraceae): A Potential Biological Control Agent Against *Myzus persicae* (Homoptera: Aphididae) on Spinach. *Jornal of Kansas Entomological Society,* 65:196–99.

Elliot SL, Blanford S, Thomas MB. 2002. Host-pathogen Interaction in a Varying Environment, Behavioural Fever and Fitness.*Proc. Biol. Sci.* 269:1599–607.

Evans HC. 1989. Mycopathogens of Insects of Epigeal and Aerial Habitats. In *Insect-Fungus Interactions,* ed. N Wilding, NMCollins, P Hammond, JFWebber, pp. 205–38. San Diego: Academic.

Febvay G, Decharme M, Kermarrec A.1984. Digestion of Chitin by the Labial Glands of *Acromyrmex octospinosus* Reich (Hymenoptera, Formicidae). *Canadian Journal of Zoology,* 62:229–34.

Furlong MJ and Pell JK. 1997. The Influence of Environmental Factors on the Persistence of *Zoophthora radicans* Conidia. *Journal of Invertebate Pathology,* 69: 223–33.

Gao Q, Jin K, Ying S-H, Zhang Y, Xiao G, *et al.* 2011. Genome Sequencing and Comparative Transcriptomics of the Model Entomopathogenic Fungi *Metarhizium anisopliae* and *M. acridum.* PLoS Genetics, 7(1): pgen.1001264.

Glare T.R., Inwood A.J., 1998. Morphological and Genetic Characterization of Beauveria from Newzealand. *Mycological Research,* 102(2): 250-256.

Glare, T. 2010. Entomopathogenic Fungi and their Role in Regulation of Insect Populations. *Insect Control: Biological and Synthetic Agents,* p. 11.

Gul H T, Saeed S and Ahmad Khan F Z. 2014. Entomopathogenic Fungi as Effective Insect Pest Management Tactic: A Review. Applied Sciences and Business Economics, 1(1): 10-18.

Hajek AE. 1989. Food Consumption by *Lymantria dispar* (Lepidoptera: Lymantriidae) Larvae Infected with *Entomophaga maimaiga* (Zygomycetes: Entomophthorales). *Environmental Entomology,* 18: 723–27.

Hare J.D., Andreadis T.G. 1983.Variation in the Susceptibility of *Leptinotarsa decemlineata* (Coleoptera: Chrysomelidae) when Reared on Different Host Plants to the Fungal Pathogen *Beauveria bassiana* in the Field and Laboratory, *Environmental Entomology,* 12: 1891–1896.

Hoffman O. 1891. *Die Schlaffsucht (Flacherie) der Nonne (Liparis monacha)nebst einem Anhang.* Frankfurt: Weber Humber, R. A. 2008. Evolution of Entomopathogenicity in Fungi. *Journal of Invertebrate Pathology,* 98: 262-266.

Inglis, G. D., Ivie, T. J., Duke, G. M and Goettel M. S. 2000. Influence of Rain and Conidial Formulation on Persistence of *Beauveria bassiana* on Potato Leaves and Colorado Potato Beetle Larvae. *Biological Control,* 18(1): 55-64.

Jin Kai, Zhang Y, Fang W, Luo Z, Yonghong Zhou and Yan Peil. 2010. Carboxylate Transporter Gene *JEN1* from the Entomopathogenic Fungus *Beauveria bassiana* Is Involved in Conidiation and Virulence. *Applied and Environmental Microbiology,* 76: 254–263.

Kaltenpoth, M, Gottler, W, Herzner, G., Strohm, E. 2005. Symbiotic Bacteria Protect Wasp Larvae from Fungal Infestation. Current Biology, 15: 475-479.

Kiuchi M., Yasui H., Hayasaka S., Kamimura M. 2003. Entomogenous fungus *Nomuraea rileyi* Inhibits Host Insect Molting by C22-oxidizing Inactivation of Hemolymph Ecdysteroids. Archives of Insect Biochemistry and Physiology. 200, 52: 35–44.

Klich, M. A. 2007. *Aspergillus flavus*: the Major Producer of Aflatoxin. *Molecular plant pathology,* 8(6): 713-722.

Klingen I., Hajek A., Meadow R., Renwick J.A.A. 2002, Effect of Brassicaceous Plants on the Survival and Infectivity of Insect Pathogenic Fungi, *Bio Control,* 47: 411–425.

Kramer JP, Steinkraus DC. 1981. Culture of *Entomophthora muscae in vivo* and Its Infectivity for 6 Species of Muscoid Flies. *Mycopathologia,* 76:139–43.

Kramm KR, West DF, Rockenbach PG.1982. Termite Pathogens: Transfer of the Entomopathogen *Metarhizium anisopliae* Between *Reticulitermes* sp. Termites. *Journal of Invertebate* Pathology, 40:1–6.

Leger, R.J., Bidochka, M.J. and Roberts, D.W. 1994. Isoforms of the Cuticle-Degrading *Pr*1 Proteinase and Production of a Metalloproteinase by *Metarhizium anisopliae. Archives of Biochemistry Biophysics,* 313: 1-7.

Lin, L., Fang, W., Liao, X., Wang, F., Wei, D. and St. Leger, R.J. (2011) The *MrCYP*52 Cytochrome P450 Monooxygenase Gene of *Metarhizium robertsii* Is Important for Utilizing Insect Epicuticular Hydrocarbons. *PLoS ONE,* 6: e28984.

Ludek Z, Watson D W, Stuart B. Krasnoff B and Coby Schala. 2002. Effect of the Entomopathogenic Fungus, *Entomophthora muscae* (Zygomycetes: Entomophthoraceae), on Sex Pheromone and Other Cuticular Hydrocarbons of the House Fly, *Musca domestica. Journal of Invertebrate Pathology,* 80: 171–176.

Milner R.J., Prior C. 1994. Susceptibility of the Australian Plague Locust, *Chortoicetes terminifera,* and the Wingless Grasshopper, *Phaulacridium vittatum,* to the Fungi *Metarhizium* spp. *Biological control,* 4:132–137.

Moguel CJ., Gonzαlez-Barajas, M., Mier, T., Reyes Montes, M.R., Aranda, E. and Toriello, C. 2007. Virulence Testing and Extracellular Subtilisin-Like (*Pr*1) and Tripsina-Like (*Pr*2) Activity during Propagule Production of *Paecilomyces fumosoroseus* Isolates from Whiteflies (Homoptera: Aeyrodidae). *Revista Iberoamericana de Micología,* 24: 62-68.

Mohammadbeigi A and Port G. 2015. Effect of Infection by *Beauveria bassiana* and *Metarhizium anisopliae* on the Feeding of *Uvarovistia zebra. Journal of Insect Science,* 15(1): 88-92.

Ohbayashi T, Iwabuchi K. 1991. Abnormal Behavior of the Common armyworm *Pseudaletia separata* (Walker) (Lepidoptera:Noctuidae) Larvae Infected with An Entomogenous Fungus, *Entomophaga aulicae,* and a Nuclear Polyhedrosis virus. *Applied Entomology and Zoology,* 26: 479–585.

Olesen US. 1984. Effect of Humidity and Temperature on *Entomophthora muscae* Infecting the House Fly, *Musca domestica,* and the Increase of Survival of the Flyby Behavioral Fever. MSc thesis. Univ.Copenhagen, Denmark.

Panteleev, D.Y, Goryacheva, I.I., Andrianov, B.V, Reznik, N.L., Lazebny, O.E.; Kulikov, A.M. 2007. The Endosymbiotic Bacterium Wolbachia Enhances the Nonspecific Resistance to Insect Pathogens and Alters Behavior of *Drosophila melanogaster*. Russian journal of Genetics, 43: 1066-1069.

Pedrini N, Urquiza A O, Bonnet C, Zhang S and Keyhani N O. 2013. Targeting of Insect Epicuticular Lipids by the Entomopathogenic Fungus *Beauveria bassiana*: Hydrocarbonoxidation within the Context to the Host-pathogen Interaction. *Frontiers in Microbiology,* 4: 1-18.

Pereira RM, Stimac JL. 1992. Transmission of *Beauveria bassiana* within Nests of *Solenopsis invicta* (Hymenoptera, Formicidae) in the Laboratory. *Environmental Entomology*, 21:1427–32.

Pereira RM. 1993. Ant Behavior and Microbial Pathogens (Hymenoptera: Formicidae). *Florida Entomologist*, 76: 63–74.

Perez S, Barranco-Florido, Navarro S R, Francisco C M and Lopez. 2014. Enzymes of Entomopathogenic Fungi,Advances and Insights. *Advances in Enzyme Research*, 2: 65-76.

Poprawski T.J and Jones W.J. 2000. Host Plant Effects on Activity of the Mitosporic Fungi Beauveria bassiana and *Paecilomyces fumosoroseus* against Two Populations of *Bemisia* Whiteflies (Homoptera: Aleyrodidae), *Mycopathologia*, 151:11-20.

Prasanna L, Eijsink V.G.H, Meadow R. and Gåseidnes, S. 2013. A Novel Strain of *Brevibacillus laterosporus* Produces Chitinases That Contribute to Its Biocontrol Potential. *Applied Microbiology Biotechnology*, 97: 1601-1611.

Ramanujam B, Rangeshwaran R, Sivakmar G, Mohan M and Yandigeri M S. 2014. Management of Insect Pests by Microorganisms. *Proceeding Indian National Science Academy*, 80 No. 2 June 2014. Spl. Sec. pp. 455-471.

Reddy GVP, Furlong MJ, Pell JK, Poppy GM. 1998. *Zoophthora radicans* Infectioninhibits the Response to and Production of Sex Pheromone in the Diamondback Moth. *Journal of Invertebate* Pathology, 72:167–69.

Restif O and Koella J.C. 2004. Concurrent Evolution of Resistance and Tolerance to Pathogens, The American Naturalist, 164: 90-102.

Roitberg B D. 1987. Adaptive Suicidal Behavior in Pea Aphids. *Nature*, 328: 797–99.

Rosengaus RB, Jordan C, Lefebvre ML,Traniello JFA. 1999. Pathogen Alarm Behaviorin a Termite: A New Form of Communication in Social Insects. *Naturwissens chaften*, 86:544–48.

Santiago-Alvarez C., Maranha E.A., Maranha E., Quesada-Moraga E. 2006. Host Plant Influences Pathogenicity of Beauveria Bassiana to Bemisia Tabaci and Its Sporulation on Cadavers, *Bio Control*, 51:519-532.

Shah PA, Evans HC. 1997. *Sorosporella*:a Cryptic Pathogen of Grasshoppers and Locustsin Africa. *Mycologist*, 11:106–110.

Shah, P. A., & Pell, J. K. 2003. Entomopathogenic Fungi as Biological Control Agents. *Applied Microbiology and Biotechnology*, 61(5-6), 413-423.

Shahid A A, Qayyum rao A, Bakhsh A and Husnain T. 2012. Entomopathogenic Fungi as Biological Controllers: New Insights into their Virulence and Pathogenicity. Archives of Biological Science, 64(1): 21-42.

Siebeneicher S R, Vinson S B, Kenerley CM. 1992. Infection of the Red Imported Fire ant by *Beauveria bassiana* Through Various Routes of Exposure. *Journal of Invertebate* Pathology, 59: 280–85.

Silva, W.O.B., Santi, L., Scharank, A. and Vainstein, M.H. 2010. *Metarhizium anisopliae* Lipolytic Activity Plays a Pivotal Role in *Rhipicepthalus* (*Boophilus*) *microplus* Infection. *Fungal Biology*, 144:10-15.

Singkaravanit, S., Kinoshita, H., Ihara, F., & Nihira, T. 2010. Cloning and Functional Analysis of the Second Geranylgeranyl Diphosphate Synthase Gene Influencing Helvolic Acid Biosynthesis in *Metarhizium anisopliae*. *Applied Microbiology and Biotechnology*, 87(3): 1077-1088.

Spatafora, J. W., Sung, G. H., Sung, J. M., Hywel, J. N. L., and J.F.White Jr. 2007. Phylogenetic Evidence for an Animal Pathogen Origin of Ergot and the Grass Endophytes. *Molecular Ecology*, 16: 1701-1711.

Steinhaus EA. 1949. *Principles of Insect Pathology*. New York: McGraw Hill, pp. 185-210.

Steinkraus DC, Kramer JP. 1988. *Entomophthora Entomophthora scatophagae* Desc. ampl. Zygomycetes,Entomophthorales), a Fungal Pathogen of the Yellow Dung Fly, *Scatophaga stercoraria* (Diptera, Anthomyiidae). *Mycotaxon*, 32: 105–13.

Steinkraus DC, Mueller AJ, Humber RA.1993. *Furia virescens* (Thaxter) Humber(Zygomycetes, Entomophthoraceae) Infections in the Armyworm, *Pseudaletia unipuncta* (Haworth) (Lepidoptera, Noctuidae)in Arkansas with Notes on Other Natural Enemies. *Journal of Entomological Science*, 28: 376–86.

Sun M.H. and Liu, X.Z. 2006. Carbon Requirements of Some Entomopathogenic and Mycoparasitic Hyphomycetesas Fungal Biocontrol Agents. *Mycopathology*, 161: 295-305

Supakdamrongkul, P., Bhumiratana, A. and Wiwat, C. 2010. Characterization of an Extracellular Lipase from the Biocontrol Fungus, *Nomuraea rileyi* MJ, and Its Toxicity Toward *Spodoptera litura*. *Journal of Invertebrate Pathology*, 105: 228-235.

Tanabe, Y., O'Donnell, K., Saikawa, M., & Sugiyama, J. 2000. Molecular Phylogeny Of Parasitic Zygomycota (Dimargaritales, Zoopagales) Based on Nuclear Small Subunit Ribosomal DNA Sequences. *Molecular Phylogenetics and Evolution*, 16(2): 253-262.

Vandenberg J.D., Ramos M., Altre J.A. 1998. Dose-response and Age and Temperature Related Susceptibility of the Diamondback Moth (Lepidoptera: Plutellidae) to Two Isolates of *Beauveria bassiana* (Hyphomycetes: Moniliaceae). *Environmental Entomology*, 27:1017–1021.

Wang C and Raymond L. 2007. The MAD1 Adhesin of *Metarhizium anisopliae* Links Adhesion with Blastospore Production and Virulence to Insects and the MAD2 Adhesin Enables Attachment to Plants. *Eukaryotic Cell*, 6(5): 808–816.

Wang C and Raymond L. 2014. Genomics of Entomopathogenic Fungi. *The Ecological Genomics of Fungi*, First Edition. Edited by Francis Martin. Published by John Wiley & Sons, pp. 243-260.

Watson DW, Mullens BA, Petersen JJ. 1993. Behavioral Fever Response of*Musca domestica* (Diptera: Muscidae)to Infection by *Entomophthora muscae* (Zygomycetes: Entomophthorales). *Journal of Invertebate* Pathology, 61: 10–16.

Xia J, Huang Z and Qiongbo–Hu. 2013. Histopathological Study of *Plutella xylostella* Infected by Three Entomopathogenic Fungal Species. *Advances in Entomology*, 1(2): 15-19.

Xiao GH, Ying S-H, *et al.* 2012. Genomic Perspectives on the Evolution of Fungal Entomopathogenicity in *Beauveria bassiana*. *Scientific Reorts*, 2: 483.

Yamazaki K, Sugiura S, Fukasawa Y.2004. Epizootics and Behavioral Alteration in the Arctiid Caterpillar *Chionarctianivea* (Lepidoptera: Arctiidae) Caused by an Entomopathogenic Fungus, *Entomophaga aulicae* (Zygomycetes: Entomophthorales). *Entomological Science*, 7: 219–23.

Zhang S, Widemann E, Bernard G, Lesot A, Pinot P, Pedrini N and Keyhani N O. 2012. CYP52X1, Representing New Cytochrome P450 Subfamily, Displays Fatty Acid Hydroxylase Activity and Contributes to Virulence and Growth on Insect Cuticular Substrates in Entomopathogenic Fungus *Beauveria bassiana*. *The Journal of Biological Chemistry*, 287(16): 13477–13486.

Zhukovskaya, Yanagawa A and Brian TF.2013. Review Grooming Behavior as a Mechanism of Insect Disease Defense. *Insecta*, 4: 609-630.

Advances in Microbiology: *Applications & Significance* Pages 123-132
Edited by: Dr. Pawan Kumar 'Bharti'
ISBN: 978-93-86841-97-1
Edition: 2019
Published by: Discovery Publishing House Pvt. Ltd., New Delhi (India)

7

Fastening Degradation of Rice Crop Residues Using Biotechnological Approach

[1]Dr. Pawan Kumar 'Bharti'

ABSTRACT

Rice residue burning is the biggest problem of north India, because its culprit of air pollution generation over NCR especially in winters. It is the prime need of the hour to resolve the problem in an eco-friendly manner.

The main target of the study is to resolve the above said problem by using biotechnological approach. In the process, the degradation of the crop residue is enhanced with the help of fungus species in moist conditions. Selected waste material from sugar industry is incorporated in the field to utilize it in the form of feed material of fungus species, which provide conditioning to soil quality also. On this basis, an eco-friendly process is developed for the better management of rice crop residue in agriculture fields in a sustainable manner.

Key words: Rice straw burning, bio-degradation, biotechnological approach, Fungi, Rice stubble

Introduction

In India, rice wheat cropping system generates huge quantities of crop residues. Majority of rice and wheat in North West India is harvested by combine harvester leaving residues in the field. The residues of cereal crops are mainly used as cattle feed. Rice straw and husk are used as domestic fuel or in boilers for parboiling rice. Management of rice straw, rather than wheat straw is a serious problem, because there is very little turn-around time between rice harvest and wheat sowing and due to the lack of proper technology for recycling and the higher silica content than other crops. Several management options are available to farmers for the gainful management of crop residues are livestock feed, mushroom cultivation, incorporation, surface retention and mulching, biochar and baling and removing the straw. Farmers use different straw management practices as per the situation (Kumar *et al.*, 2015).

[1] R&D Division, Shriram Institute for Industrial Research 19, University Road, Delhi-110 007, India

The practices in current use, for utilizing rice residue, include livestock fodder, livestock bedding, in-situ incorporation, composting, generating electricity, mushroom cultivation, roof thatching, biogas (anaerobic digestion), furnace fuel, biofuel, and paper and pulp board manufacturing (Rathoure and Bharti, 2018). Presently these options together utilize <15% of the total rice residue produced in NW India. Of the various available options, electricity generation, production of bio-oil, gasification and on-farm utilization of rice residue are the major practices in current use.

Burning of farm waste causes severe pollution of land and water on local as well as regional and global scales. It is estimated that burning of paddy straw results in annual nutrient losses to the tune of 3.85 million tonnes of organic carbon, 59,000 t of nitrogen, 20,000 t of phosphorus and 34,000 t of potassium at the aggregate (Kumar *et al.*, 2015). This also adversely affects the nutrient composition of the soil. When crop residue is burnt existing minerals present in the soil are destroyed, which adversely hampers the cultivation of the next crop. Straw carbon, nitrogen and sulphur are completely burnt and lost in the atmosphere in the process of burning (Bharti, 2017). These results in the emission of smoke which when added to the gases present in the air like methane, nitrogen oxide and ammonia can cause severe atmospheric pollution. These gaseous emissions can pose health risks, aggravating asthma, chronic bronchitis and decreased lung function. Burning of crop residue also contributes indirectly to increased ozone pollution.

The main aim of the study is to develop a process for accelerated degradation of rice crop residues using biotechnological approach having the following objectives:

- To create environmental conditions for accelerated crop residues bio-degradation.
- Optimization of process and parameters standardization of degradation process.
- Standardize the efficiency and performance of degradation process in term of soil quality characteristics.

Pollution Due to Burning

The major pollutants emitted by crop residue burning - CO_2, CO, CH_4, N_2O, NO_x, SO_2, black carbon, non-methyl hydrocarbons (NMHC), volatile organic compounds (VOC) and particulate matter (PM2.5 and PM10), contribute enormously to global warming, environmental degradation and impacts on human health. Extensive crop burning resulted in Delhi air becoming the most polluted in the World in the first week of November 2016, compelling the Government to declare Delhi air pollution an emergency (Agarwal *et al.*, 2008).

Apart from the damage caused by air pollution, burning of rice residue also results in loss of soil organic matter and plant nutrients and adversely affects soil health. About 90% of N and S and 15-20% of P and K contained in rice residue are lost during burning. Burning of 23 million tonnes of rice residues in NW India leads to a loss of about 9.2 million tonnes of C equivalent (CO2-equivalent of about 34 million tonnes) per year and a loss of about 1.4×105 t of N (equivalent to Rs 200 crores) annually. In addition, in-field burning of crop residues also destroys the beneficial micro-flora and fauna of soil causing adverse impact on soil health (Kumar *et al.*, 2015).

Table 7.1: Major Pollutants Emitted During Crop Residue Burning (Singh *et al.*, 2008)

Category	Pollutants	Source
Particulars	SPM (PM100)	Incomplete combustion of in organic material, particle on burnt soil
	RPM (PM10)	Condensation after combustion of gases and incomplete combustion of organic matter
	FPM (PM2.5)	
Gases	CO	Incomplete combustion of organic matter
	NO_2	Oxidation of N2 in air at high temperature
	N_2O	
	O_3	Secondary pollutant, form due to Nitrogen Oxide and Hydrocarbon
	CH_4/Benzene	Incomplete combustion of organic matter
	PAHS	Incomplete combustion of organic matter

SPM Suspended particulate matter; *PM* particulate matter; *FPM* fine particulate matter

One tonne of straw on burning releases 3 kg of particulate matter, 60 kg of CO, 1,460 kg of CO_2, 199 kg of ash and 2 kg of SO_2 (Gupta *et al.* 2004). The major pollutants that are emitted during crop residue burning are given in Table 7.1. Further, in the year 2000, around 78 million tonnes of rice and 85 million tonnes of wheat straw were generated in India of which around 17–18 million tonnes ended up being burnt in the field Singh *et al.* (2008).

Current Scenario

Presently, crop residue are being burnt and creating major problem of winter smog in north India especially over NCR, which creates problems and attract everyone's attention every almost year. It's really one of the big problems and need urgent solution for the betterment of society, environmental quality and ultimately human health. Hence, the proposed work has very high significance for society as well as for entire nation.

Table 7.2: Total Quantity of Crop Stubble Generated in India as Per Different Studies

Sl.No.	Study and year	Total quantity of crop residue produced in India
1.	Garg (2008)	133,138 Gg
2.	Mandal *et al.* (2004)	350 × 106 kg year^{-1}
3.	Gupta *et al.* (2004)	347 million tonnes (2000)
4.	Agarwal *et al.* (2008)	184,902 Gg

Table 7.3: End Use of Stubble by the Farmers

Sl.No.	End use	Rice (percentage of total stubble production)	Wheat (percentage of total stubble production)
1.	Fodder	7	45
2.	Soil incorporation	1	<1
3.	Burnt	81	48
4.	Rope making	4	0
5.	Miscellaneous	7	7

Source: Government of Punjab (2007)

Production and consumption activities generate pollution and waste, and atmospheric environment can absorb pollution/waste up to a limit. Agriculture is one of the important production activities and crop residue burning generates a significant amount of air pollution. Atmospheric environment can absorb this pollution in a particular geographic region given its assimilative capacity. If the burning activities remain confined within the assimilative capacity, the pollution does not create harmful effects. Therefore, in the initial stages when the production and burning activities are limited, pollution caused through these activities is not considered a problem. However, due to technological advancements in the agricultural sector, waste concentration has gone beyond the assimilative capacity of the environmental limit, thereby distorting the balance (Bisen and Rahangdale, 2017).

Table 7.4: Chemical Composition in Rice Straw (Agarwal *et al.* (2008)

Sl.No.	Constituents	Percentage composition
1.	Organic matter	82.0
2.	Crude protein	4.0
3.	Crude fibre	37.0
4.	Ash	18.0

Burning of farm waste causes severe pollution of land and water on local as well as regional and global scales. It is estimated that burning of paddy straw results in annual nutrient losses to the tune of 3.85 million tonnes of organic carbon, 59,000 t of nitrogen, 20,000 t of phosphorus and 34,000 t of potassium at the aggregate (Kumar *et al.*, 2015). This also adversely affects the nutrient composition of the soil. When crop residue is burnt existing minerals present in the soil are destroyed, which adversely hampers the cultivation of the next crop. Straw carbon, nitrogen and sulphur are completely burnt and lost in the atmosphere in the process of burning (Borah *et al.*, 2015). This result in the emission of smoke, which when added to the gases present in the air like methane, nitrogen oxide and ammonia can cause severe atmospheric pollution. These gaseous emissions can pose health risks, aggravating asthma, chronic bronchitis and decreased lung function. Burning of crop residue also contributes indirectly to increased ozone pollution.

Material and Methodology

Experimental Setup

3 quadrates of almost same area are selected for the experimental work. The quadrates must be in situ conditions and having rice stubble and crop residue, which is generally remain in field for open burning. The quadrates are maintained submerged condition for experiment. Nitrogenous fertilizer and selected fungi are to be applied into the quadrates to fastening the degradation rate of lingo-cellulosic crop residue of rice fields.

Nitrogenous Material

A suitable nitrogenous organic material received from sugar industry (Press mud & bio-methanated effluent water) will be used to create the condition favorable.

Microorganisms

Fungi including the deuteromycetes, Aspergillus terreus, Trichoderma reesei; the basidiomycetes, Armillaria sp., Polyporus sp., and Phanerochaete chrysosporium will be obtained from the Microbiology Laboratory or will be arranged from any suitable reference laboratory.

Media and Culture Conditions

Stock cultures of fungi will be maintained at 4°C on commercially prepared Potato Dextrose Agar (PDA, Merck). The vegetative mycelia of fungi were inoculated in 250-ml Erlenmeyer flasks containing 1.0 g of milled agricultural residues (<2 mm) in 100 ml distilled water. Agricultural residues are rice (Oryza sativa) straws. All inoculated cultures will be incubated at 28°C with (120 rev min^{-1}) agitation.

Biodegradation Measurements

After stipulated period of time, filtration of culture media, agricultural residues and fungal active biomasses remaining on the filter paper will be dried in an oven at 75°C. Weight, crude fiber (CF), neutral detergent fiber (NDF) and acid detergent fiber (ADF) losses of each sample will be calculated with respect to their blanks. Crude fiber, NDF, and ADF of these samples were measured according to the gravimetric methods (Sinegani *et al.*, 2005).

Gravimetric methods for the analysis of dietary fiber have been divided into two groups. The first (detergent acid and neutral methods, ADF and NDF) consists in the gravimetric determination of residues previously treated with acid and neutral detergent solutions. These methods determine the insoluble fraction and their individual components (Van Soest´s methods). The second group uses amylolytic and/or proteolytic enzymes determination of insoluble and soluble fraction. Although, the first methods sometimes leads to overestimation due to the incomplete removal of starch, proteins and fats (Robertson and Horvath, 1992), in this study samples will be analyzed for acid and neutral detergent fibers by the method of Van Soest (Van Soest and Wine, 1967, 1968) and crude fiber by the gravimetric method #7071 described in AOAC (1984, 1995). After the treatments, all samples will be ashed for 2 hours at 550°C, cooled and weighed. Crude Fiber, ADF, and NDF will be assayed without residual ash.

Biodegradation and Digestibility

Biodegradation of crop residues by fungi is dependent on the plant and fungus species. Residues reduction varied markedly with plant species. However, there was a relatively good relation between residues biodegradation and fungi lignocellulolytic enzyme activities. The deuteromycetes grew fast and produced more hemicellulolytic and cellulolytic enzymes in easily degradable plant residues like wheat, barley, and pea. Therefore, they reduced more of these crop residues. The basidiomycetes Armillaria sp., Polyporus sp. and Phanerochaete chrysosporium could produce equal or higher amounts of the lignocellulolytic enzyme on the plant residues with high lignin and C/N ratio (result not shown) compared to the other fungi. Consequently, the basidiomycetes degraded these plant residues more.

Digestibility of agricultural residues in animal feeding is deeply dependent on the amounts and types of their fibers. Biological treatment of agricultural residues is a new method for improvement of digestibility. Therefore, the capacity of a few fungi in biodegradation of some agricultural residues will be studied. Losses of crude fiber (CF), neutral detergent fiber (NDF) and acid detergent fiber (ADF) of rice will be investigated in agitated submerged culture vis-à-vis soil characteristics during biodegradation by fungi. Biodegradation of the plant residues is dependent on the plant and fungus species (Sinegani *et al.*, 2005).

The incorporation of the straw in the soil will have a favorable effect on the soil's physical, chemical and biological properties such as pH, organic carbon, water holding capacity and bulk density of the soil. On a long-term basis it has been seen that it increases the availability of zinc, copper, iron and manganese content in the soil and it also prevents the leaching of nitrates. By increasing organic carbon it increases bacteria and fungi in the soil.

Solutions

Various modern inputs were introduced in Punjab to harvest the rice crop within such a short period of time. One such input which has become the most popular implement in the rice-wheat cropping system is the use of the combined mechanized harvester (CMH). The use of the combined harvester has increased at a tremendous rate in Punjab. Almost 80 % of the rice crop is harvested using this implement in Punjab. However, the use of the combined harvester has in reality exacerbated the problem of crop residue management. The use of combined harvesters leaves behind a large amount of rice residue to be burnt in the open fields. The combined harvester spreads the rice residue in the fields which is difficult to collect. It is widely perceived that farmers find it the easiest and the most economical way of getting rid of the rice stubble through burning it. Also, the shortage of time for sowing the wheat crop, after the rice crop harvest, leaves farmers with no other option but to burn it (Kumar *et al.*, 2015).

Thus, burning has emerged as the standard method of rice residue/stubble management in the combine harvested rice-wheat cropping system that is practised on a broad scale in the state of Punjab in northwest India. Every year almost 15 million tonnes of paddy straw are generated in Punjab. Of this, according to various estimates, on an average, almost 7–8 million tonnes of rice residue are set on fire in open fields (NAAS, 2017).

Rice residue burning results in extensive impacts both on and off farm, e.g., losses in soil nutrients, soil organic matter, production and productivity, air quality, biodiversity, and water and energy efficiency and on human and animal health. In India, air pollution from residue burning can be severe, with impacts on human health by directly causing or exacerbating a range of health hazards and contributing to the incidence of traumatic road accidents through significantly reduced visibility. One of the recognized threats to the rice-wheat cropping system sustainability is the loss of soil organic matter as a result of burning. The straw collected from the fields is of great economic value as livestock feed, fuel and industrial raw material. In northern India, wheat straw is preferred while in Southern India paddy straw is fed to livestock (Hegde 2010). The residue generated from the rice wheat cropping system can be put to many uses, but this is possible if the residue is separated from the grain and carried out of the field. Burning reduces the availability of straw to livestock, which is already in short supply by more than 40 %. However, in the case of combine harvesting, most of the residue is left in the field for burning adversely affecting overall sustainability of the rice-wheat cropping system

(Thakur 2003). Zero tillage after stubble burning is now being adopted by many farmers. In 2005–2006, around 10 % of the total area sown under wheat was by using zero till machines. Apparently less than 1 % of farmers incorporate the paddy straw because in the case of incorporation more tillage operations are required than after burning (Singh *et al.* 2008). The options for crop residue management may include developing systems to plant residue into bailing and removal for use as animal feed or for industry. Enhanced decomposition of machine-harvested straw to improve nutrients in the soil can be useful. The use of microbial sprays that can speed up decomposition of residue is also an option. The option of planting into residue needs further investigation of inorganic nitrogen and its adverse effect due to nitrogen deficiency.

Lignocellulosic materials are the most abundant agricultural residues in the world. They are constantly being replenished by photosynthesis. Thus, microorganisms able to degrade these compounds, including fungi as well as actinomycetes and other bacteria, have an important role in increasing their digestibility. Biological treatment of agricultural residues is a new method for the improvement of their digestibility (Jalk *et al.*, 1998).

Although cellulolytic fungi occur in all major fungal taxa (Coughlan, 1985), there are relatively few groups of microorganisms that can produce the ligninolytic enzymes. The most efficient lignin degrading microorganisms are the white-rot fungi (Falcon *et al.*, 1995; Orth and Tien, 1995). Hence much of the research on the lignin-degrading enzyme systems has centered upon the enzymes of the white-rot fungi specially Phanerochaete Chrysosporium. However, there is considerable documentation on the bioremediation and biodegradation of the lignin-related compounds by the imperfect fungi (Betts and Dart, 1988; Iyayi and Dart, 1982). The major objective of this study is to characterize and directly compare the biodegradation capacities of a number of saprophytic fungi on agricultural residues.

Significance

Residue waste of rice crop is being burnt in north India and creating major environmental problem and it's really one of the big problems and need urgent solution for the betterment of society, environmental quality and ultimately human health. Currently, not much degradation measures are being used in Punjab and crop residues are being burnt openly, which not only creates air pollution but also degrading soil quality characteristics too.

Hence, it's a very wonderful idea to manage the rice crop residues in situ using biotechnological approach and by modifying environmental conditions. The proposed process has a great potential to utilize the beneficial elements of crop residues, by promoting sustainable agriculture practice as well as pollution abatement. Once the process is optimized at various stages including bench, semi-pilot and in-situ, it can be used agriculture fields. This eco-friendly process will make benefit the agriculture yields, soil quality and environmental conservation.

REFERENCES

Agarwal, S., Trivedi, R. C. & Sengupta, B. (2008): Air Pollution Due to Burning of Agricultural Residue. *Indian Journal of Air Pollution Control*, 8(1), 51–59.

AOAC (1984). Official Methods of Analysis, 14th edn. Association of Official Analytical Chemists, Washington, DC, USA.

AOAC (1995). Official Methods of Analysis, 16th edn. Association of Official Analytical Chemists, Washington, DC, USA.

Betts WB, Dart RK (1988). The Biodegradation of Lignin-related Compounds by Aspergillus flavus. *J. Gen. Microbiol.* 134: 2413-2420.

Bisen N. and Rahangdale CP (2017): Crop Residues Management Option for Sustainable Soil Health in Rice-wheat System: A Review. *International Journal of Chemical Studies.* 5(4): 1038-1042.

Boraha Nilay, Rajen Baruaa, Dhrubajyoti Natha, Kailash Hazarikab, Amrita Phukona, Kasturi Goswamia, Deben Chandra Baruac (2016): Low Energy Rice Stubble Management through in Situ Decomposition. *Procedia Environmental Sciences* 35: 771-780.

Bharti, P.K. (2017): Organic Farming, *Current Science*, 112(8): 1617.

Coughlan M (1985). The Properties of Fungal and Bacterial Cellulases with Comment on their Activities and Application. *Biotechnol. Genet.Engr. Rev.* 3: 39-109.

Falcon MA, Rodriguez A, Carnicero A, Regalado V, Perestelo F, Milstein O, Fuente GL (1995). Isolation of Microorganisms with Lignin Transformation Potential from Soil of Tenerife Island. *Soil Biol. Biochem.* 27: 121-126.

Garg, S. C. (2008). Traces Gases Emission from Field Burning of Crop Residues. Indian Journal of Air Pollution Control, viii(1), 76–86.

Gupta P. K., Sahai, S., Singh, N., Dixit, C. K., Singh, D. P., Sharma, C. (2004). Residue Burning in Rice-wheat Cropping System: Causes and Implications. *Current Science*, 87(12), 1713–1715.

Government of Punjab. (2007). State of Environment. Chandigarh: Punjab State Council of Science and Technology.

Hegde N. G. (2010). Forage Resource Development in India. In: Souvenir of IGFRI Foundation Day, November, 2010. www.baif.org.in.

Iyayi CB, Dart RK (1982). The Biodegradation of p-Coumaryl Alcohol by Aspergillus flavus. *J. Gen. Microbiol.* 128: 1473-1482.

Jalk D, Nerud R, Siroka P (1998). The Effectiveness of Biological Treatment of Wheat Straw by White Rot Fungi. *Folia Microbiol.* 43: 687-689.

Kumar P.; Kumar S. and Joshi L. (2015): The Extent and Management of Crop Stubble. In: Socioeconomic and Environmental Implications of Agricultural Residue Burning: A Case Study of Punjab, India. *Springer Briefs in Environmental Sciences, SpringerOpen*, pp: 144 (ISBN 978-81-322-2014-5).

Mandal, K. G., Misra, A. K., Hati, K. M., Bandyopadhyay, K. K., Ghosh, P. K., & Mohanty, M. (2004). Rice Residue Management Options and Effects on Soil Properties and Crop Productivity. *Food, Agriculture and Environment*, 2, 224–231.

NAAS (2017): Innovative Viable Solution to Rice Residue Burning in Rice-Wheat Cropping System through Concurrent Use of Super Straw Management System-fitted Combines and Turbo Happy Seeder. Policy Brief No.2, *National Academy of Agricultural Sciences, New Delhi*. P:16.

Orth AB, Tien M (1995). Biotechnology of Lignin Biodegradation. In: Kuck (Ed). The mycota II. Genetics and Biotechnology. *Springer- Verlag Berlin Heidelberg CO*. pp. 289-302.

Rathoure, A.K. and Bharti, P.K. (2018): Emerging Trends in Bioremediation Success: Implication and Application, *Brillion Publication, Delhi*, pp. 330.

Sinegani, A. A. Safari; Emtiazi, G.; Hajrasuliha, S. and Shariatmadari H. (2005): Biodegradation of Some Agricultural Residues by Fungi in Agitated Submerged Cultures. *African Journal of Biotechnology*. 4 (10): 1058-1061.

Thakur, T. C. (2003). Crop Residue as Animal Feed: Addressing Resource Conservation Issues in Rice–wheat Systems of South Asia, A Resource Book. Rice Wheat Consortium for Indo-Gangetic Plains (CIMMYT), March, 2003.

Van Soest PJ, Wine RH (1967). Use of Detergents in the Analysis of Fibrous Feeds. IV. Determination of Plant Cell-wall Constituents. *J. Assoc. Off. Anal. Chem.* 50: 50-55.

Van Soest PJ, Wine RH (1968). Determination of Lignin and Cellulose in Acid-detergent Fiber with Permanganate. *J. Assoc. Off. Anal. Chem.* 51: 780-785.

Advances in Microbiology: *Applications & Significance* Pages 133-154
Edited by: Dr. Pawan Kumar 'Bharti'
ISBN: 978-93-86841-97-1
Edition: 2019
Published by: Discovery Publishing House Pvt. Ltd., New Delhi (India)

8

Endophytic Microbes
A Novel Approach for Plant Disease Management

[1]Joginder Pal, [2]Satish K. Sharma,
[3]Ranjna Sharma, [4]Monica Sharma and [5]Sonia Kaushal

ABSTRACT

Endophytes constitute the group of microorganisms that usually inhabit the plant host intercellularly but sometimes intracellularly without causing any apparent noticeable symptoms. These microorganisms are extremely diverse in their habitat concern and found virtually in all the living tissues of every plant species on earth. The endophytic microbes maintain a variety of relationships, ranging from symbiotic to slightly pathogenic. Enhanced host plant resistance to various phytopathogens has been reported in several host plant and endophytic interactions. Endophytes nowdays are gaining attention as a subject due to their wide applications in plant pathology which made them valuable tool in crop performence and management of plant diseases. These microorganisms are present in a much more protected environment than rhizosphere and therefore explored the excellent source of potential biocontrol agents. Endophytic microorganisms are able to provide many functional mechanisms besides being preventing the deleterious effects of pathogenic microorganisms. The widely recognised plant disease management mechanisms mediated by fungal and bacterial endophytes are discussed in this review.

Key words: Endophytes, symbiotic, rhizosphere, biocontrol agents.

Introduction

Endophytes has been known since the end of the 19th century and are first distinguished from epiphytic microorganisms by DeBary (1887).These microbes are known to colonize internal plant tissues without inducing apparent symptoms of disease.and represent a large diversity of microbial adaptations that have developed in special and hidden environments. In general, approximately 300,000-500,000 plant species growing in unexplored area on the earth are host to one or more endophytes (Strobel, 2006). Recently, more importance is given to endophytes research because of declining global biodiversity, disappearance of species and ecosystem, etc. (Gimenez *et al.*,

[1,5] Department of Plant Pathology, Dr. Y.S. Parmar University of Horticulture and Forestry Nauni, Solan-173230 (Himachal Pradesh), INDIA

2007). The intimate association of these microorganisms with host plants offers a unique oppurtinity for their potential application in plant protection and biological control. The term endophytes refers to internal colonization of plants by fungal or bacterial microbes, which made these microbes precious for agriculture and a tool to advance crop performance (Azevedo *et al.*, 2000). Charles Bacon and his colleagues found that leaves and stems of the pasture grass systemically colonized by a fungus (*Neotyphodium coenophialum*), can be beneficial to their plant hosts by increasing their tolerance to biotic and abiotic stresses.

In 1980's, Dr. C. Reed Funkat at Rutrers university investigated the potential insect resistance of endophytes infected rye grass plants. Carroll (1986) used it for those organisms that cause asymptomatic infections within plant tissues, excluding pathogenic and mycorrhizal fungi whereas, Shimanuki (1987) first recorded an endophyte and showed that timothy (*Phleum pratense*) plants infected with the choke fungus, *Epichloe typhina*, were resistant to the fungus *Cladosporium phlei*. Endophytic microorganisms comprises especially of fungi and bacteria that colonize internal tissues without causing visible damage to their hosts (Petrini, 1991). Wilson (1995) defined endophytes as the those fungi that live internally and remain asymptomatic for atleast part of their life cycle. Studies on these microorganisms from plant species are recently becoming more frequent, since these fungi and bacteria have been studied for biological control and production of compounds with pharmacological properties. Later on, all microorganisms residing inside plants without producing visible symptoms were categorized as endophytes (Azevedo *et al.*, 2000).

Bacon and White (2000) defined endophytes as 'microbes that colonize living internal tissues of plants without causing any immediate, overt negative effect. There are many reports demonstrating that many bioactive compounds could be produced by endophytic microoganisms (Haung *et al.*, 2001). Furthermore, the endophytic microorganisms are not considered as saprophytes since they are associated with living tissues and contribute to the well being of plants. Endophytes are broad spectrum or more diverse in range than the pathogenic microorganisms present in living plant tissues. They primarily presents in the roots and the aerial parts (leaves, bark, petiole, inflorescence) of plants and are different from phytopathogenic microorganisms because they are not deterimental and do not cause diseases to plants. These microbes are distinct from epiphytic microorganisms because they later live on the surface of plant organs and tissues but the endophytic microorganisms inhabit the living plant tissues (Hallmann *et al.*, 1997). The larger endophytic populations were reported in roots followed by leaves, stem, twigs, flowers and other aerial plant parts (Lamb *et al.*, 1996; Hallmann *et al.*, 2006).

Endophytes offers a wide range of benefits to plants such as control of pathogen suppresion inside the plants directly by the production of antibiotics

(Sturtz *et al.*, 1999), indirectly by induction of plant resistance response and promoting growth (Barka *et al.*, 2002; Kang *et al.*, 2007), reducing diseases severity (Kloepper *et al.*, 2004; Senthilkumar *et al.*, 2007), inducing defense mechanisms (Bakker *et al.*, 2007) and competition for nutrients (Puente *et al.*, 2009). Endophytes-host relationships ranging from mutualistic to slightly pathogenic, therefore both either endophytes as well as host plants get benefits from the relationships. Endophytes gains energy, shelter and nutrient as well as protection from environmental stress whereas, plant Growth promotion (enhanced nutrient uptake), increased tolerance to harsh environments (e.g. drought tolerance) and induced resistance to pests and diseases (Schulz and Boyle, 2005).

Endophytes get an edge over their rhizospheric antagonists-counterpartson association of their abiliy to enter the host system without stimulating pathogens induced vulnerability responses but triggering host defense pathways (Conn *et al.*, 2008). Endophytes may be fungi, bacteria or actinomycetes which colonizes internal living tissues of plants either as obligate or in facultative associated with lower and higher plants without causing any immediate negative or external symptom to host and shows the beneficial effects to their host plant (Padhi *et al.*, 2013). Fungal endophytes benefit plants by promoting plant growth and involves various mechanisms of plant protection including production of antibiotics, induction of plant resistance, seceretion of lytic enzymes, hyperparasitism and stimulation of plant secondary metabolites (Gao *et al.*, 2010). On the other hand, bacterial endophytic microorganisms generally responds by producing phytohormones, fixing nitrogen, solubilizing phosphate, production of antibiotic compounds and suppression of phytopathogens by competence of invasion sites (Lin *et al.*, 2013).

Recently endophytes are viewed as outstanding source of secondary metabolites that acts as a store house of bioactive compound and provide a broad variety of bioactive secondary metabolites with unique structure. The important bioactive compounds elicited by these microbes includes alkaloids, benzopyranones, flavonoids, phenolic acids, quinones, steroids, terpenoids, tetralones, xanthones etc. (Tan and Zou, 2001). Such bioactive metabolites have wide-ranging applications as agro-chemicals, antibiotics, immunosuppressants, antiparasitics, antioxidants, and anticancer agents therefore, contributing largely in various fields of industrial, agriculture and pharmaceutical (Strobel, 2003).

Being internal colonizers, endophytes provide a barrier against the invading pathogens directly or through the production of bioactive compounds (Thomas and Upreti 2014; Podolich *et al.*, 2015). Besides this, antibiotics produced by these microorganisms has unique activity to suppresses many phytopathogens.Natural products produced by various endophytic microbes also acts as immuno suppressive agent, antidiabetic agents, insecticidal agents, antioxidant agents, antiviral agents, products of plant growth and development, antibiotics and anticancerous agents. Endophytic fungi *Gliocladium* spp. found effective in reducing mean population from soil and root of tomato plant when it was treated at 10^6 cfu/ml (Amin, 2014; Gomez-Lama Cabanas *et al.*, 2014). This article reviews the plant disease management mechanisms of endophytes i.e. how plants be benefited with endophytisms.

Fungal Endophytes in Plant Disease Management

Endophytic fungi are broad spectrum microorganisms which colonizes the plants without causing any symptoms and proven an effective biological control agents against a variety of fungal pathogens. They are widespread in all the kingdom fungi but most of them belong to phylum Ascomycota. These are often closely related to fungi which are known to cause disease, either in healthy tissues or as seconday invaders of damaged tissues (Schardl *et al.*, 1997). This suggests that the endophytes may have evolved from the pathogens or vice-versa. The intensive work regarding fungal endophytes suggested that they have a potential to produce antimicrobial compounds and control various plant pathogens. (Duijff *et al.*, 1997; Sturz and Matheson, 1996), and nematodes (Hallmann *et al.*, 1998). Schulz *et al.* (2002) isolated and screened 6500 endophytic fungi from plants for biologically active metabolites and found positive correlation between bio-activity and biotope. Many endophytic fungi are known to produce antimicrobial substances. Arnold *et al.* (2003) showed that fungal leaf endophytes protect *Theobroma cacao* against *Phythophthora* diseases, and similarly Lee *et al.* (2009) also revealed that the endophytic *Fusarium verticillioides* reduces disease severity of *Ustilago maydis* on maize. *Gliocladium catenulatum* has been found effective in controlling the witches broom disease of cacao reducing the disease incidence upto 70% at seedling stage during *in vitro* and *in vivo* studies (Rubini *et al.*, 2005).

Shahasi *et al.* (2006) has isolated nine endophytic *F. oxysporum* and screened them for the production of secondary metabolites which was antagonistic to *Radopholus similis* in the culture. Fungal endophytes induced ISR may also associate with the expression of pathogenesis related genes. *F. solani,* isolated from the root tissues of tomato elicited induced systemic resistance against the tomato foliar pathogen, *Septoria lycopersici* and triggered PR genes, PR5 and PR7 expression in the roots (Kavroulakis *et al.*, 2007).

Mejia *et al.* (2008) studied fungal endophytes isolated from healthy *Theobroma cacao* tissues and carried *in vitro* screening for antagonism against major pathogens of cacao. Of the tested endophytic morphospecies, they found that 40% (21/52), 65% (28/43) and 27% *in vitro* antagonism against *Moniliophthora roreri* (frosty pod rot), *Phytophthora palmivora* (black pod rot) and *Moniliophthora perniciosa* (witches broom), respectively. The observed reduction in pod loss due to *Phytophthora* spp., and sporulation by *M. roreri*, supports the potential of fungal endophytes as biological control agents. Guo *et al.* (2009) isolated 47 endophytic fungi from liverwort *Scapania verrucosa* and tested them against *Pyricularia oryzae* for their antifunal activity, where they found strain T11 having strong capability to be developed as antifungal agent. Microbial predations are the mode of action of endophyte to suppress the plant pathogens. *Trichoderma* produces a range of enzymes that are directly used against the cell walls of fungi to utilize the fragment of pathogens (Gao *et al.*, 2010).

Mahapatra and Banerjee (2010) had evaluated endophytes of petiole, bark and leaf isolated from *Alstonia scholaris* (L.) R.Br. for their antibacterial activity and noted *Curvularia* sp., *Aspergillus* sp. and an unidentified fungus shows significant activity. A new a-tetralone derivative (3S)-3,6,7- trihydroxy-a-tetralone together with cercosporamide, b-sitosterol and trichodermin was reported to be produced by *Phoma sp.* endophytic in *Arisaema erubescens*. These isolated compounds exhibited antifungal and antibacterial activity against pathogenic fungi *Fusarium oxysporum, Rhizoctonia solani, Colletotrichum gloeosporioides* and *Magnaporthe oryzae* as well as against two plant pathogenic bacteria *Xanthomonas campestris* and *Xanthomonas oryzae* (Wang *et al.*, 2012).

Orole and Adejumo (2009) reported the effect of endophytic isolates of fungi on different test pathogens viz., *Fusarium oxysporum, Fusarium pallidoroseum, Fusarium verticillioides* and *Cladosporium herbaru* and found that *Acremonium* spp. showed the highest potential (80 to 90%) under *in vitro* conditions.They are ubiqitous and occur within all known plant host order, family genera and species (Su *et al.*, 2010; Sun *et al.*, 2011). Amin *et al.* (2013) isolated four endophytic isolates from maize i.e. *Aspergillus* sp., T*richoderma* sp., *Beauveria* sp., *Gliocladium* sp., and evaluated them as seed treatment at planting and as flour formulation on rhizosphere (20 days after planting). The result showed that the average downy mildew disease intensity on the plots treated with *Beauveria* sp. was consistently lower than the control plots.

Mode of Action of Endophytic Fungi

The colonization of plant tissues by endophytic fungi occurs in a manner similar to those of plant pathogens and mycorrhizae. In order to colonize the plant, endophytes find their way through cracks formed at the emergence of lateral roots or at the zone of elongation and differentiation of roots. Fungal endophytes have the ability to produce numerous extracellular enzymes; such as pectinases, cellulases, lipases, amylases, laccases, and proteinases. These fungal enzymes play the key role in biodegradation and hydrolysis processes which are significantly important mechanisms against pathogenic infection. It has also been proposed that cellulolytic and pectinolytic enzymes produced by endophytes are involved in the infection process (Sunitha *et al.*, 2013). Entry and mode of entry of entry of fungi is given in the Figure 8.1:

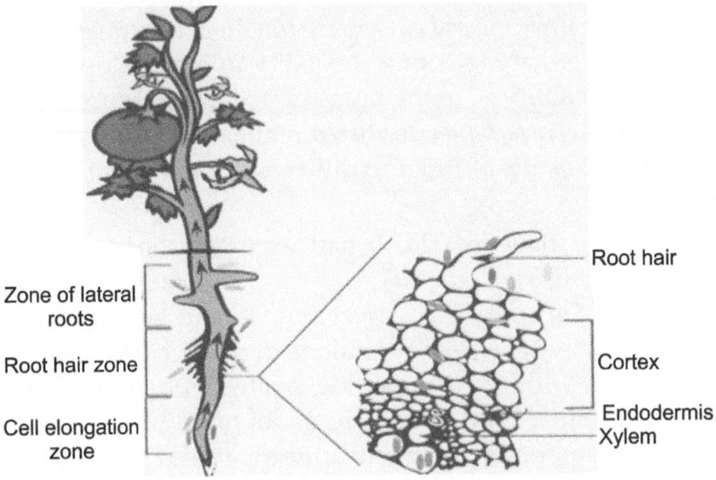

Fig 8.1. Entry and colonization of endophytic fungi (Malfanova *et al.*, 2013)

Endophyte and Pathogenicity

Several researchers reported that endophytes may become latent pathogen due to changes in developmental stages of host and fungus, environmental factors such as CO_2 accumulation or O_2 depletion and host defense responses (Saikkonen *et al.*, 2002). Mutation of pathogenic *Colletotrichum magna* resulted in the loss of a virulence factor and transformed into an endophytic fungus. Hence, parasitism is an exception in plant-endophytes interactions. Existence of balanced antagonism between the virulence of the colonizing endophyte and the plant defence response has been reported to be a key factor involved in endophytic relationship without producing any apparent symptom (Macia-Vicente *et al.*, 2009).

How Does the Endophyte Manage to Exist and Grow within its Host Without Causing Visible Disease Symptoms?

Asymptomatic colonization of endophytes is a balanced antagonistic interaction between host plant and endophyte. Once the host-endophyte interaction becomes imbalanced either disease results in the host plant or the plant defense machinery kills the pathogenic endophytic fungus. Whether the interaction is balanced or imbalanced depends on the virulence of the fungus and the defense of the host, and both virulence and defense being variable and influenced by environmental factors, nutritional status and developmental stages of the partners. A general interaction between host plant and endophytes is described in the Figure 8.2.

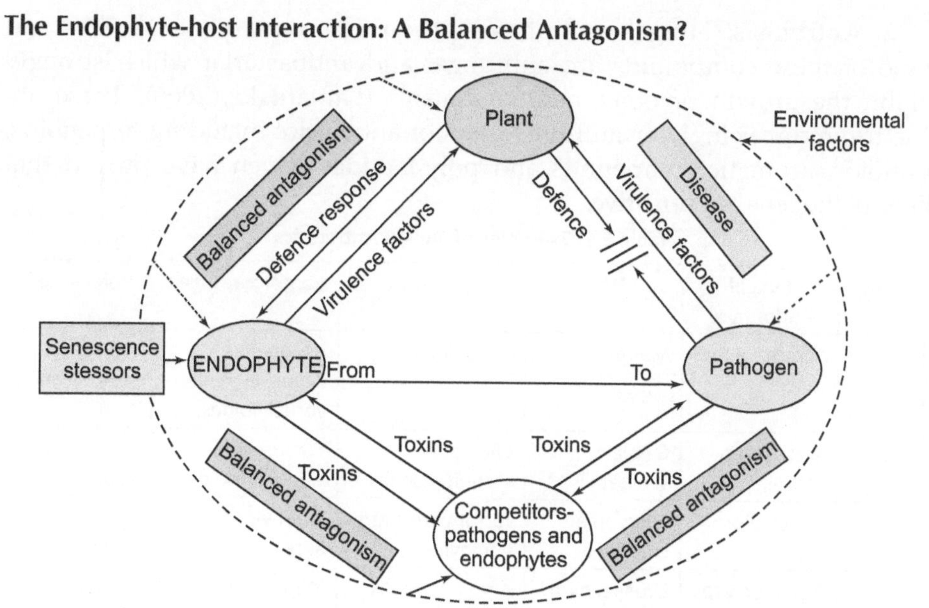

Fig. 8.2. A Balance of antagonisms between endophytic virulence and plant defense response results in asymptomatic colonization (Schulz and Boyle, 2005).

Mechanism of Action of Endophytic Fungi

Type	Mechanism
Direct	Hyperparasitism/Predation
	Antibiotics
Indirect	Promotion of plant growth and physiology
	Stimulation of plant secondary metabolites
	Induction of plant resistance and protection from abiotic stresses

Direct Mechanism

1. Hyperparasitism/Predation: In hyper parasitism, the pathogen is directly attacked by a specific endophyte that kills it or its propagules (Tripathi *et al.*, 2008). Fungal endophytes parasitize around hyphae of pathogens by various means as twisting, penetrating the hyphae of pathogens and secreting lyase to decompose cell wall of pathogens. Microbial predations are the mode of action of endophyte to suppress the plant pathogens. *Trichoderma* produces a wide range of enzymes that are directly used against the cell walls of fungi to utilize the fragment of pathogens and are also able to parasitize *Trichoderma* are able to parasitize hyphae of plant pathogen such as *Rhizoctonia solani* and many of these observations are linked with biocontrol (Gao *et al.*, 2010; Grosch *et al.*, 2006).

2. Antibiosis: Fungal endophytes produce secondary metabolites and some of these compounds are antifungal and antibacterial which strongly inhibit the growth of other microorganisms (Gunatilaka, 2006). These are able to produce single or multiple kinds of antibiotics including terpenoids, alkaloids, aromatic compounds and polypeptides which have proved that plant pathogens are sensitive.

Table 8.1: Examples of Fungal Antibiotics

S.No.	Fungal endophyte	Host	Antibiotic	Target pathogen	Reference
1.	Acremonium zeae	Maize	Pyrrocidines	Aspergillus flavus, Fusarium verticillioides	Wicklow et al., 2005
2.	Verticillium sp.	Cassia spectabilis	Cadinane sesquiterpenes	Cladosporium cladosporioides	Silva et al., 2006
3.	Gliocladium sp.	Eucryphia cordifolia	Tetrohydrofuran, Aciphyllene	Staphylococcus aureus	Ly et al., 2008
4.	Ampelomyces sp.	Urospermum picroides	Altersolanol A	Staphylococcus aureus	Ly et al., 2008

Indirect Mechanism

1. Promotion of plant growth and physiology: An increase in plant growth will prevent a variety of abiotic and biotic stresses, reflecting plant vigor or persistence and considered as a potential protection to pathogen challenge (Kuldau and Bacon, 2008). *Colletotrichum* sp., an endophytic fungus in *Artemisia annua* produces substances like indole acetic acid (IAA) to regulate plant processes (Lu *et al.*, 2000). It is reasonable to believe that enhancement of plant growth induced by fungal endophytes will increase indirect protection to pathogens. It has been also reported that *Aspergillus flavus, A. niger, Fusarium oxysporum, Penicillium corylophilum, P. cyclopium, P. funiculosum* and *Rhizopus stolonifer* have the capacity to produce gibberllic acid (GAs) and IAA. Reduced content of stress responsive abscisic acid suggest lesser stress convened to endophyte associated plants (Khan *et al.*, 2012).

2. Stimulation of plant secondary metabolites: Endophytes provide a broad variety of bioactive secondary metabolites with unique structure, including alkaloids, benzopyranones, flavonoids, phenolic acids, quinones, steroids, terpenoids, tetralones, xanthones, and others . Such bioactive metabolites find wide-ranging application as agrochemicals, antibiotics, immune suppressants, antiparasitics, antioxidants, and anticancer agents (Strobel, 2003).

3. Induction of plant resistance: Endophytic fungi are becoming essential for protecting host plant from diseases and damages inflicted by various biotic factors and also impart enhanced tolerance to abiotic stresses (Siegel *et al.*, 1990;

Vega *et al.*, 2008). Pathogenesis related proteins (PR proteins) comprises of a variety of enzymes, some of which may act directly to lyses the invading cells, including chitinase and 1, 3-glucanases (Fukuda and Shinshi,1994). *Fusarium solani* isolated from root tissues of tomato elicited induced systemic resistance against the tomato foliar pathogen *Septoria lycopersici* and triggered PR genes, PR 5 and PR7 expression in roots (Kavroulakis *et al.*, 2007). *Citrullus lanatus* and *Cucumis sativus* exposed to a non pathogenic mutant of *Colletotrichum magna* exhibited high levels lignin deposition, peroxidase activity and phenyl alanine, ammonia lyase activity and obtained the protection against disease caused by *Colletotrichum orbiculare* and *Fusarium oxysporum* (Redman *et al.*, 1999).

Piriformospora indica, a new root colonizing endophytic fungus was discovered by Varma *et al.*, 1999. *P. indica* colonizes various monocot and dicot plants and convey several benefits to host plants such as better tolerance to various biotic and abiotic stresses. In low NaCl salt stress condition, the endophyte *Piriformospora indica*-infected barley plants showed higher than non-infected barley plants (Waller *et al.*, 2005). The contribution of *P. indica* symbiosis to improve plant drought and salinity tolerance might point towards the natural habitat of its desert origin (Sherameti *et al.*, 2008).

Ting *et al.* (2009) observed that endophytes isolated from roots of wild banana elicited the production of host enzyme related to induced resistance. A significant increase in all levels of enzyme and biochemical markers assayed (peroxidase, polyphenoloxidase, phenyalanine ammonia lyase, phenol content and lignothiolycolic acid) was observed in inoculated plantlets than control. As a result, the endophyte pre-treated plantlets recorded lower percentage of disease incidence and severity, suggesting the possible role of induced host resistance triggered by the endophyte UPM31P1. Amin *et al.* (2013) isolated four endophytic fungi i.e. *Aspergillus* sp., *Trichoderma* sp, *Beauveria* sp., *Gliocladium* sp., from maize and were evaluated as seed treatment at planting and as flour formulation on rhizosphere 20 days after planting. The result showed that the average downy mildew disease intensity on the plots treated with *Beauveria* sp., was consistently lower than the control plots.

Bacterial Endophytes in Plant Disease Management

Endophytic bacteria can be defined as those bacteria that colonize the internal tissue of the plant showing no external sign of infection or negative effect on their host (Holliday, 1989; Schulz and Boyle, 2006).Endophytic bacteria have the ability to promote growth and inhibit plant disease, and as they are in intimate contact with the plant they are an attractive choice as biological control agents. Sturz *et al.*, (1999) found that 61 of 192 endophytic bacterial isolates from potato stem tissues were effective biocontrol agents against *Clavibacter michiganensis* subsp. *sepedonicus*. Bivi *et al.* 2011 isolated twenty endophytic bacteria from

from symptomless oil palm roots but only seven isolates showed inhibitory effect by suppressing the mycelial growth of *Ganoderma boninense*. The isolated bacteria were screened *in vitro* by dual culture assay and culture filtrate test for their antagonistic properties towards *G. boninense*. Four bacterial endophytes (EB2, EB4, EB5 and EB6) were established to have potential as biocontrol agents suppressed the fungal growth by an average of 56.65, 91.45, 69.48 and 97.95%, respectively on Nutrient Agar (NA) medium. Thirty one endophytic bacteria belonging to *Pseudomonas, Bacillus, Enterobacter, Klebsiella, Acetobacter Burkholderia, Rhizobium* and *Xanthomonas* were isolated from soybean and were screened *in vitro* for the antagonistic activity against soil-borne fungal pathogens of soybean viz., *Rhizoctonia solani, Fusarium oxysporum, Sclerotium rolfsii*. The effective antagonists were further screened for their plant growth promoting (PGP) activity viz., production of plant growth siderophores and HCN. Five isolates JDB 3 (*Pseudomonas sp.), JDB 5 (Pseudomonas sp.), JDB 9 (Bacillus sp.), JDB 11 (Bacillus sp.) and JDB 14 (Bacillus sp.) were found to* exhibit maximum number of PGP traits and possess dual abilities i.e. antagonistic and plant growth promotion with the view of plant health and productivity (Dalal and Kulkarni, 2013). Nagendran *et al*., 2013 isolated twenty-nine bacterial endophytes from different plant sources and tested their efcacy against *R. solani* inciting sheath blight in rice. He found that *Bacillus subtilis* var. *amyloliquefaciens* (FZB24) caused a maximum 36% inhibition of *R. Solani* and higher concentration of defence-related enzymes, peroxidase, polyphenol oxidase and phenylalanine ammonia lyase and total phenols were produced in plants than in the untreated control plants.

Gholami *et al*. (2013) studied eight different endophytic bacteria for their biocontrol activity and found that *Bacillus subtilis* subsp. *subtilis* (96.66%) showed highest percent inhibition of mycelial growth against *Colletotrichum lindemuthianum*, while disease severity was in the range of 40 to 76.80% against anthracnose of bean when compared to control.Nineteen bacterial endophytic strains were isolated from red fruit of chilli and were screened for their antagonistic potential against *Colletotrichum gloeosporioides*, cause of anthracnose of chilli. Ten strains i.e. CEFR-1, CEFR-3, CEFR-4, CEFR-4, CEFR-5, CEFR-6, CEFR-7, CEFR-9, CEFR-10, CEFR-11 and CEFR-12 were identified as fungal antagonistic strains against *Colletotrichum* and were proved to be the most promising biocontrol isolates (Allu *et al*., 2014).

Entry and Mode of Action of Endophytic Bacteria

The preferable sites of bacterial attachment and subsequent entry are wounds and the apical root zone such as the cell elongation and the basal root hair zone. For active penetration, endophytic bacteria have cell wall degrading enzymes (Pectinases and cellulolytic enzymes) which hydrolyze the plant's exodermal cell walls. Hydrolytic enzymes, pectinases and cellulases play a role in the mechanisms by which endophytic bacteria penetrate into and persist in the host plant which hydrolyze the plant's exodermal cell walls (Hallmann *et al.*, 1997; Reinhold-Hurek and Hurek, 1998). Also many proteins involved in defense pathways in plants (Norman-Setterblad *et al.*, 2000). The expression of endoglucanase, the main cellulase responsible for hydrolysis of β (1!4) linkage in cellulose, was detected *ad planta e.g. Azoarcus* sp. *BH72* (Reinhold-Hurek *et al.*, 2006). A general entry and colonization of endophytic bacteria is described in Figure 8.3.

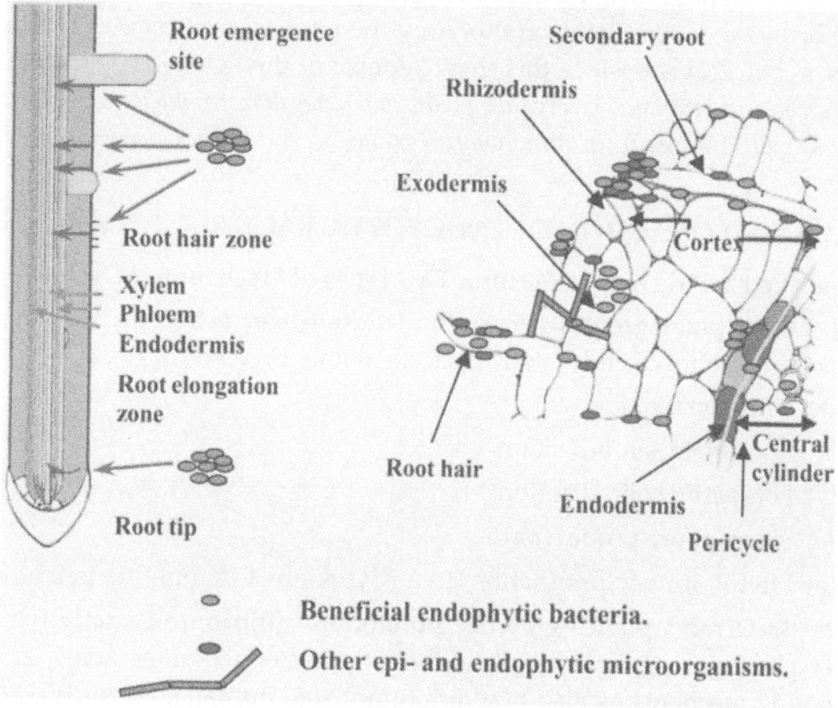

Fig. 8.3. Entry and colonization of plant by endophytic bacteria (Reinhold-Hurek and Hurek (1998) and Compant (2007).

"Main colonization used by endophytes seems to be rhizosphere and reach the rhizosphere by chemotaxis followed by attachment:Type IV pili, lipopolysaccharide and exopolysaccharide are shown to play roles in attachment of endophytes. At the sites of passive penetration bacteria form biofilms around the roots to protect root tissues from the pathogens.The preferred site of attachment and subsequent entry is the wound and the apical root zone such as the cell elongation zone and the root hair zone. Lateral roots are generally considered as the main 'doors' for bacterial penetration to move deeper inside and occupy the intercellular space of the cortex. For penetration, they produce Hydrolytic enzymes such as pectinases and cellulolytic enzymes which hydrolyse the exodermal walls whereas, enzymes such as endoglucanases and exoglucanase enzymes (β- glucosidase) was identifid to be key player for colonization and spreading through the intercellular space of root cortex by distrupting the endodermal barrier. Bacterial flagella and plant transpiration stream seem to further support their movements inside plants. However, only few endophytes are able to colonize aerial vegetative plants part" (Reinhold *et al.*, 2006).

Plant endophytic bacteria mainly colonize the plant cortex where they cross the exodermal barier e.g. *Paenibacillus polymyxa in Arabidopsis* (Timmusk *et al.*, 2005) or move deeper inside and occupy the intercellular space of the cortex (Gasser *et al.*, 2011) Besides this they colonize of the xylem e.g. *Pseudomonas fluorescens* and *reproductice organ e.g. Gluconobacter diazotrophicus* on sugarcane (James *et al.*, 2002) and for *Streptomyces galbus* on rhododendron (Suzuki *et al.*, 2005).

MECHANISM OF ACTION OF ENDOPHYTIC BACTERIA

Endophytic Bacteria Mainly Perform Two Types of Mechanism of Action

1. Direct plant growth promotion (Biofertilizer activity): Direct plant promotion activity of endophytic bacteria mainly involves:

(*i*) Nitrogen fixation

(*ii*) Phosphate solubilization

(*iii*) Potassium solubilization

(*iv*) Siderophore production

(*v*) Phytohormone production (IAA, Cytokinin, GA and Ethylene)

2. In-Direct plant growth promotion (Biocontrol activity): In-Direct plant growth activity of endophytic bacteria besides being growth promoting mechanisms also play important role in management of various phytopathogens. It involves:

(*i*) Antibiotic production

(*ii*) Hydrolytic enzyme production

(*iii*) Induced systemic resistance (ISR)

(*iv*) Exopolysaccharide production

Broadly, the mechanism of action of endophytic bacteria mainly involves the following steps:

1. Biological control of phytopathogens (antagonism by production of enzymes, antibiosis and by competition).
2. Plant growth promotion (by Biological nitrogen fixation, phosphate solubilization, siderophore production and regulation of phytohormone).

3. Elicitors of Induced systemic resistance.
4. Increase tolerance against abiotic stresses.

1. Biological Control of Phytopathogens

(*a*) Production of Enzymes: Hydrolytic enzymes produced by some biocontrol PGPR lyses specifically fungal cell walls, and thereby prevent phytopathogens from proliferating e.g. *Pseusdomonas stutzeri* produces chitinase that lyse cell wall of *Fusarium solani* (Hilda and Fraga, 1999).

(*b*) Antagonism by Competition: Competition for space (niches) and nutrients is another mechanism of endophytes e.g. high inoculum level of *Pseudomonas syringae* protected pears against *Botrytis cinerea* and *Penicillium expansum*. Bacteria are capable of multiplying on the leaf surface to form a large population and could compete successfully with pathogens for these sites and often reduce disease.

(*c*) Antibiosis: Microbial toxins/substances that can kill the other microorganisms. Important antibiotics produced by bacterial endophytes against fungal pathogens reported by various workers are listed below:

Table 8.2: Examples of Bacterial Endophytes Antibiotics

S.No.	Name of Endophyte	Antibiotics	Activity	Reference
1.	*Pseudomonas fluorescens* F113	2, 4-diacetyl phloroglucinol	*Pythium* spp.	Shanahan *et al.*, 1992
2.	*Bacillus subtilis* AU195	Bacillomycin D	*Aspergillus flavus*	Moyne *et al.*, 2001
3.	*Lysobacter sp.* strain SB-K88	Xanthobaccin A	*Aphanomyces cochlioides*	Islam *et al.*, 2004
4.	*Pantoea agglomerans* C9-1	Herbicolin	*Erwinia amylovora*	Sandra *et al.*, 2001
5.	*B. subtilis* BBG100	Mycosubtilin	*Pythium aphanidermatum*	Leclere *et al.*, 2005
6.	*P. fluorescens* Pf-5	Pyrrolnitrin	*Pythium ultimum* and*R. solani*	Thomashow *et al.*, 1990

2. Plant Growth Promotion

(*a*) Nitrogen Fixation: The atmospheric N_2 is converted into plant-utilizable forms by biological N2 fixation (BNF) which changes nitrogen to ammonia by nitrogen fixing microorganisms using a complex enzyme system known as nitrogenase e.g. *Azospirillum* in rice plant (Kim and Rees, 1994: Ladha and Reddy, 2003), *Rhizobium leguminosarum* in rice (Yanni *et al.*, 1997). Combination of nitrogen-fixing bacteria (viz., *Rhizobium trifolii* and *Burkholderia* MG43) and reduced amount of chemical fertilizer can achieve overall yield equivalent to the yield that was obtained from recommended full dose of chemical fertilizer (Bhattacharjee *et al.*, 2008).

(*b*) Phosphate solubilization: Some bacterial endophytic microorganisms also possessed the ability to convert insoluble phosphorus (P) to an accessible form, like orthophosphate (PO_4^{2-}).*Burkholderia, Enterobacter, Pantoea, Pseudomonas, Azotobacter* etc (Park *et al.*, 2005). However, most of the bacterial genera solubilize phosphate through the production of organic acids such as gluconate, ketogluconate, acetate, lactate, oxalate, tartarate, succinate, citrate and glycolate (Khan *et al.*, 2012).Examples: *Burkholderia, Enterobacter, Pantoea, Pseudomonas, Azotobacter* etc (Park *et al.*, 2005).

(*c*) Production of phytohormone: The endophytic bacteria helps in production of phytohormone which contribute largely in the plant growth promotion. Some important growth hormones are IAA (Shin *et al.*, 2007; Syamsia *et al.*, 2015), GA (Khan *et al.*, 2012), auxins and cytokinins (Dalal and Kulkarni, 2013).Plant growth promotion as a result of IAA has been documented in several plants in recent years (Spaepen *et al.*, 2007).Cytokinin produced by *Bacillus megatarium* UMCV1, a rhizospheric bacterium, was found to promote biomass production in *Arabidopsis thaliana* through the inhibition of primary root growth followed by increased lateral root formation and root hair length of host plant (López-Bucio *et al.*, 2007). The role of phytohormone produced by associative bacteria in the promotion of plant growth during stress conditions such as salinity or draught has also been demonstrated recently (Egamberdieva *et al.*, 2008).

(*d*) Siderophore production: Siderophore are high-affinity iron chelating compounds secreted by microorganisms. Siderophore chelate ferric ion with high affinity, allowing its solubilization and extraction from most mineral or organic complexes. Bacterial siderophores classified into four main classes carboxylate, hydroxamates, phenol catecholates and pyoverdines. *Pseudomonas fluorescens* produces pyoverdines type of siderophore which inhibit the growth of *Fusarium oxysporum* (Lemanceau *et al.*, 2009).

3. Induction of Plant Resistance

Systemic acquired resistance (SAR) and induced systemic resistance (ISR) are two forms of induced resistances. SAR, induced by pathogen infection, is mediated by salicylic acid and associated with the accumulation of pathogenesis-related (PR) proteins. Whereas, ISR is induced by some non pathogenic rhizobacteria, is mediated by jasmonic acid or ethylene and is not associated with the accumulation of PR protein (Tripathi *et al.*, 2008).

Table 8.3: Endophytic Strains that have been Reported to Induced Systemic Resistance

S.No.	Strains	Effects reported	Reference
1	IN937a *Bacillus amyloliquefaciens*	Reduced incidence and severity of vegetable diseases caused by *CMV, Scleritium rolfsii* and *Rhizoctonia solani*	Jetiyanon *et al.*, 2002
2	IN 937 b *Bacillus subtilis*	Reduced incidence of *CMV* on tomato	Zehnder *et al.*, 2001
3	90-166*Serratia marcescens*	Reduced incidence of Fusarium wilt of tomato caused by *F. oxysporum* f.sp. *cucumerium*	Liu *et al.*, 1995

4. Endophytic Bacteria Conferring Abiotic Stress Tolerance in Crop Plants

Endophytic bacteria emerge a series of abiotic stress tolerance mechanisms against various phytopathogenic microorganisms. Some important bacterial endophytes with their beneficial mechanisms against various type of stress with respect to specific hosts are listed below:

Table 8.4: Examples of Bacterial Endophytes against Various Types of Abiotic Stresses

S.No.	Organism	Crop	Type of stress	Mechanism	Reference
1.	*Pseudomonas* sp.	Pea	Drought	Decreased ethylene production	Arshad *et al.*, 2008
2.	*Pseudomonas* AMK-P6	Sorghum	Heat	Induction of heat shock protein	Ali *et al.*, 2008
3.	*Bacillus* sp.		Drought, High Temperature	Soil aggregation	Sandhya *et al* ., 2009
4.	*Bacillus megaterium*	Trifolium	Drought	IAA and proline production	Marulanda *et al.*, 2010

Conclusion

Endophytes represent diversity of microbial adaptations that have been developed in special and hidden environment. These microorganisms are the best partners of plants and can accelerate host plant growth, resistance and improve their immunity against various plant pathogens. Because of their different mechanisms, they can be used successfully as potential biological control agents. It is conceivable that the application of endophytes could be an advantage over the other methods of plant disease management. Since, they are present in a much more protected environment than rhizospheric bacteria and other biocontrols and therefore, likely to be less vulnerable to changing environmental conditions. The major impact of adoption of such beneficial microorganisms in the field of agriculture is the reduction of use of different agro-chemcials such as pesticides, chemical fertilizers, etc. which are the cause of environmental pollution and therefore can be described as a non-hazardous strategy to reduce crop damage caused by plant pathogens.

REFERENCES

Ali, S.S., Kasoju, N., Luthra, A. and Singh, A. (2008). Indian Medicinal Herbs as Sources of Antioxidants. *Food res. Int* 41:1-15.

Allu, S., Kumar, N.P. and Audipudi, A.V. (2014). Isolation, Biochemical and PGP Characterization of *Pseudomonas aeruginosa* Isolated from Chilli Red Fruit Antagonistic against Chilli Anthracnose Disease. *International Journal of Current Microbiology and Applied Science* 3: 318-329.

Aly, A.H., Edrada, E.R., Wray, V., Muller, W.E.G., Kozytska, S. and Hentschel, U. (2008). Bioactive Metabolites from the Endophytic Fungus *Ampelomyces* sp. Isolated from the Medicinal Plant *Urospermum picroides*. *Phytochemistry* 69: 1716-1725.

Amin, N., Daha, L., Nasruddin, A., Junaed, M. and Andi, I. (2013). The Use of Endophytic Fungi as Biopesticide against Downy Mildew *Perenosclerospora* spp. on Maize. *Natural and Applied Sciences* 4: 2223-9944.

Amin, N., Daha, L., Nasruddin, A., Junaed, M. and Andi, I. (2014). The Use of Endophytic Fungi as Biopesticide against Downy Mildew *Perenosclerospora spp.* on Maize. *Natural and Applied Sciences* 4: 2223-9944.

Arnold, A.E., Mejia, L.C., Kyllo, D., Rojas, E.I., Maynard, Z., Robbins, N. and Herre E.A. (2003). Fungal Endophyte Limit Pathogen Damage in a Tropical Tree. PNAS 100: 15649-15654.

Arshad, M., Shaharoona, B. and Mahmood, T. (2008). Inoculation with Plant Growth Promoting Rhizobacteria Containing ACC-deaminase Partially Eliminates the Effects of Water Stress on Growth, Yield and Ripening of *Pisum sativum* L. *Pedosphere* 18: 611-620.

Azevedo, J.L., Maccheroni, W., Pereira, J.O. and Araujo, W.L. (2000). Endophytic Microorganisms: A Review on Insect Control and Recent Advances on Tropical Plants. *Electronic Journal of Biotechnology* 3: 1-36.

Bacon, C.W. and Hinton, D.W. (1996). Symptomless Endophytic Colonization of Maize by *Fusarium moniliforme*. *Can J Botany* 74: 1195-1202.

Bacon, C.W. and White, J.F. (2000). Microbial Endophytes. Marcel Dekker, New York, pp. 341-388.

Bakker, P.A., Pieterse, H.M. and Van Loon, L.C. (2007). Induced Systemic Resistance by Fluorescent *Pseudomonas* spp. *Phytopathology* 97: 239-243.

Barka, E.A., Gognies, S., Nowak, J., Audran, J.C. and Belarbi, A. (2002). Inhibitory Effect of Endophyte Bacteria on *Botrytis cinerea* and Its Influence to Promote the Grapevine Growth. *Biological Control* 24: 135-142.

Bhattacharjee, R.B., Singh, A. and Mukhopadhyay, S.N. (2008). Use of Nitrogen-xing Bacteria as Biofertiliser for Non-legumes: Prospects and Challenges. *Appl Microbiol Biotechnol* 80: 199-209.

Bivi, M.R., Farhana, M.S., Khairulmazmi, A. and Idris, A. (2010). Control of *Ganoderma boninse*: A Causal Agent of Basal Stem Rot Disease on Oil Palm with Endophyte Bacteria *In Vitro*. *International Journal of Agriculture and Biology* 6: 833-839.

Carroll, G. (1986). Fungal Endophytes in Stems and Leaves: From Latent Pathogen to Mutualistic Symbiont. *Ecology* 69: 2-9.

Compant, S., Reiter, B., Sessitsch, A., Nowak, J., Clement, C. and Barka, E. (2007). Endophytic Colonization of *Vitis vinifera* L. by Plant Growth-promoting Bacterium *Burkholderia* sp. strain PsJN. *Appl. Environ. Microbiol.*, 71: 1685-1693.

Conn, V.M., Walker, A.R. and Franco, C. M., (2008). Endophytic Actinobacteria Induce Defense Pathways in *Arabidopsis thaliana*. *Molecular and Plant Microbe Interaction* 21: 208-218.

Dalal, J. and Kulkarni, N. (2013). Antagonistic and Plant Growth Promoting Potentials of Indigenous Endophytic Bacteria of Soybean (*Glycine max* (L) Merril). *Curr. Res. Microbiol. Biotechnol* 2: 62-69.

De Bary, A. (1887). Comparative Morphology and Biology of Fungi. Mycotozoa and Bacteria. Clarendon Press, Oxford.1966. Reprinted by Johnson Reprint Corporation, NewYork.

Duijff, B.J., Gianinazzi-Pearsonand, V. and Lemanceau, P. (1997). Involvement of the Outer Membrane Lipopolysaccharides in the Endophytic Colonization of Tomato Roots by Biocontrol *Pseudomonas fluorescens* Strain WCS417r. *New Phytol* 135: 325-334.

Egamberdiyeva, D., Kamilova, F., Validov, S., Gafurova, L., Kucharova, Z. and Lugtenberg, B. (2008). High Incidence of Plant Growth-stimulating Bacteria Associated with the Rhizosphere of Wheat Grown in Salinated Soil in Uzbekistan. *Environ. Microbiol.* 10: 1-9.

Fukuda, Y. and Shinshi, H. (1994). Characterization of a Novel cis-acting Element that is Responsive to Fungal Elicitor in the Promoter of a Tobacco Class I Chitinases Gene. *Plant Molecular Biology* 24: 485-493.

Gao, F.K., Dai, C.C. and Liu, X.Z. (2010). Mechanism of Fungal Endophytes in Plant Protection Against Pathogens. *African Journal of Microbiology Research* 4: 1346-1351.

Gasser, I., Cardinale, M., Müller, H., Heller, S., Eberl, L., Lindenkamp, N., Kaddor, C., Steinbüchel, A. and Berg, G. (2011). Analysis of the Endophytic Lifestyle and Plant Growth Promotion of Burkholderia terricola ZR2-12. *Plant and Soil* 347: 125- 136.

Gholami, A.S., Shahsavani, S. and Nezarat N. (2013). The Effect of Plant Growth Promoting Rhizobacteria (PGPR) on Germination, Seedling Growth and Yield of Maize. *World Acad. of Sci., Eng. and Technol* 3: 9-14.

Gimenez, C., Cabrera, R., Reina, M. and Coloma, A. (2007). Fungal Endophytes and their Role in Plant Protection. *Curr. Organic Chem.*, 11: 707-720.

Gomez-Lama Cabanas, C., Schilirò, E., Valverde-Corredor, A. and Mercado-Blanco, J. (2014). The Biocontrol Endophytic Bacterium *Pseudomonas fluorescens* PICF7 Induces Systemic Defense Responses in Aerial Tissues upon Colonization of Olive Roots. *Frontier Microbiology* 5: 427-431.

Grosch, R., Scherwinski, K., Lottmann, J. and Berg, G. (2006). Fungal Antagonists of the Plant Pathogen *Rhizoctonia solani*: Selection, Control Efficacy and Influence on the Indigenous Microbial Community. *Mycological Research* 110: 1464-1474.

Gunatilaka, A.A.L. (2006). Natural Products from Plant-associated Microorganisms: Distribution, Structural Diversity, Bioactivity, and Implications of their Occurrence. *Journal of National Production* 69: 509-526.

Guo, L.D., Huang, G.R. and Wang, Y. (2008). Seasonal and Tissue Age Influences on Endophytic Fungi of *Pinus tabulaeformis* (Pinaceae) in Dongling Mountain, Beijing. *J Integr Plant Biol.* 50: 997-1003.

Hallmann, J., Quadt-Hallmann, A., Mahaffee, W.F. and Kloepper, J.W. (1997). Bacterial Endophytes in Agricultural Crops. *Canadian Journal of Microbiology* 43: 895-914.

Hallmann, J., Quadt-Hallmann, A., Mahaffee, W.F. and Kloepper, J.W. (2006). Bacterial Endophytes in Agricultural Crops. *Canadian Journal of Microbiology* 43: 895-914.

Hilda, R. and Fraga, R. (1999). Phosphate Solubilizing Bacteria and their Role in Growth Promotion. *Biotechnological Advancement* 17: 319-339.

Holliday, P. (1989). A Dictionary of Plant Pathology. Cambridge University Press, Cambridge.

Islam, M., Morgan, J., Doyle, M.P., Phatak, S. C., Millner, P. and Jiang, X. (2004). Fate of *Salmonella enterica* Serovar Typhimurium on Carrots and Radishes Grown in Fields Treated with Contaminated Manure Composts or Irrigation Water. *Appl. Environ. Microbiol.* 70:2497-2502.

James, E.K., Gyaneshwar, P., Mathan, N., Barraquio, W.L., Reddy, P.M., Iannetta, P.P., Olivares, F.L. and Ladha J.K. (2002). Infection and Colonization of Rice Seedlings by the Plant Growth-promoting Bacterium *Herbaspirillum seropedicae* Z67. *Mol Plant Microbe Interact* 15: 894-906.

Jetiyanon, K. and Kloepper, J.W. (2002). Mixtures of Plant Growth-promoting Rhizobacteria for Induction of Systemic Resistance against Multiple Plant Diseases. *Biol Control* 24: 285–291.

Kang, S.H., Cho, H.S., Cheong, H., Ryu, C.M., Kim, J.F. and Park, S.H. (2007). Two Bacterial Entophytes Eliciting Both Plant Growth Promotion and Plant Defense on Pepper (*Capsicum annuum* L.). *Journal of Microbiol Biotechnology* 17: 96-103.

Kavroulakis, N.S., Zervakis, G.I., Ehaliotis, C., Haralampidis, K. and Papadopoulou, K.K. (2007). Role of Ethylene in the Protection of Tomato Plants Against Soil-borne Fungal Pathogens Conferred by an Endophytic *Fusarium solani* Strain. *Journal of Experimental Botany* 58: 3853-3864.

Keem, J. and Rees, D.C. (1994). Nitrogenases and Biological Nitrogen Fixation. Biochemistry 33: 389-397.

Khan, A.L., Hamayun, M., Kang, S.M., Kim, Y.H., Jung, H.Y., Lee, J.H. and Lee, I.J. (2012). Endophytic Fungal Association via Gibberellins and Indole Acetic Acid can Improve Plant Growth Potential in Abiotic Stress: An Example of *Paecilomyces formosus* LHL10. *BMC Microbiol* 12: 3-5.

Khan, M.S.A., Zaidi, P.A., Wani, M. (2009). Role of Plant Growth Promoting Rhizobacteria in the Remediation of Metal Contaminated Soils *Environ Chem Lett* 7: 1-19.

Kloepper, J.W., Ryu, C.M. and Zhang, S. (2004). Induced Systemic Resistance and Promotion of Plant Growth by *Bacillus* spp. *Phytopathology* 94: 1259-1266.

Kuldau, G. and Bacon, C. (2008). Clavicipitaceous Endophytes: Their Ability to Enhance Resistance of Grasses to Multiple Stresses. *Biological Control* 46: 57-71.

Ladha, J.K. and Reddy, P.M. (2003). Nitrogen Fixation in Rice Systems: State of Knowledge and Future Prospects. *Plant Soil* 252: 151-167.

Ladha, J.K. and Reddy, P.M. (2000). The Quest for Nitrogen Fixation in Rice. Proceedings of the Third Working Group Meeting on Assessing Opportunities for Nitrogen Fixation in Rice, 9–12 Aug. 1999, IRRI, Los Banos, Laguna, Philippines, 354p.

Lamb, T.G., Tonkyn, D.W. and Kluepfel, D.A. (1996). Movement of *Pseudomonas aureofaciens* from the Rhizosphere to Aerial Plant Tissue. *Canadian Journal of Microbiology* 42: 1112-1120.

Leclère, V., Bechet, M., Adam, A., Guez, J.S., Wathelet, B. and Ongena, M. (2005). Mycosubtilin Overproduction by *Bacillus subtilis* BBG100 Enhances the Organism's Antagonistic and Biocontrol Activities. *Appl. Environ. Microbiol.* 71: 4577-4584.

Lee, K., Pan, J.J. and May, G. (2009). Endophytic *Fusarium verticillioides* Reduces Disease Severity Caused by *Ustilago maydis* on Maize. FEMS Microbiol.Lett. 299(1): 31- 37.

Lemanceau, P., Bauer, P., Kraemer, S. and Briat, J.F. (2009). Iron Dynamics in the Rhizosphere as a Case Study for Analyzing Interactions Between Soils, Plants and Microbes. *Plant Soil* 321: 513-535.

Lin, T., Zhao, L., Yang, Y., Guan, Q. and Gong, M. (2013). Potential of Endophytic Bacteria from *Sophora alopecuroides* Nodule in Biological Control against Verticillium wilt Disease. *Australian Journal of Crop Science* 7: 139-146.

Liu, L., Kloepper, J.W. and Tuzun, S. (1995). Induction of Systemic Resistance in Cucumber Against Fusarium Wilt by Plant Growth-Promoting Rhizobacteria. *PhytoPath.* 5: 695-698.

Lopez-Bucio, J., Campos-Cuevas, J.C., Hernandez-Calderon, E., Velasquez Becerra, C., Farias-Rodriguez, R., Macias-Rodriguez, L.I. and Valencia-Cantero, E. (2007). *Bacillus megaterium* Rhizobacteria Promote Growth and Alter Root System Architecture Through an Auxin-and Ethylene-independent Signaling Mechanism in *Arabidopsis thaliana. Molecular Plant-Microbe Interactions* 20: 207-217.

Lu, H., Zou, W.X., Meng, J.C., Hu, J. and Tan, R.X. (2000). New Bioactive Metabolites Produced by *Colletotrichum* sp., An Endophytic Fungus in *Artemisia annua. Plant Science* 151: 67-73.

Macia-Vicente, J.G., Jansson, H.B., Talbot, N.J., and Lopez-Llorca, L.V. (2009). Real-time PCR Quantification and Live-cell Imaging of Endophytic Colonization of Barley (*Hordeum vulgare*) Roots by *Fusarium equiseti* and *Pochonia chlamydosporia.* New Phytologist, 182: 213-228.

Malfanova, N., Kamilova, F., Validov, S., Chebotar, V. and Lugtenberg, B. (2013). Is L-arabinose Important for the Lifestyle of *Pseudomonas* spp.? *Arch Microbiol. Ecol.* 60:157-166.

Mahapatra, S. and Banerjee, D. (2010). Diversity and Screening for Antimicrobial Activity of Endophytic Fungi of *Alstonia scholaris. Acta Microbial Immunol Hung* 57: 215-223.

Marulanda, A., Azcón, R., Chaumont, F., Ruiz-Lozano, J. and Aroca, R. (2010). Regulation of Plasma Membrane Aquaporins by Inoculation with a Strain in Maize (L.) Plants Under Unstressed and Salt-stressed Conditions. *Planta* 2: 533-543.

Mejýa, L.C., Rojas, E.I., Maynard, Z., Bael, S.V., Elizabeth M, Arnold, A., Hebbar, P., Samuels, G.J., Robbins, N. and Herre, E.A. (2008). Endophytic Fungi as Biocontrol Agents of *Theobroma cacao* Pathogens. *Biological Control* 46: 4-14.

Moyne, A.L., Shelby, R., Clevel, T.E. and Tuzun, S. (2001). Bacillomycin D: An Iturin with Antifungal Activity Against *Aspergillus flavus. J Appl Microbiol.* 90: 622-629.

Nagendran, K., Karthikeyan, G., Faisal, P.M., Kalaiselvi, P., Raveendran, K. P. and Reguchander, T. (2013). Exploiting Endophyte Bacteria for the Management of Sheath Blight Disease in Rice. *Biological Agriculture and Horticulture* 13: 249-258.

Norman-Setterblad, C., Vida,l S. And Palva, E.T. (2000). Interacting Signal Pathways Control Defense Gene Expression in Arabidopsis in Response to Cell Wall-Degrading Enzymes from *Erwinia carotovora. Mol. Plant-Microbe Interact.* 13: 430-438.

Orole, O.O. and Adejumo, T.O. (2009). Activity of Fungal Endophytes against Four Maize wilt Pathogens. *Afr. J. Microbiol. Res.* 3 (12): 969-973.

Padhi, L., Mohanta, Y.K. and Panda, S.K. (2013). Endophytic Fungi Withgreat Promises: A Review. *Journal of Advanced Pharmaceutical Education and Research* 3: 152-170.

Park, J.H., Cho,i G.J., Lee, H.B., Kim, K.M., Jung, H. S., Lee, S.W., Jang, K.S., Cho, K.Y. and Kim, J.C. (2005). Griseofulvin from *Xylaria* sp. Strain F0010, An Endophytic Fungus of *Abies holophylla* and Its Antifungal Activity Against Plant Pathogenic Fungi. *Journal of Microbiology and Biotechnology* 15: 112-117.

Petrini, O. (1991). Fungal Endophytes of Tree Leaves. In Microbial Ecology of Leaves (Andrews, J.H. and Hirano, S.S., eds), pp. 179-197.

Podolich, O., Ardanov, P., Zaets, I., Pirttila, A.M. and Kozyrovska, N. (2015). Reviving of the Endophytic Bacterial Community as a Putative Mechanism of Plant Resistance. *Plant Soil* 38: 367-377.

Puente, M.E., Li, C.Y. and Bashan, Y. (2009). Endophytic Bacteria in Cacti Seeds can Improve the Development of Cactus Seedlings. *Environ and Experimental Botany* 66: 402-408.

Redman, R.S., Freeman, S., Clifton, D.R., Morrel, J., Brown, G.S. and Rodriguez, R.J. (1999). Biochemical Analysis of Plant Protection Afforded by a Non-pathogenic Endophytic Mutant of *Colletotrichum magna* (teleomorph: *Glomerella magna*. *Plant Physiology* 119: 795-803.

Reinhold-Hurek, B. and Hurek, T. (1998). Interactions of Gramineous Plants with *Azoarcus* spp. and Other Diazotrophs: Identification, Localization, and Perspectives to Study their Function, *Critical Reviews of Plant Sciences* 17: 29-54.

Reinhold-Hurek, B. and Hurek, T. (1998). Life in Grasses: Diazotrophic Endophytes. *Trends Microbiol.* 6: 139-144.

Reinhold-Hurek, B. and Hurek, T. (2006). Endophytic Associations of *Azoarcus spp.* In *Associative and Endophytic Nitrogen-Fixing Bacteria and Cyanobacterial Associations*, ed. CElmerich,WENewton, pp. 191-210. Berlin: Springer.

Reinhold-Hurek, B., Maes, T., Gemmer, S., Van Montagu, M. and Hurek, T. (2006). An Endoglucanase is Involved in Infection of Rice Roots by the Non-cellulose-metabolizing Endophyte *Azoarcus* sp. strain BH72. *Molecular and Plant-Microbe Interaction* 19: 181-188.

Rubini, M.R., Silva-Ribeiro, R.T., Pomella, A.W.V., Maki, C.S., Araujo, W.L., Dos Santos, D.R., and Azevedo, J.L. (2005). Diversity of Endophytic Fungal Community of Cacao (*Theobroma cacao* L.) and Biological Control of *Crinipellis perniciosa,* Causal Agent of Witches' Broom Disease. *Int J Biol Sci* 1: 24-33.

Saikkonen, K., Ion, D. and Gyllenberg, M. (2002). The Persistence of Vertically Transmitted Fungi in Grass Metapopulations. *Proceeding of Biological Science* 269: 1397-1403.

Sandhya, V., Ali, S.Z., Grover, M., Reddy, G. and Venkateswarlu, B. (2009). Alleviation of Drought Stress Effects in Sunflower Seedlings by Exopolysaccharides Producing *Pseudomonas putida* Strain P45. *Biol Fertility Soil* 46:17–26.

Sandra, A.I., Wright, C.H., Zumoff, L.S. and Steven, V.B. (2001). *Pantoea agglomerans* Strain *EH318* Produces Two Antibiotics that Inhibit *Erwinia amylovora* Under *in vitro*. *Applied and Environmental Microbiology* 144:633-642.

Schardl, C.L., Leuchtmann, A., Chung, K.R., Penny, D and Siegel, M.R. (1997). Coevolution by Common Descent of Fungal Symbionts (*Epichloe* spp.) and Grasshosts. *Molecular Biology and Evolution* 14:133-143.

Schulz, B. and Boyle C. (2005). The Endophytic Continuum. *Mycological Research* 109: 661-686.

Schulz, B. and Boyle, C. (2006). What are Endophytes? Microbial Root Endophytes (Schulz BJE, Boyle CJC & Sieber TN, eds). Speringer-Verlag pp. 1-13.

Schulz, B., Boyle, C., Draeger, S., Römmert, A.K. and Krohn, K. (2002). Endophytic Fungi: A Source of Novel Biologically Active Secondary Metabolites. *Mycological Research* 106: 996-1004.

Senthikumar, M., Govindasamy, V. and Annapurna, K. (2007). Role of Antibiosis in Suppression of Charcoal Rot Disease by Soybean Endophyte *Paenibacillus* sp. HKA-15. *Curent Microbiology* 55: 25-29.

Shahasi, A., Dubois, Y., Viljoen, A., Nico, L., Ragama, P. and Niere, B. (2006). *In vitro* Antagonism of Endophytic *Fusarium oxysporum* Isolates Against the Burrowing Nematode *Radopholus similis*. *Nematol.*, 8(4): 627-636.

Shanahan, P., Sullivan, D.J., Simpson, P., Glennon,, J.D. and Gara, F. (1992). Isolation of 2,4-diacetylphloroglucinol from a Fluorescent Pseudomonad and Investigation of Physiological Parameters Influencing its Production. *Appl Environ Microbiol* 58: 353-358.

Sherameti, I., Tripathi, S., Varma, A. and Oelmüller, R. (2008). The Root-colonizing endophyte *Piriformospora indica* Confers Drought Tolerance in *Arabidopsis* by Stimulating the Expression of Drought Stress–related Genes in Leaves. *Mol Plant Microbe Interact* 21: 799-800.

Shim, S.H., Gloer, J.B. and Wicklow, D.T. (2006). Penifulvins B-E and a Silphinene Analogue: Sesquiterpenoids from a Fungicolous Isolate of *Penicillium griseofulvum* . *J Nat Prod.* 69: 1601-1605.

Shimanuki, T. (1987). Studies on the Mechanisms of the Infection of Timothy with Purple Spot Disease Caused by *Cladosporium* (Gregory) de Vries. *In:* Res. Bull. 148 *Hokkaido Natl. Agric. Exp. Sta.* pp. 1-56.

Siegel, M.R., Latch, G.C.M., Bush, L. P., Fannin, F.F., Rowan, D.D., Tapper, B.A., Bacon, C.W. and Johnson, M.C. (1990). Fungal Endophyte Infected Grasses: Alkaloid Accumulation and Aphid Response. *Journal of Chemical Ecology* 16: 3301-3315.

Silva, G.H., Teles, H.L. and Zanardi, L.M. (2006). Cadinane Sesquiterpenoids of *Phomopsis cassiae,* An Endophytic Fungus Associated with *Cassia spectabilis* (Leguminosae). *Phytochemistry* 67: 1964-9.

Spaepen, S., Vanderleyden, J. and Remans, R. (2007). Indole-3-acetic Acid in Microbial and Microorganism-plant Signalling. *FEMS Microbiol. Rev.* 31: 425-448.

Strobel, G. (2003). Endophytes as Sources of Bioactive Products. *Microbes and Infection* 5: 535-544.

Strobel, G. (2006). *Muscodor albus* and Its Biological Promise. *Journal of Indian Microbiology and Microbiology* 33: 514-522.

Sturz, A.V. and Matheson, B.G. (1996). Populations of Endophytic Bacteria which Influence Host-resistance to *Erwinia*-Induced Bacterial Soft Rot in Potato Tubers. *Plant Soil* 184: 265-271.

Sturz, C., Matheson, A. and Buchanan, N. (1999). "Endophytic Bacterial Communities in the Periderm of Potato Tubers and Their Potential to Improve Resistance to Soil-borne Plant Pathogens." *Plant Pathology* 48: 360-69.

Su, Y.Y., Guo, L.D. and Hyde, K.D. (2010). Response of Endophytic Fungi of *Stipa grandis* to Experimental Plant Function Group Removal in Inner Mongolia steppe, China. *Fungal Divers* 43: 93-101.

Sun, X., Guo, L.D. and Hyde, K.D. (2011). Community Composition of Endophytic Fungi in *Acer truncatum* and their Role in Decomposition. *Fungal Divers* 47: 85-95

Sunitha, V.H., Devi, D.N. and Srinivas, C. (2013). Extracellular Enzymatic Activity of Endophytic Fungal Strains Isolated from Medicinal Plants. *World Journal of Agricultural Sciences* 9: 1-2.

Suzuki, A., Kanaoka, M., Isogai, A., Murakoshi, S., Ichinoe, M. and Tamura, S. (1977). Bassianolide, a New Insecticidal Cyclodepsipeptide from *Beauveria bassiana* and *Verticillium lecanii. Tetrahedron Letters* 25: 2167-2170.

Suzuki, T., Shimizu, M., Meguro, A., Hasegawa, S., Nishimura, T. and Kunoh, H., (2005). Visualization of Infection of an Endophytic Actinomycete *Streptomyces galbus* in Leaves of Tissue-cultured Rhododendron. *Actinomycetologica* 19: 7-12.

Tan, R.X. and Zou, W.X. (2001). Endophytes: A Rich Source of Functional Metabolites. *National Prodeeding of Reproduction* 18: 448-459.

Thomas, P. and Upreti, R. (2014).Testing of Bacterial Endophytes from Non-host Sources as Potential Antagonistic Agents against Tomato Wilt Pathogen *Ralstonia solanacearum. Advanced Microbiology* 4: 656-666.

Thomashow, L.S., Weller, D.M, Bonsall, R.F. and Pierson, L.S. (1990). Production of the Antibiotic Phenazine-1-carboxylic Acid by Fluorescent *Pseudomonas* Species in the Rhizosphere of Wheat. *Appl Enviorn Microbiol* 56: 908-912.

Timmusk, S., Grantcharova, N. and Wagner, E.G.H. (2005). *Paenibacillus polymyxa* Invades Plant Roots and Forms 578 biofilms. *Appl Environ Microbiol* 71: 7292-7300.

Ting, A.S.Y., Meon, S., Kadir, J., Radu, S. and Singh, G. (2009). Induced Host Resistance by Non-pathogenic Fusarium Endophyte as a Potential Defence Mechanisms in Fusarium wilt Management of Banana. *Pest technology* 56: 441-467.

Tripathi, S., Kamal, S., Sheramati, I., Oelmuller, R. and Verma, A. (2008). Mycorrhizal Fungi and Other Root Endophytes as Biocontrol Agents Against Root Pathogens. *Mycorrhiza* 281-306.

Varma, A., Verma, S., Sudha Sahay, N., Butehorn, B. and Franken, P. (1999). *Piriformospora indica*, a Cultivable Plant-growth-Promoting Root Endophyte. *Applied Environmental Microbiology* 65: 2741-2744.

Vega, F.E., Posada, F., Aime, M.C., Pava-Ripoll, M., Infante, F. and Rehner, S.A. (2008). Entomopathogenic Fungal Endophytes. *Biol. Control* 46: 72- 82.

Waller, F., Achatz, B., Baltruschat, H., Fodor, J., Becker, K., Fischer, M., Heier, T., Huckelhoven, R., Neumann, C., Wettstein, D., Franken, P. and Kogel, K.H., (2005). The Endophytic Fungus *Piriformospora indica* Reprograms Barley to Salt-stress Tolerance, Disease Resistance and Higher Yield. *Proc Natl Acad Sci* USA 102: 13386-13391.

Wang, L.W., Xu, B.G., Wang, J.Y., Su, Z.Z., Lin, F.C. and Zhang, C.L. (2012). Bioactive Metabolites from *Phoma* Species, an Endophytic Fungus from the Chinese Medicinal Plant *Arisaema erubescens*. *Appl. Microbiol. Biotechnol.* 93: 1231-1239.

Wicklow, D.T., Roth, S., Deyrup, S.T. and Gloer, J.B., (2005). A Protective Endophyte of Maize: *Acremonium zeae* Antibiotics Inhibitory to *Aspergillus flavus* and *Fusarium verticillioides. Mycological Research* 109: 610-618.

Wilson, D. (1995). Endophyte-the evolution of the term, the clarification of its use and definition. *Oikos* 73: 274-276.

Yanni, Y.G., Rizk, R. Y., Corich, V., Squartini, A., Ninke, K., Philip-Holingsworth, S., Orgambide, G., Bruijn, F.J., Stoltzfus, J., Buckley, D., Schmidt, T. M., Mateos, P. F., Ladha, J.K. and Dazzo, F.B. (1997). Natural Endophytic Association Between *Rhizobium leguminosarum* bv. *trifoli* and Rice Roots and Assessment of Potential to Promote Rice Growth. *Plant Soil* 194: 99-114.

Zehnder, G.W., Murphy, J.F., Sikora, E.J. and Kloepper, J.W. (2001). Application of Rhizobacteria for Induced Resistance. *Eur J Plant Pathol* 107: 39-50.

Advances in Microbiology: ***Applications & Significance*** **Pages 155-177**
Edited by: ***Dr. Pawan Kumar 'Bharti'***
ISBN: 978-93-86841-97-1
Edition: **2019**
Published by: **Discovery Publishing House Pvt. Ltd., New Delhi (India)**

9

Fluorescent Pseudomonads

Potent Bacterial Antagonist for Sustainable Agriculture

[1]Reshma P., [2]Naik M.K. and [3]Esakkimuthu M.

ABSTRACT

Free living, root colonizing bacteria (rhizobacteria) have been studied for the past century as possible inoculants for increasing plant productivity. Plant Growth Promoting Rhizobacteria (PGPR) are characterized by a number of functions which include improvement of plant establishment, increased availability of plant nutrients, enhancement of nutrient uptake, improvement of soil structure and protection against diseases. They survive in seed or soil, multiply in the rhizosphere in response to the exudates rich in carbohydrates and aminoacids attach to root surfaces and become endophytic by colonizing in root cortex region. Rhizobacteria are distributed in the rhizosphere in a log normal pattern and are sporadically dispersed along roots. More specifically, the soil borne fluorescent Pseudomonads have received particular attention throughout the global science because of their catabolic versatability, excellent root colonizing abilities and their capacity to produce a wide range of antifungal metabolites. It is in this regard, the present study is undertaken for the identification and exploitation of antibiotic genes like 2,4-DAPG, pyoluteorin, pyrrolnitrin and pyoverdin genes in indigenous fluorescent Pseudomonads isolates as they have broad spectrum activity against various phytopathogens and also their role in induction of systemic resistance and subsequently plant growth promotion activity.

Keywords: Antagonist, Fluorescent Pseudomonads, PGPR, Rhizobacteria and systemic resistance.

Introduction

In commercial agriculture, crop protection against phytopathogens relies heavily on agro-chemicals. Use of commercial insecticides and pesticides offers an effective control strategy, but the approach is not only expensive but also poses adverse effects on human health, environment and is lethal to other beneficial bacteria. At this juncture, environment-friendly approach

[1,3] University of Agricultural Sciences, Raichur, Karnataka 584104, India
[2] Kerala Agricultural University, RARS, Pilicode, Kerala, India

to control pathogens for agricultural sustainability is the need of the hour. Biological control employing phylloplane, rhizospheric microflora or indigenous endophytic bacterial flora seems to be promising against plant pathogens without adverse environmental effects. The cost, convenience, efficacy and reliability of biological controls are important considerations, in comparison with the alternative disease control strategies and hence are expected to play an important role in Integrated Pest Management (IPM) systems. Biological control of soil-borne diseases by plant growth-promoting rhizobacteria is a well-established phenomenon and has been shown to play a major role in suppression of several plant pathogens (Handelsman and Stabb, 1996). Plant growth promoting rhizobacteria (PGPR) are rhizosphere-competent bacteria that aggressively colonize plant roots and have ability to multiply and colonize across the ecological niches found on the roots at all stages of plant growth, in the presence of a competing microflora (Antoun and Kloepper, 2001). The control of phytopathogenic fungi depends on a wide variety of traits, such as the production of antifungal metabolites and lytic enzymes, induction of systemic resistance and high competitive maintenance in the rhizosphere which are considered to be important pre-requisites for the optimal performance of PGPR towards plant pathogen (Haas and Defago, 2005). The bacterial secondary metabolites play a critical role in bacterium-host interactions. Secondary metabolites produced by beneficial bacteria prevent infection by altering the environment and improving their ability to compete with pathogens, by inhibiting the activity of pathogens, or by triggering host defenses (Raaijmakers *et al.,* 2002). Among the various PGPR, fluorescent *Psuedomonas* is considered as the most important as they have both plant growth promotion activity and production of antifungal secondary metabolite. In recent years, several plant root-colonizing *Pseudomonas* spp. have shown to be a potent biocontrol agent in various plant-pathogen systems (Thomashow and Weller, 1996). The production of antifungal secondary metabolites like 2,4-diacetylphloroglucinol (2,4-DAPG/ DAPG or Phl), pyoluteorin (Plt), hydrogen cyanide, phenazines or pyrrolnitrin (PRN) is a prominent feature of many biocontrol fluorescent *Pseudomonas* spp. (Raaijmakers and Weller, 1998). Indian soils are considered to be poor in such 2,4-DAPG gene possessing isolates but the fact that as many as 9 isolates were obtained having 2,4-DAPG gene indicated to the possibility of exploiting the rhizospheric soils for obtaining wide ranging antibiotic and other useful traits (Naik *et al.,* 2012). Therefore, the present study was particularly aimed at identifying the location of the antagonistic gene(s) like 2,4-DAPG, Phenazines, pyoverdine and pyoluteorine in fluorescent Pseudomonads using PCR based approach.

Fluorescent Pseudomonads also play a major role in plant growth promotion and induced systemic resistance. Induced resistance is a state of enhanced defensive capacity developed by a plant when appropriately stimulated (Van Loon *et al.*, 1998). The utilization of plants own defense mechanism is the subject of interest in management of pest and diseases. Induced resistance is generally systemic and can be triggered by pathogens, certain chemicals, and even non-pathogenic rhizosphere bacteria. Inducing the plant's own defense mechanisms by prior application of a biological inducer is thought to be a novel plant protection strategy (Ramamoorthy *et al.*, 2001). The use of fluorescent Pseudomonads for inducing systemic resistance against phytopathogens have been well documented. Plant growth promotion is mediated by these rhizobacteria through different mechanism which includes production of lytic enzymes such as chitinase and β-1,3 glucanase and other enzymes such as phenylalanine ammonia lyase and polyphenol oxidases (Anand *et al.*,2010). Isolation and exploitation of indigenous strains with more than one antimicrobial compounds having multiple and broad spectrum action will be beneficial to farming community which will go a long way in ensuring sustainable crop protection. Hence, in the present investigation selected potential isolates were screened for their capacity to induce systemic resistance in rice crop against sheath blight fungus *Rhizoctonia solani*. Rice sheath blight is one of the major biotic production constraint in rice growing countries of the world and ranks next to blast in causing economical loss (Ou, 1985). Currently, no economically viable control measures are available to tackle the disease. Chemical means of management are expensive and not ecofriendly. So in this context, management through biocontrol agent which can promote growth and induce defense related enzymes against pathogen is more enterprising. The major factor that goes into success of biocontrol programme is the effectiveness with which the biocontrol agents are delivered to the environment. This requires preparation of formulations and is very important for effective implementation of biocontrol agents against various crop diseases (Prasad and Rangeshwaran, 2000). Formulations are usually prepared as carrier-based inoculants containing effective microorganisms. Incorporation of microorganisms in carrier material enables easy-handling, high effectiveness and long-term storage. Compatibility study of biocontrol agent with commonly used fungicides, insecticides and plant extracts can be useful for the successful integration of these formulations as an essential component in Integrated Pest Management in an agro-ecosystem.

Formulations and Shelf Life of Fluorescent Pseudomonads in Different Carrier Materials

Commercial application of *Pseudomonas fluorescens* either to increase crop health or to manage plant disease depends on the development of efficient formulations with suitable carriers that support the survival of bacteria for a considerable length of time. These carriers may be either organic or inorganic in nature. It should be economically feasible and easily available to be beneficial to farming community. Kloepper and Schroth (1981) demonstrated the pototentiality of talc to be used as a carrier material for formulating rhizobacteria. Fluorescent Pseudomonads did not decline in talc mixture with 20% xanthum gum after storage for two months at 4°C. *P. fluorescens* isolate Pf1 survived up to 240 days in storage. The initial population of Pf1 in talc based formulation was 37.5 x 107 cfu/g and declined to 1.3 × 107 cfu/g after eight months of storage. Ammendment of sucrose (0.72M) in King's B medium increased population and shelf life of *P. fluorecsens* (P7NF, TL3) in talc based formulation up to 12 months (Cesar and Burr, 1991). The various organic carriers used for development of formulation include peat, talc, lignite, kaololinite, pyrophyllite, zeolite, montmorillonite, alginate, pressmud, sawdust and vermiculite, etc. The carriers increase the survival rate of bacteria by protecting it from dessication and death of cells (Heijnen *et al.*, 1993). Montmorillonite, zeolite and vermiculite with smaller particle size increased the survival rate of *P. fluorescens* (2-79RN10, W4F393) compared to kaolinite, pyrophyllite and talc with bigger particle size. The carriers with smaller particle size have increased surface area, which increased coverage of bacterial cells (Dandurand *et al.*, 1994).

According to Vidhyashekaran and Muthamilan (1995) studied the shelf life of *P. fluorescens* (Pf1) in various carriers and recorded shelf life for a period of eight months with a viable load of bacteria in vermiculite of 1 × 106 cfu/g, 2.8 x 106 cfu/g in peat based formulation, 1 × 106 cfu/g in farm yard manure and 1.3 × 107 cfu/g in talc. They also recorded a shelf life of Pf1 for four months with a viable load of bacteria as 2.8 × 106 cfu/g in both kaolinite and lignite.

Various powder formulations of two efficient *P. fluorescens* strains were developed and it was noted that their shelf life in vermiculite, lignite and kaolinite formulations were short. Unformulated bacterial suspensions could not be stored even for ten days and their efficacy was completly lost. Hence they concluded that development of powder formulations of *P. fluorescens* might aid in large scale application in farmers field (Vidhyashekaran *et. al.*, 1997). Amer and Utkhede (2000) recorded the shelf life of *P. putida* for 45 days in talc and the bacterial load was 1.0 × 103 cfu/g. Sivakumar *et. al.* (2000) reported that of the various carrier materials studied for the survival of *P. fluorescens*, peat and talc maintained the highest population level of 19.5 × 10 7 and 18.3 × 107 cfu/g. *P. fluorescens* BRG100 survived best in oat flour and the addition of 20 per cent (wt/wt) maltose extended the shelf life of the product to more than 32 weeks (Daigle *et. al.*, 2002). *P. putida* strain 30 and 180 survived upto six months in talc based formulations. Shelf life of *P. chloraphis* (PA23) and *B. subtilis* (CBE4) in peat carriers was retained for more than six months (Nakkeran *et al.*, 2004). Shelf life of a highly antagonistic *P. fluorescens* strain PfT-8 was evaluated in seven different carrier formulations viz., talc, lignite, peat, lignite+ flyash, wettable powder, bentonite-paste and polyethylene glycol (PEG) paste for upto six months of storage at ambient room temperature. The formulations were stable upto at least two months of storage at ambient temperatures. Peat, lignite, lignite + flyash, bentonite paste based formulations maintained higher populations than others and also showed greater biocontrol potential. However, the population decreased in all formulations with time (Jayaraman *et. al.*, 2007). Bora and Bora (2008) reported that the population of *P. fluorescens* in bioformulations prepared from the two substrates significantly increased after storage (27.5 cfu/g to 128.5 cfu/g). The formulation of vermicompost, CMC and mannitol recorded the highest population of *P. fluorescens* at 30, 60, 90, 120, 150 and 180 days after inoculation. Assay on population dynamics of *P. fluorescens* and *Trichoderma harzianum* from two different substrates viz, vermicompost and wheat bran after different days of storage revealed that both the subsrates, the population density of *P. fluorescens* significantly increased upto 45 days of storage in both the substrates. Manikandan *et al.* (2010) developed liquid formulation of *P. fluorescens* strain (Pf1) in nutrient broth medium with the addition of different carrier chemicals such as trehalose, polyvinylpyrrolidone and glycerol. Among them, glycerol amendment maintained the greater population level of Pf1 up to six months of storage.

Manjunath *et al.* (2011) reported that talc is the best carrier material to support the longer shelf life at both room temperature and refrigerator temperature, which maintained 20.66 × 107 and 11.33 × 107 cfu/g respectively after one year of storage. The BCAs can provide effective control if the delivery system of the microorganism in a formulation is efficient enough to support survival of recommended count of viable propagules of the biocontrol agents. There are different techniques of cell immobilization such as pellet, granular and liquid formulations that have been evaluated and employed to develop carriers for the field application of biocontrol agents. Khan *et al.* (2011) described a novel process to produce biopesticides of *Trichoderma harzianum, Bacillus. subtilis* and *P. fluorescens* Migula by taking 1 part of stock culture (sawdust: soil: 5% molasses, 15:5:1) of the biocontrol agents and 20 parts carrier (flyash: soil: 5% molasses mixture, 5:3:1) (w/w). The greatest CFU counts of the microorganisms were recorded at 25°C or room temperature during 2–12 weeks of 32 weeks long shelf life test. Powder or granular carriers for biocontrol agents are more useful than gelant or liquid formulations, and compatible with existing farm machinery (Khan, 2008). Sivakumar *et al.* (2012) reported that peat formulation of *P. fluorescens* Pf51 and *Bacillus. subtilis* Bs 45 supported survival of both the strains up to 270 days with a viable population of 4.3 × 107 cfu /g and 6.2 × 107 cfu/ g respectively. Rajalaxmi *et al.* (2012) also reported that among the carrier materials talc was best suited for both *P. fluorescens* and *P. putida* isolates with 12 × 107 and 10 × 107 cfu/g respectively up to 300 days of storage. The powder formulations available are less expensive as they were developed from the low cost agriculture/industrial wastes or by-products and their handling is also easy.

Compatibility of Fluorescent Pseudomonads with Fungicides, Insecticides, Botanicals and Fungal Bioagent *Trichoderma* in the form of Consortium

It is essential to work out the compatibility of bioagents with other insect pest and disease management chemicals since the bioagents are to be integrated and practiced in agro-ecosystem approach. Even otherwise bioagent alone will not be able to solve the problem of pest and diseases in isolation. Moreover, in the present circumstances variety of interventions are made in pest management. Rhizobacteria showing antagonism against *Aphanomyces cochlioides* were tested for compatibility with seed treatment fungicides, thiram and hymexazol. Integration of the Pseudomonads with thiram in a pellet without Hymexazol was also feasible (Walker *et al.*, 2001). The effect of carbendazim and thiophanate-methyl on the growth of *Trichoderma viride* (Tv 33, Tv 48, and Tv 52), *T. harzianum* (Th 5 and Th 62), and *Pseudomonas. fluorescens* (ARR 1G, ARR 2, ARR 10, CHAO, EP1, FP7, KKM 1, KKM 2, Pf1, VPT 2, VPT 4, and VPY 10) isolates was evaluated *in vitro*. Carbendazim and thiophanate-methyl at 100 ppm enhanced the growth of *P. fluorescens* isolates; the antagonistic bacteria multiplied even when the fungicide rate was increased to 500 ppm. *P. fluorescens* + thiophanate methyl resulted in the highest plant survival rate (81.67%) (Malathi *et al.*, 2002). Jayakumar *et. al.* (2003) studied the compatibility of *P. fluorescens* with avermectin, carbofuran 3G and *Trichoderma viride* for the management of *Rotylenchulus reniformis* in bhendi which revealed that avermectin + *P. fluorescens* and avermectin + *T. viride* combination gave the maximum reduction in *R. reniformis* soil population (by 71.01%) and root nematode population (by 66.89%). The application of *P. fluorescens* (2.5 kg/ha) singly and in combination with carbofuran 3G significantly improved plant growth (Senthilkumar and Ramakrishnan, 2004). Plants treated with *P. fluorescens* (1.25 kg/ha) + carbofuran 3G (0.5 kg a.i./ha) recorded the highest fruit weight per plant (184.48%) Moreover, the compatibility of the most efficient strain 51 with some fungicides, which are commonly sprayed on greenhouse was investigated under *in vitro* conditions. The fungicides did not adversely affect the colonial development of bacteria at concentrations as high as 100 μg ml-1 *in vitro* (Gore and Altin, 2006). Khan and Gangopadhyay (2008) studied the *in vitro* sensitivity of *P. fluorescens* towards fungicides. They reported that carboxin, chlorothalonil and carbendazim were least toxic to *P. fluorescens* strain PFBC-25, while captan was most inhibitory to this strain. The EC50 values of carbendazim, corboxin and chlorothalonil to PFBC-25 were 251.2, 199.5 and 190.6 ppm respectively while it was 49.0 ppm in case of captan. Laha and Venkatraraman (2001) have noted the compatibility of *P. fluorescens* with carbendazim while studying sheath blight management in rice.

Compatibility of fluorescent Pseudomonads with plant products was reported by Loganathan *et al.* (2004). They tested the aqueous chloroform and methanol extracts of leaves of *Vitex negundo* against *B. subtilis* NCIM 2063 and *Pseudomonas sp.* and found that methanolic and chloroform extracts are detrimental against both the bacteria. No inhibitory activity of aqueous extract was noticed. Eftekhar *et al.* (2005) investigated the anti-bacterial activity of the methanolic extracts (at 0.75, 1.25 and 2.5 mg/ ml) of the aerial parts of *Datura innoxia* and *D. stromonium* against *B. subtilis* and *Pseudomonas sp.*, where *D. innoxia* extract showed dose- dependent antibacterial activity against *B. subtilis* (highest at 2.5 mg/ml). *D. stramonium* had slight antibacterial activity at 2.5 mg/ml and the lower concentrations were not effective. Both were ineffective against *Pseudomonas sp.* Kumar and Palakshappa (2009) reported the compatibility of *Pseudomonas fluorescens* with castor cake, pongamia cake, neem cake, safflower cake and their efficacy against *Alternaria porri* and *A. alternata* using poisoned food technique. The greatest inhibition of the mycelia growth of *A. alternata* and *A. porri* was exhibited by groundnut cake, followed by castor cake. Manjunatha *et. al.* (2011) reported compatibility of *P. fluorescens* with carbendazim, thiram among fungicides, Imidacloprid and Carbofuran among insecticides at 0.1 and 0.2 per cent concentration. Among plant products like NSKE, garlic bulb extract, *Tulsi* extract, nimbicine and Eucalyptus extract, *Pseudomonas fluorescens* was compatible with NSKE, garlic bulb extract and *Tulsi* extract at 2.5 and 5.00 per cent concentrations. Archana *et al.* (2012) studied the compatibility of Azoxystrobin 23 SC with bacterial and fungal biocontrol agents and insecticides under *in vitro* and glass house conditions, respectively. The bacterial biocontrol agents *viz., Pseudomonas fluorescens* and *Bacillus subtilis* were compatible with azoxystrobin 23 SC even at a high concentration of 300 ppm whereas fungal biocontrol agent *Trichoderma viride* was inhibited by Azoxystrobin 23 SC at a concentration of above 15 ppm. Among the four insecticides tested for compatibility, all insecticides were physically compatible with Azoxystrobin 23 SC at 125, 250 and 500 g ai ha-1 whereas Dichlorovos was biologically incompatible even at the lowest concentration tested.

According to Rajalaxmi *et al.* (2012) reported that among pesticides, *P. fluorescens* and *P. putida* was compatible with Carbendazim, Hexaconazole and Propiconazole whereas with Indoxacarb and Novaluron were incompatible. The combination of biocontrol agents that are compatible with each other is a strategic approach to control the plant disease and pest. Latha *et al.* (2011) studied the compatibility of fungal (*Trichoderma*) and bacterial biocontrol agents (*Pseudomonas* and *Bacillus*) individually and in combinations with oil cakes, organic manures and micronutrients for their efficacy against collar and root rot pathogen, *Lasiodiplodia theobromae* under *in vitro*, glasshouse and field conditions. The study revealed that the isolate of *T. viride* (Tv1), *P. fluorescens* (Pf1) and *B. subtilis* (Bs16) were compatible with each other and also with neem cake and zinc sulphate.

Molecular Characterization of Siderophore and Other Antibiotic Genes such as Phenazines, Pyoluteorine and Pyrrolnitrin

Fluorescent Pseudomonads produce different secondary metabolites including a range of antibiotic compounds which have been scrutinized mainly by genetic techniques for biocontrol activity. However, success in the fields is limited due to variable results. Isolation and characterization of the genes from microbes antagonistic to the different phytopathogens will enable us to understand the molecular mechanism involved in biological control approaches. Therefore it is important to understand the genes involved in antagonism to fungal pathogens so as to develop efficient biocontrol agent. Antibiotics include a chemically heterogeneous group of small organic molecules of microbial origin that, at low concentrations, are deleterious to the growth or metabolic activities of other microorganisms (Thomashow and Weller, 1996). Antifungal compounds include 2,4-diacetylphloroglucinol (Phl), Pyoleuteorin (Plt), Pyrrolnitrin (Prn), HCN, Phenazines (Phz) all contribute to disease suppression in various pathogen host plant systems. Howell and Stipanovic (1980) first established the importance of antibiotic production in the suppression of seedling pathogens such as *Pythium ultimum* causing damping off in cotton using *Pseudomonas fluorescens* Pf-5. A number of disease suppressive antibiotic compounds have been characterized including N-containing heterocycles such as phenazines, pyroll type antibiotics, pyo-compounds and indole derivatives. *P. fluorescens* produces the antibiotics 2,4-diacetylphloroglucinol (DAPG), Phenazine-1-carboxylic acid (PCA), salicylic acid (Sal) and Pyochelin (Pch) which inhibit a broad spectrum of plant pathogenic fungi, bacteria, nematode (Raaijmakers and Weller, 1998., Boruah and Kumar, 2002). Carine *et al.* (2012) reported that production of DAPG and HCN by *Pseudomonas sp.* LBUM300 contributes to the biological control of bacterial canker of tomato.

Molecular Characterization of Phl (DAPG) Gene

Certain plant-associated strains of fluorescent *Pseudomonas* spp. are known to produce the antimicrobial antibiotic 2, 4-diacetylphloroglucinol (DAPG). It has anti-bacterial, anti-fungal, anti-viral and anti-helminthic properties and has played a significant role in the biological control of tobacco, wheat, and sugar beet diseases (Velusamy *et al.*, 2006). DAPG is the major determinant in the biological control of a range of plant pathogens by many fluorescent *Pseudomonas* spp. *Phl A, B, C, D* genes are responsible for the production of DAPG in *P. fluorescens* (Abbas *et al.*, 2002). A 4.8Kb chromosomal DNA region from *P. fluorescens* carrying *Phl* biosynthetic gene is used as a probe to determine *Phl* biosynthetic locus conserved within *Phl* producing *Pseudomonas* strains of world wide origin. The *Phl* producers have considerable phenotypic and genotypic diversity. Two phenotypically distinct groups are detected. The first group produces *Phl*, pyoluteorin, and hydrogen cyanide and consisted of

13 strains from almost all locations sampled in the United States, Europe, and Africa. The second produced only *Phl* and HCN and consisted of 32 strains from the U.S. and European soils. *Phl* producing fluorescent *Pseudomonas* spp. are the key components of the natural biological control that operates in take-all suppressive soils. The production of antifungal compounds plays an important role in the suppressive properties of *P. fluorescens* strain CHAO and it is suggested that over production of these compounds may have deleterious effect on plants (Bencini *et al.*, 1983).

The antibiotic 2, 4-DAPG (*Phl*) is an important factor in the biological control of many soil borne diseases by fluorescent *Pseudomonas* sp. A 6.5 kb genomic DNA fragment from *P. fluorescens* Q2-87 conferred production of *Phl*. The size of the genomic region involved in *Phl* production and the consistency and specificity with which these sequences transferred *Phl* biosynthetic capability support the conclusion that the 6.5-kb fragment contains the *Phl* biosynthetic locus (Bangera and Thomashow, 1996). McSpadden *et al.* (2001) developed the new primers for the easy detection of *Phl-D* +ve strains based on cloning and sequence analysis of *Phl-D* open reading frame from five genotypically distinct strains of *P. fluorescens.* Velusamy and Gnanamanickam (2003) screened 637 fluorescent bacterial strains which were obtained from rice rhizosphere samples collected from various places in Karnataka, Kerala and Tamil Nadu, India. Of these, 278 strains showed antibiosis to *Xanthomonas oryzae* pv. *oryzae*, the causal agent of rice bacterial blight, in laboratory bioassays, and only 27 strains produced 2,4-diacetylphloroglucinol (2,4-DAPG), as confirmed by PCR analysis and chromatography. While 6 of the 27 strains recorded more than 50 per cent reduction in bacterial blight incidence, application of strain PTB9, a rice-associated bacterium, reduced bacterial blight by 64.5 per cent. These results suggest that 2, 4-DAPG production in crop rhizosphere is yet another important mechanism that reduces the severity of bacterial blight in rice.

Research evidenced by Velusamy *et al.* (2006) reported that a sub population of 27 strains of plant-associated *Pseudomonas fluorescens* screened in a batch of 278 strains of fluorescent Pseudomonads produced DAPG. The DAPG production was detected by a PCR-based screening method that used primers Phl2a and Phl2b and amplified a 745-bp fragment characteristic of DAPG. This compound inhibited the growth of the devastating rice bacterial blight pathogen *Xanthomonas oryzae pv. oryzae* in laboratory assays and suppressed rice bacterial blight up to 59-64 per cent in net-house and field experiments. Futhermore, among the 193 isolates studied from Tungabadra Project Area in Raichur, 9 isolates were found to be 2,4-DAPG +ve these indigenous isolates were collected from crop rhizosphere of sorghum, chickpea, pigeonpea, greengram and one endophyte isolate from chickpea roots. Detection of 2,4-DAPG gene in endophytic region is first report from this region (Manjunath *et al.*, 2011; Naik *et al.*, 2012 and Rajalaxmi *et al.*, 2012). Indian soils are considered to be poor in such 2,4-DAPG gene possessing isolates but the fact that 9 isolates were obtained having 2,4-DAPG gene indicated to the possibility of exploiting the rhizospheric soils for obtaining wide ranging antibiotic and other useful traits for emerging pest and diseases.

Molecular Characterization of Plt (Pyoluteorine) Gene

Pyoluteorin (Plt) is a phenolic polyketide with resorcinol ring which is produced by fluorescent Pseudomonads. The ring is linked to a bichlorinated pyrrole moiety. Biosynthesis of pyrrole moiety is unknown (Kitten *et al.*, 1998 and Nowak-Thompson *et al.*, 1999). It was first isolated from *P. aeruginosa* (Takeda, 1958) followed by *P. fluoresens* Pf-5 and CHAO (Bender *et al.*, 1999). Plt has bactericidal, herbicidal and fungicidal properties in particular against Pythium spp, Maurhofer *et al.* (1994). Application of Plt to cotton seeds suppressed cotton damping-off (Howell and Stipanovic, 1980). Ten genes, *Plt LABCDEFG* are involved in the biosynthesis of Plt. Among the ten genes, *pltB* and *pltC* encode type 1 polyketide synthetase, *plt*G encodes a thio esterase, three halogenases are coded by *pltA, pltD* and *pltM*. Among the *plt* gene products, PltR is similar to LysR family of the transcriptional activators (Pierson *et al.*, 1998 and Nowak-Thompson *et al.*, 1999). Furthermore, PltR acts as a positive transcriptional activator linked to *phzI* loci of the Phz biosynthetic locus (Pierson *et al.*, 1998; Chin A-Woeng *et al.*, 2001). Primers to detect PltBf and PltBr is a 773-bp segment from PltB, genes involved in the biosynthesis of Plt, Plt primers were developed from *P. fluorescens* BL915 and Pf-5 sequences, respectively (Mavrodi *et al.*, 2001). Plt biosynthesis is positively autoregulated by Plt itself and repressed by another antibiotic antibiotic 2,4-DAPG (Brodhagen *et al.*, 2004)

Molecular Characterization of PvdA (Pyoverdine) Siderophore Gene: Siderophore Synthesis by Fluorescent Pseudomonas Isolates

Siderophores are one of the green fluorescent pigment produced by *Pseudomonas* sp that play a vital role in controlling several plant disease. They function as biocontrol agent by depriving the pathogens from iron nutrition thus resulting in increased yield of crops. Pyoviridines, pyochelin, salicylic acid and quinolobactins are the major siderophores produced by fluorescent pseudomonas. Kloepper *et al.* (1980) first demonstrated the importance of siderophores. Several species of fluorescent Pseudomonads like *P. fluorescens, P. putida, P. aeruginosa, P. chlororaphis* produce siderophores and there is evidence that a number of plant species can absorb bacterial Fe^{+3} siderophore complexes. Fluorescent yellow green siderophores have been named as pyoverdines (PVDs) or pseudobactins. Besides PVD, *P. aeruiginosa* produces another siderophore called pyocehelin with a lower affinity for iron (Cox *et al.*, 1981). Siderophores are low molecular weight compounds that are produced under iron limiting condition, which chelate the ferric ion (Fe^{+3}) with a high specific activity and serve as vehicles for the transport of Fe+3 into a microbial cell (Neilands, 1981). Dave and Dube (2000) examined siderophore production by six rhizobacterial fluorescent pseudomonads (P1-P6), among the isolates P2 showed the maximum (0.44) CAS activity (OD at 630 nm) and it was least in Pf6 (0.37). Yeole and Dube (2000) reported the production of siderophore by *Pseudomonas* isolates under iron deficient condition.

According to Sharma *et al.* (2007) determined the siderophore production by *P. aeruginosa* in chrome azurol S (CAS) assay and antifungal activity of the strain against three phytopathogenic fungi, *viz., F. moniliformae, A. solani,* and *H. halodes* assay by poison food technique. The test isolates inhibited the growth of *F. monoliformae* (92%), *A. solani* (89%) and *H. halodes* (80%). A scale based on the size of the orange zone created due to siderophore production was developed to determine the ability of fluorescent *Pseudomonas* isolates for siderophore production on the CAS agar medium, among 92 isolates collected from crop rhizosphere in Raichur, 6 isolates were reported to be high producers of siderophore (>4 mm orange zone surrounding bacterial growth), 7 isolates were moderate producers (2-4 mm orange zone), 41 isolates were low producers (<2 mm orange zone) and 38 isolates did not produce any siderophore (Manjunath *et. al.*2011).

Molecular Detection of PvdA (pyoverdine) Siderophore Gene

Pvd is a fluorescent dihydroxyquinoline derivative connected to a small peptide and contain s hydroxamate and catecholate residues to chelate ferric ions, Fe^{+3}. The genes *PvdA, PvdD, PvdE* are responsible for *Pvd* synthesis (Visca *et al.,* 1994). Takase *et al.* (2000) has amplified the *PvdA* gene (on the DNA fragment corresponding to base positions 753 to 2272 of Genebank sequence Z25465) from the chromosomal DNA of *P. aeuroginosa* strain PAO1 by PCR. The entire nucleotide sequence of the *PvdA* gene, from which the primary structure of the encoded polypeptide was deduced, was determined. The *PvdA* structural gene is 1,278 bp (Visca *et al.,* 1994). Chris *et al.* (2004) reported the functional characterization of an aminotransferase PvdH which is required for pyoverdine siderophore biosynthesis in *P. aeruginosa* PA01.

Molecular Characterization of Phz (phenazine) Gene

Phenazines (Phz) are N-containing heterocyclic pigments synthesized by *Pseudomonas* (Leisinger and Margraff, 1979). Weinberg (1970) reported that *Pseudomonas fluorescens* produced PCA (Phenazine-1-carboxylic acid), whereas *Pseudomonas aureofaciens* 30-84 not only produced PCA but also lesser amounts of 2-hydroxyphenazines. The major phenazine derived by *Pseudomonas aeruginosa* was pyocyanin (1- OH-5-methyl phenazine). Smirnov and Kiprianova (1990) showed that bacterization of wheat seeds by *Pseudomonas fluorescens* strains 30-84 and 2-79 provided primary protection against *Gauemannomyces graminis tritici* on account of release of phenazine. Almost all phenazines exhibited broad spectrum activity against bacteria and fungi. *P. fluorescens* 2-79 is among the first few strains from which purified phenazine compounds were shown to have antifungal activity (Gurisiddaiah *et al.*, 1986). Genes encoding the phenazine biosynthetic enzymes are arranged in one core operon, phzABCDEFG, in most producer Pseudomonads, including *P. chlororaphis* 30-84 (Pierson and Thomashow, 1992; Delaney *et al.*, 2001). The phzD gene is known to code for an essential enzyme in phenazine biosynthetic pathway in different bacteria.

Molecular Characterization of Prn (Pyrrolnitrin) Gene

Pyrrolnitrin was identified as a broad spectrum antifungal metabolite produced by many fluorescent and non-fluorescent strains of the genus *Pseudomonas* (Kirner, 1998). It was first described by Arima *et al.* (1964). This highly active metabolite has been primarily used as a clinical antifungal agent for treatment of skin mycoses against dermatophytic fungi, particularly members of the genus *Trichophyton*. A phenyl pyrrol derivative of pyrrolnitrin has been developed as an agricultural fungicide. Elander *et al.* (1968) reported that isopyrrolnitrin, oxypyrrolnitrin and mono-dechloropyrrolnitrin have lower antifungal activities than pyrrolnitrin. Schnider *et al.* (1995) reported that pyrrolnitrin actively persists in soil for at least 30 days. It did not readily diffuse and was released only after lysis of host bacterial cells. This property of slow release facilitated protection against *Rhizoctonia solani* as the cells died. Chang *et al.* (1981) reported that the biocontrol agent, *Pseudomonas fluorescens* BL915 contained four gene clusters involved in the biosynthesis of antifungal molecule, pyrrolnitrin, from the precursor tryptophan. The pyrrolnitrin (prn) operon has been completely sequenced, prnABCD genes which encode different enzymes of the pathway have been identified. Zhang *et al.* (2006) detected antibiotic genes in *P. chlororaphis* PA23, *Pseudomonas sp* strain DF41, *B.amyloliquifaciens* BS6. 30 primers were used to amplify PCA, 2,4DAPG, Pyoluteorine, Pyrrolnitrin and zwittermycin. Fungal antagonists PA23 contain PCA and Prn. This was confirmed by high performance liquid chromatography (HPLC). Upadhyay and Srivastava (2010) reported a unique combination of phenazine and pyrrolnitrin biosynthesis gene from the strain Psd. PhzCD for phenazine and prnC for pyrrolnitrin has been PCR amplified, cloned sequenced and phylogenetic relation has been derived. Biosynthesis of a unique combination of antibiotics will provide a competitive edge to this strain in rhizosphere.

Induction of Systemic Resistance by Fluorescent Pseudomonads

Rhizobacteria that establish positive interaction with plant roots are called plant growth promoting rhizobacteria (PGPR). These bacteria exert beneficial effects which include plant growth promotion and biological disease control. The important traits of PGPR include production of exopolysaccharides, plant hormones, siderophores, bacteriocins, fixation of atmospheric nitrogen, solubilization of phosphorus and antibiotic resistance. Fluorescent Pseudomonads are among the most effective rhizosphere bacteria due to their (Kloepper *et al.*, 1980) strong competitive behaviour, colonization potential and sustainability (Glick, 1995). Resistance inducing rhizobacteria offer an excellent alternative in providing a natural, effective, safe, persistent and durable protection. One classical biotic inducer is the plant growth promoting bacterium, *Pseudomonas fluorescens* Migula (Iavicoli *et al.*, 2003). Induced resistance is a state of enhanced defensive capacity developed by a plant when appropriately stimulated (Van Loon *et al.*, 1998). Induced resistance is generally systemic and can be triggered by pathogens, certain chemicals, and non-pathogenic rhizosphere bacteria. Inducing the plant's own defense mechanisms by prior application of a biological inducer is thought to be a novel plant protection strategy (Ramamoorthy *et al.*, 2001). The use of fluorescent Pseudomonads for inducing systemic resistance against phytopathogens have been well documented.

Mechanism of Induced Systemic Resistance (ISR)

Fluorescent Pseudomonads bring about ISR through fortifying the physical and mechanical strength of the cell wall and as well as changing the physiological and biochemical reaction of host leading to synthesis of defense chemicals against the challenge pathogen.

Biochemical and Physiological Changes in PGPR Treated Plants

PR (Pathogenesis Related) Proteins

Pathogenesis related proteins are the proteins produced in the plants in the event of pathogen attack. PR proteins play important role in disease resistance, seed germination and also help the plant to adapt to the environmental stress. These include β-1,3 glucanase, Chitinases, Thaumatine like protein and glycine rich proteins. Normally ISR by PGPR is associated with the accumulation of PR proteins (Viswanathan and Samiyappan, 1999), synthesis of phytoalexin and other secondary metabolites (Van Peer and Schippers, 1988). The performance of PGPR in inducing systemic resistance has been successful against certain pathogens, pests and nematodes under field conditions. Colonization of bean root by fluorescent bacteria is correlated with induction of PR proteins and systemic resistance against *Botrytis cinerea* (Zdor and Anderson, 1992). Maurhofer *et al.* (1994) reported that ISR by *P. fluorescens* strain CHAO against tobacco necrosis virus (TNV) in tobacco was associated with accumulation of PR proteins namely β-1,3 glucanases and endochitinases. They also established that ineffective strain P3 did not accumulate PR proteins indicating involvement of PR proteins in induction of resistance. In pea, seed treatment with *P. fluorescens* strain 63-28 produced hydrolytic enzymes such as chitinases and β-1, 3 glucanases. These host lytic enzymes accumulate at the site of penetration of the fungus, *F. oxysporum* f. sp. *pisi* resulting in the degradation of fungal cell wall (Benhamou and Chet, 1996). Inoculation of tomato plants with the same strain has similarly induced the production of plant chitinases when challenged with the wilt pathogen, *F. oxysporum f. sp. radicislycopersici* (M' Piga *et al.*, 1997). ISR has been correlated with a two-fold increase in activity of pathogenesis-related peroxidase and chitinase proteins. Two peroxidase and one chitinase (35 kDa) isoforms have been induced in the PGPR-treated plant inoculated with the rice sheath blight pathogen, *Rhizoctonia solani* (Nandakumar, 2001). Similarly, in sugarcane, PGPR-mediated ISR against *C. falcatum*, enhanced levels of chitinase and peroxidase were noticed and specific induction of two new chitinase isoforms were found when inoculated with *C. falcatum* (Viswanathan and Samiyappan, 1999).

Peroxidases

Peroxidases are another set of enzymes induced in the host while host pathogen interface. Peroxidases catalyses the last step in biosynthesis of lignin and other oxidative phenols (Bruce and West, 1989). Bradley *et al.* (1992) reported that increased PO activity is correlated with resistance in many species including barley, cucurbits, cotton, tobacco, wheat and rice. These enzymes are involved in polymerization of proteins and lignin into plant cell wall thus creating a physical barrier that could prevent pathogen penetration into cell wall. Seed treatment and seedling dip with *P. fluorescens* induced early and enhanced PO activity in rice palnts (Nayar, 1996).

Peroxidases has been implicated in the regulation of plant cell elongation in plants treated with *P. corrugate* strain 13 and induction of isoperoxidase that play important role in ISR (Chen *et al.*, 2000). In groundnut increased activity of PO was observed due to application of *P. fluorescens* and PO isoforms were expressed at high levels (Meena, 2000). Two peroxidase isoforms have been induced in the PGPR treated rice plants inoculated with the sheath blight pathogen, *Rhizoctonia solani*. These enzymes are also part of the response of plant defense pathogen (Nandakumar *et al.*, 2001). High level of expression of PO was reported in reported in *P. fluorescens* (Pf1) treated tomato plants challenge inoculated with *Fusarium oxysporium f.sp lycopersici* (Raamamoorthy *et al.*,2001). Inoculation resulted in four isoforms of PO in PGPR treated green gram plants inoculated with root rot pathogen *Macrophomina phaseolina* (Sarvanakumar, 2002). Mathiyazhagan (2003) reported that the bacterial antagonist *B. subtilis* isolate (BSCBE4) induced three isoforms PO1,PO2, PO3 while only PO2 and PO3 was expressed in *Phyllanthus amarus* treated with *P. chlororaphis* (PA23) and challenged against the pathogen *Corynesoria cassicola*. Kamalakannan (2004) observed that the soil application of biocontrol agents such as *Trichoderma* species and bacterial isolates like *P. fluorescens* induced plant to synthesize more amount of peroxidases than the untreated Coleus plants. Kavitha (2004) reported that the peroxidases activity was maximum on the fourth day after challenge inoculation in turmeric rhizome but an increase in the activity was observed upto sixth day after inoculation in case of turmeric leaves pretreated with the consortia formulation of *P. chlororaphis* (PA23) and *Bacillus subtilis* (9CBE4), which was challenged with *Pythium aphanidermatum*. Anand *et al.* (2010) reported the increased activity of defense related enzymes mainly peroxidase, phenylammonia lyase, total phenol and β1,3 glucanase due to application of *P. fluorescens* isolates in chilli plants challenge inoculated with *F. solani* both at short durations (0, 1, 3, 5, 7, 9) and long durations(30, 60 and 90th day).

Polyphenol Oxidases (PPO)

PPO catalyses the biosynthesis of oxidative phenols (Avdiushko *et al.*, 1993). It accumulates upon wounding in plants. Biochemical approaches to understand PPO function and regulation are difficult because the quinoid reaction products of PPO could be detected in cucumber leaf in octadeacanoid defense signal pathway (Constabel *et al.*, 1995). PGPR untreated canes after pathogen inoculation showed comparatively lesser induction of PPO isoforms than the PGPR treated palnts (Vishwanathan, 1999). Chen *et al.* (2000) reported that PPO was stimulated by PGPR or by pathogen, but the wounds on split roots did not influence PPO activity compared to intact control in 13 days. The increased activation of PPO could be detected in the cucumber leaf in the vicinity of lesions caused by some foliar pathogens. Induction of high PPO activity was noticed in rice against sheath blight pathogen *Rhizoctonia solani* when treated with *P. fluorescens* (Radjacommare, 2000). Activation of PPO was stimulated with root application of *P. corrugate* 13 and *P.aureofaciens* in cucumber roots in response to infection by *Pythium aphanidermatum* and was correlated with disease resistance (Chen *et al.*, 2000). Induction of a new and unique PPO1 isoform and higher level expression on PPO2 was noticed in *P. fluorescens* treated tomato plants in response to infection by *F.oxysporium f. sp lycoperscici* (Ramamoorthy *et al.*, 2001). Mathiyazhagan (2003) reported that combined application of biocontrol agents as seed soaking and foliar spray on *P. amarus* recorded the maximum PPO activity on 4th day after challenge inoculation with the pathogen *C. cassicola* in turmeric rhizome PPO activity was maximum on the 4th day due to the application of *P. chlororaphis* (PA23) and *B. subtilis* (CBE4) when challenge inoculated with *P. aphanidermatum* (Kavitha, 2004). Rao *et al.* (2007) studied the effect of *P. fluorescens* strain Migula on sunflower particularly the activity of defense related enzymes like peroxidase, polyphenol oxidase and catalase in treated seeds increased activity of these enzymes in bioprimed seeds may help in conferring resistance against seed borne infections like *Alternaria* causing Alternaria blight of sunflower .

Phenylalanine ammonia lyase activity (PAL)

PAL is the key enzyme in inducing synthesis of salicylic acid (SA) which induces systemic resistance in many plants. In Rice ZB8 PAL gene was found to be induced by the elicitor treatment in rice cells (Li *et al.*, 1993). Seed treatment and seedling root dipping with PGPR induced early and enhanced level of PAL in rice plants (Nayar, 1996) Induction of enzymes such as PAL and peroxidases and the accumulation of such phenolics as lignin can occur in response to insect and pathogen attack, exposure to oxidizing pollutants, mechanical stimulation are thought to function in resistance of plants to damage by the stresses. PAL plays an important role in the biosynthesis of phenolics and phytoalexins (Daayf *et al.*, 1997). The gene was cloned and transgenic rice palnts expressing PAL ZB8 showed systemic resistance against rice pathogens (Lamb *et al.*, 1996). PAL catalyses the deamination of L-phenylalanine to transcinnamic acid which is the first step in the biosynthesis of large class of plant natural products based on phenyl propane skeleton including lignin monomers as well as certain classes of phytoalexins. Podile and Laxmi (1998) demonstrated systemic increase in the PAL activity in pigeon pea seedlings after treatment of seeds with *B.subtilis* strain AF1. Plants treated with *Pseudomonas* strains had initially higher level of PAL but these levels were lower in control (Chen *et al.*, 2000). Sivakumar and Sharma (2003) reported the increased activity of peroxidase, polyphenol oxidase and phenylalanine ammonia lyase activity when maize leaf sheaths were inoculated with the pathogen and plants were raised from *P. fluorescens* treated seeds. Muthuswamy *et. al.* (2005) showed the increased activity of peroxidase (PO), polyphenol oxidase (PPO), phenyalanine ammonia lyase (PAL) in black gram by using *P. fluorescens* isolates of Endo2 and Endo 35 when challenge inoculated with *Macrophomina phaseolina*. Anand *et al.* (2010) reported the increased activity of defense related enzymes mainly peroxidase, phenylammonia lyase, total phenol and β1,3 glucanase due to application of *P. fluorescens* isolates in chilli plants challenge inoculated with *F.solani* both at short durations (0, 1, 3, 5, 7, 9) and long durations(30, 60 and 90th day). ISR by PGPR is also dependent on bacterial determinants like lipopolysaccharides, siderophores and salicylic acid production. It is likely that most of naturally occurring biological control results from mixtures of antagonists rather than from high populations of a single antagonist. Similarly, application of a mixture of introduced biocontrol agents would more closely mimic the natural situation and might broaden the spectrum of biocontrol activity and enhance the efficacy and reliability of control (Duffy and Weller, 1995). Sundaramoorthy *et al.* (2012) studied the combined effect of *P. fluorescens* (Pf1) and *Bacillus subtilis* (EPCO16, EPC5) in the ability to stimulate PO and PPO in chilli plants inoculated with *F. solani* causing wilt disease. Increased PO and PPO activities were observed in EPCO16+ EPC5 + Pf1 mixtures treated plants inoculated with *F. solani* compared to untreated control plants. The activities of β -1,3-glucanase and chitinase increased in plants treated with bio-formulation mixture (EPCO16 + EPC5 + Pf1) up to 9 days after *F. solani* inoculation, and declined thereafter. The native-PAGE analysis of enzyme extract from the mixture of EPCO16 + EPC5 + Pf1 treated plants inoculated with *F. solani* expressed three isoforms PO1, PO2 and PO3. A higher induction and a new isoform of PPO were observed in plants pretreated with mixtures of EPCO16 + EPC5 + Pf1 strains and inoculated with *F. solani*.

Conclusion

Therefore, indiscriminate use of inorganic chemical components viz., fertilisers and pesticides in farming practices have pose serious environmental problems. Fluorescent Pseudomonads are rhizosphere competent bacteria that control soil borne plant diseases and also promote plant health. Secondary metabolites produced by these bacteria play crucial role in control of plant pathogens. Utilization of soil microbacteria to induce plant growth and control of plant diseases seems to be a promising against plant pathogens without adversely effecting environment.

REFERENCES

Abbas, A., Morrissey, J., Marquez, P. C., Sheehan, M. M., Delany, I. R. and 0 'Gara, L. F. (2002): Characterization of Interactions between the Transcriptional Repressor PhlF and Its Binding Site at the phlA Promoter in *Pseudomonas fluorescens* F113, *J. Bacteriol.*, 184(11): 3008-3016.

Amer, G. A., and Utkhede, R. S. (2000): Development of Formulations of Biological Agents for Management of Root Rot of Lettuce and Cucumber, *Can. J. Microbiol.*, 46: 809-816.

Anand, M., Naik, M.K., Ramegouda, G. and Devika Rani, G.S. (2010): Biocontrol and Plant Growth Promotion Activity of Indigenous Isolates of *Pseudomonas fluorescens, J. Mycopathol. Res.*, 48(1): 45-50.

Antoun, H. and Kloepper, J. W. (2001): Plant Growth-promoting rhizobacteria (PGPR), *Encycl. of Genetics.*, Fitzroy Dearborn, London, pp. 1477-1480.

Archana, S., Manjunath, H., Ranjitham, T.P., Prabhakar, K. and Raghuchander, T. (2012): Compatibility of Azoxystrobin 23SC with Biocontrol Agents and Insecticides, *Madras Agric. J.*, 99(4):374-377.

Arima, K., Imanaka, H., Kausaka, M., Fukuda, A. and Tameera, C. (1964): Pyrrolinitrin a New Antibiotic Substance, Produced by *Pseudomonas, Agric. Biology and Chem.*, 28: 575-576.

Avdiushko, S.A., Ye, X.S. and Kuc, J. (1993): Detection of Several Enzymatic Activities in Leaf Prints Cucumber Palnt, *Physiol. Mol. Plant Pathol.*, 42: 441-454.

Bangera, M. G. and Thomashow, L. S. (1996): Characterization of a Genomic Locus Required for Synthesis of the Antibiotic 2, 4-diacetylphloroglucinol by the Biological Control Agent *Pseudomonas fluorescens* Q2-87, *Mol. Pl. Microbiol. Interac.*, 9(2): 83-90.

Bencini, D. A., Howell, C. R. and Wild, J. R. (1983): Production of Phenolic Metabolites by a Soil Pseudomonad, *Soil Biol. Biochem.*, 15: 491-492.

Bender, C. L., Rangaswamy, V. and Loper, J. E. (1999): Polyketide Production by Plant-Associated Pseudomonads, *Annu. Rev. Phytopathol.*, 37: 175-196.

Benhamou, N. and Chet, I. (1996): Parasitism of Sclerotia of *Sclerotium rolfsii* by *Trichoderma harzinium*: Ultrastructural and Cytochemical Aspects of the Interaction, *Phytopathol.*, 86: 405-416.

Bora, L. C. and Bora, P. (2008): Vermicompost Based Bioformulation for Management of Bacterial Wilt of Tomato in Polyhouse, *J. Mycol. Plant. Pathol.*, 38: 527-530.

Boruah, H. P. D. and Kumar, B. S. D. (2002): Biological Activity of Secondary Metabolites Produced by a Strain of *Pseudomonas fluorescens, Folia Microbiol.*, 47: 359-363.

Bradley, D. J., Kjelbern, P. and Lamb, C.J. (1992): Elicitor and Wound Induced Oxidative Cross Linking of a Plant Cell Wall Proline Rich Protein: A Novel, Rapid Defense Response, *Cell.*, 70: 21-30.

Bruce, R.J. and West, C.A. (1989): Elicitation of Lignin Biosynthesis and Isoperoxidase Activity by Pectic Fragments in Suspension Cultures of Castor Bean, *Plant Physiol.*, 91: 889-897.

Caesar, A. J. and Burr, T. J. (1991): Effect of Conditioning, Betaine and Sucrose on Survival of Rhizobacteria in Powder Formulations, *Appl. Environ. Microbiol.*, 57: 168-172.

Carine, L., Gadkar, J. V., Wallon, T., Novinscak, A. and Martin, F. (2012): Production of DAPG and HCN by *Pseudomonas* sp. LBUM300 Contributes to the Biological Control of Bacterial Canker of Tomato, *Biological Control*, 102(10): 967-973.

Chang, C. J., Strans, N. A. and Wijndham, C. (1981): The Biosynthesis of the Antibiotic Pyrrolnitrin by *Pseudomonas aureofaciens, J. of Antibiotics*, 24: 555-566.

Chen, C., Belanger, R. R., Benhameu, N. and Paulitz, T. C. (2000): Defense Enzymes Induced in Cucumber Roots by Treatment with Plant Growth Promoting Rhizobacteria, *Physiol. Mol. Plant Pathol.*, 56: 13-23.

Chin-A-Woeng, T. F. C, Thomas-Oates, J. E., Lugtenberg, B. J. J. and Bloemberg, G. V. (2001): Introduction of the *phzH* Gene of *Pseudomonas chlororaphis* PCL 1391 Extends the Range of Biocontrol Ability of Phenazine-1-carboxylic Acid Producing *Pseudomonas spp*. Strains, *Mol. Pl. Microbe. Interact.*, 14: 1006-1015.

Constabel, C. P., Bergey, D. R. and Ryan, C. A. (1995): Systemin Activates Synthesis of Wound-inducible Tomato Leaf Polyphenoloxidase *via* the Octdecanoid Defense Signaling Pathway, *Proc. Natl. Acad. Sci.*, USA, 92: 407-110.

Cox, C. D., Rinehart, K. L., Moore, M. L. and Cook, J. C. (1981): Pyochelin: Novel Structure of an Iron Chelating Growth Promoter for *Pseudomonas aeruginosa, Proc. Natl. Acad. Sci.*, USA, 78: 4256-4260.

Daayf, F., Bel-Rhlid, R. and Bekabger, R. R. (1997): Methyl ester of p-coumaric acid: A Phytoalexin like Compound from Long English Cucumber Leaves, *J. Chem. Ecol.*, 29: 1517-1526.

Daigle, D. J., Connick, W. J. and Boyetchko, S. M. (2002): Formulating a Weed-suppressive Bacterium in Pesta, *Weed Technol.*, 16(2): 407-413.

Dandurand, L. M., Morra, M. J., Chaverra, M. H. and Orser, C. S. (1994): Survival of *Pseudomonas* spp. in Air Dried Mineral Powders, *Soil Biol. Biochem.*, 26: 1423-1430.

Dave, B. P. and Dube, H. C. (2000): Detection and Chemical Characterization of Siderophores of Rhizobacterial Fluorescent *Pseudomonas, Indian Phytopathol.*, 53: 97-98.

Eftekhar, F., Yousefzadi, M. and Tafakori, V. (2005): Antimicrobial Activity of *Datura innoxia* and *Datura stramonium, Fitother.*, 76(1): 118-120.

Elander, R. P., Mabe, J. A., Hamill, R. H. and Gorman, M. (1968): Metabolism of Tryptophans by *Pseudomonas aureofaciens.* VI, Production of Pyrrolnitrin by Selected *Pseudomonas* sp, Applied and Environmental Microbiology, 16: 753-758.

Glick, B. R., Karaturovic, D. M. and Newell, P. C. (1995): A Novel Procedure for Rapid Isolation of Plant Growth Promoting Pseudomonads, *Can. J. Microbiol.*, 41: 533-536.

Gore, M. E. and Altin, N. (2006): Growth Promoting of Some Ornamental Plants by Root Treatment with Specific Fluorescent Pseudomonads, *J. Biol. Sci.*, 6(3): 610-615.

Gurusiddaiah, S., Weller, D. M., Sarkar, A. and Cook, R. J. (1986): Characterisation of an Antibiotic Produced by an Strain of *Pseudomonas fluorescens* Inhibitory to *Gaeumanomyces graminis var.tritici* and *Pythium* spp, *Antimicrobial Agents Chemotherapy*, 29: 488-495.

Haas, D. and Defago, G. (2005): Biological Control of Soil-borne Pathogens by Fluorescent Pseudomonads, *Nat Rev Microbiol.*, 3: 307-319.

Handelsman, J. and Stabb, E.V. (1996): Biocontrol of Soilborne Plant Pathogens, *Plant Cell.*, 8: 1855-1869.

Heijnen, C. E., Burgers, S. L. G. E. and Van Veer, J. A. (1993): Metabolic Activity and Population Dynamics of Rhizobia Introduced into Un-amended and Betonite Amended Loamy Sand, *Appl. Environ. Microbiol.*, 59: 743-747.

Howell, C. R. and Stipanovic, R. D. (1980): Suppression of *Pythium ultimum* induced damping-off of cotton seedlings by *Pseudomonas fluorescens* and its antibiotic, pyoluteorin, *Phytopathol.*, 70: 712-715.

Howell, C. R. and Stipanovic, R. D. (1980): Suppression of *Pythium ultimum* induced damping-off of cotton seedlings by *Pseudomonas fluorescens* and its antibiotic, pyoluteorin, *Phytopathol.*, 70: 712-715.

Iavicoli, A., Boutet, E., Buchala, A. and Metraux, J. P. (2003): Induced systemic resistance in *Arabidopsis thaliana* in response to root inoculation with *Pseudomonas fluorescens* CHA0, *Mol. Pl. Microbe. Interact.*, 16: 851–858.

Jayaraman, J., Parthasarathy, T. and Radhakrishnan, N. V. (2007): Characterization of a *Pseudomonas fluorescens* strain from tomato rhizosphere and its use for integrated management of tomato damping-off, *Biocontrol.*, 52(5): 683-702.

Kamalannan, A. (2004): Development of Management Strategies for the Control of Coleus (*Coleus forskohlii*) BRIQ Root Rot Caused by *Macrophomina phaseolina* (Tassi.) Goid and *Rhizoctonia solani* (Kuhn.) *Ph.D Thesis*, TamilNadu Agricultural University, Coimbatore, India.

Kavitha, K. (2004): Molecular and bioche Kirner, S. (1998): Functions Encoded by Pyrrolnitrin Biosynthetic Genes from *Pseudomonas fluorescens*. *J. Bacteriol.*, 180: 1939-1943. Mical Approaches for the Selection of Biocontrol Agents for the Eco- Friendly Management of Turmeric Rhizome rot, *Ph.D. Thesis*, Tamil Nadu Agricultural University, Coimbatore, India.

Khan M. A. and Gangopadhyay, S. (2008): Efficacy of *Pseudomonas fluorescens* in Controlling Root Rot of Chickpea Caused by *Macrophomina phaseolina*, *J. Mycol. Pl. Pathol.*, 38: 580-587.

Khan, M.R., Majid, S., Mohidin, F.A. and Khan, N. (2011): A New Bioprocess to Produce Low Cost Powder Formulations of Biocontrol Bacteria and Fungi to Control Fusarial Wilt and Root-knot Nematode of Pulses, *Biological Control*, 59: 130-140.

Kitten, T., Kinscherf, T., McEvoy, G. and Willis, D. K. (1998): A Newly Identified Regulator is Required for Virulence and Toxin Production in *Pseudomonas syringae*, *Mol. Microbiol.*, 28: 917-929.

Kloepper, J. W. (1992): *Plant Growth Promoting Rhizobacteria as Biological Control Agents*, Marcel Decker (ed.), *Soil Microbial Ecology, Applications in Agriculture, Forestry and Environmental Management*, New York: Dekker, 255-274.

Kloepper, J. W. and Schroth, M. N. (1981): Development of Powder Formulation of Rhizobacteria for Inoculation of Potato Seed Pieces, *Phytopathol.*, 71: 590-592.

Kloepper, J. W., Leong, J., Teintze, M. and Schroth, M. N. (1980): *Pseudomonas* Siderophores: A Mechanism Explaining Disease Suppressive Soils, *Current Microbiol.*, 4: 317-320.

Kumar, T. P. and Palakshappa, M. G. (2009): Effect of Organic Amendments on Antagonists and Pathogen Causing Purple Blotch of Onion, *Karnataka J. Agril. Sci.*, 22(1): 229-230.

Lamb, T. G., Tonkyn, D. W. and Kluepfel, D. A. (1996): Movement of *Pseudomonas aureofaciens* from the Rhizosphere to Aerial Plant Tissue, *Can. J. Microbiol.*, 42: 1112–1120.

Latha, P., Anand, T., Prakasama, V., Jonathan, E.I., Pramathma. and Samiyappana, R. (2011): Combining *Pseudomonas, Bacillus* and *Trichoderma* Strains with Organic Amendments and Micronutrient to Enhance Suppression of Collar and Root Rotdisease in Physic Nut, *Appl. Soil Ecol.*, 49: 215-223.

Leisinger, T. and Margraff, R. (1979): Secondary Metabolites of Fluorescent Pseudomonads, *Microbiological Reviews.*, 43: 422-442.

Li, L., Qu, R., Kochko, A., Fauquest, C. and Beachy, R. N. (1993): An Improved Rice Transformation System using the Biolistic Method, *Plant Cell Rep.*, 12: 250-255.

Loganathan, V., Sreekanth, N., Kumar, B. S., Ubaidulla, U., Reddy, M. V. S. and Manimaran, S. (2004): Antibacterial Activity of *Vitex negundo* Linn, *Hamdard-Medicus.*, 47(3): 29-32.

Malathi, P., Viswanathan, R., Padmanaban, P., Mohanraj, D. and Sunder, A. R. (2002): Compatibility of Biocontrol Agents with Fungicides against Red Rot Disease of Sugarcane, *Sugar Tech.*, 4(3/4): 131-136.

Manikanda R., Saravanakumar, D., Rajendran, L., Raguchander, T. and Samiyappan R. (2010): Standardization of Liquid Formulation of *Pseudomonas fluorescens* Pf1 for Its Efficacy against *Fusarium* Wilt of Tomato, *Biol control.*, 54: 83-89.

Manjunath, H., Naik, M. K., Rangeshvaran, S.V. and Vagid, N. V. (2011): Deposition of Sequences of *Pseudomonas putida* Possessing 2,4-DAPG Positive Antibiotic gene, In NCBI, Gen Bank Maryland, USA. *www.ncbi.nlm.nih.gov.*

Mathiyazhagan, S. (2003): Studies on the Soil Borne Diseases of *Phyllanthus amarus* (Scham and Thom) and their Management, *M. Sc. (Ag.), Thesis,* Tamil Nadu Agric. Univ., Coimbatore, India.

Maurhofer, M., Hasse, C., Maurwly, D., Metranx, J.P. and Defago, G. (1994): Induction of Systemic Resistance of Tobacco to Tobacco Necrosis Virus by the Root Colonizing *Pseudomonas fluorescens* CHAO: Influence of the Gac A Gene and of Pyoverdine Production, *Phytopathol.*, 84: 136-146.

Mavrodi, O.V., McSpadden Gardener, B. B., Mavrodi, D. V., Bonsall, R.F., Weller, D.M. and Thomashow, L. S. (2001): Genetic diversity of phlD from 2,4-diacetylphloroglucinol-producing fluorescent *Pseudomonas* spp, *Phytopathol.*, 91: 35-43.

McSpadden-Gardener, B. B., Schroeder, K. L., Kalloger, S. E., Raaijmakers, J. M., Thomashow, L. S. and Weller, D. M. (2001): Genotypic and Phenotypic Diversity of phlD-containing *Pseudomonas* Strains Isolated from the Rhizosphere of Wheat, *Appl. Environ. Microbiol.*, 66: 1939-1946.

Meena, B. (2000): Induction of Systemic Resistance against Late Leaf Spot of Groundnut Using Fluorescent Pseudomonads, *Ph.D Thesis,* Tamil Nadu Agric. Univ., Coimbatore, India.

Muthuswamy, Ramajnujans, K. B. and Krishnan Radhika. (2005): Endophytic *Pseudomonas fluorescens* Endo2 and Endo 35 Induce Resistance in Black Gram(*Vigna mungo* L. Hepper) to their Pathogen *Macrophomina phaseolina, J. Pl. Interac.*, 1: 135-143.

Naik, M.K.,Rajalaxmi, Keshgond, Manjunath, H. and Y.S. Amaresh. (2012): Development of Indigenous Fluorescent *Pseudomonas* as Integrated Component of Sustainable Crop Management, *Proceedings of 3rd Global Conf. Plant Pathol and Food Security*, MPUAT, Rajasthan, Jan-10-13, pp. 22.

Nakkeeran, S., Kavitha, K., Mathiyazhagan, S., Fernando, W. G. D., Chandrasekar, G. and Renukadevi, P. (2004): Induced Systemic Resistance and Plant Growth Promotion by *Pseudomonas chlororaphis* strain PA-23 and *Bacillus subtilis* strain CBE4 against Rhizome Rot of Turmeric (*Curcuma longa* L.), *Canadian J. of Plant. Pathol.*, 26: 417-418.

Nandakumar, R., Babu, S., Vishwanathan, R., Raghuchander, T. and Samiyappan, R. (2001): Induction of Systemic Resistance in Rice Against Sheath Blight Disease by Plant Growth Promoting rhizobacteria, *Soil Biol. Biochem.*, 33: 603-612.

Nayar, K. (1996): Development and Evaluation of a Biopesticides Formulation for Biocontrol of Foliar Diseases of Rice, *Ph.D Thesis,* Tamil Nadu Agric. Univ., Coimbatore, India.

Neilands, J. B. (1981): Iron Absorption and Transport in Microorganisms, *Annu. Rev. Nutr.*, l: 27-46.

Nowak-Thompson, B., Chaney, N., Wing, J. S., Gould, S. J. and Loper, J. E. (1999): Characterization of the Pyoluteorin Biosynthetic Gene Cluster of *Pseudomonas fluorescens* Pf-5, *J. Bacteriol.*, 181: 2166-2174.

odhagen, M., Henkels, M. D. and Loper, J. E. (2004): Positive Autoregulation and Signaling Properties of Pyoluteorin, an Antibiotic Produced by the Biological Control Organism *Pseudomonas fluorescens* Pf-f, *Appl. Environ. Microbiol.*, 70: 1758-1766.

Ou, S. H. (1985): *Rice Diseases*. Commonwealth Mycological Institute, Kew survey, England, pp. 256-368.

Pierson, L. S. Wood, D. W., Pierson, E. A. and Chancey, S. T. (1998): N-acylhomo Serine Lactone-mediated Gene Regulation in Biological Control by Fluorescent Pseudomonads: Current Knowledge and Future Work, *Eur. J. Pl. Pathol.*, 104: 1-9.

Pierson, L. S., and Thomashow, L. S. (1992): Cloning and Heterologus Expression of the Phenazine Biosynthetic Locus from *Pseudomonas aureofaciens, Eur. J. Pl. Pathol.*, 30-84. 5: 330-339.

Podile, A. R. and Laxmi, V. D. V. (1998): Seed Bacterization with *Bacillus subtilis* AF1 Increases Phenalanine Ammonia Lyase and Reduce the Incidence of Fusarial Wilt in Pigeon Pea, *J. Phytopathol.*, 146: 225-259.

Prasad, R. D. and Rangeshwaran, R. (2000): Effect of Soil Application of a Granular Formulation of *Trichoderma harzianum* on *Rhizoctonia solani* Incited Seed Rot and Damping Off of Chickpea, *J. Mycol. and Plant Pathol.*, 30: 216-220.

Raaijmakers, J. M., Vlami, M and de Souza, J. T. (2002): Antibiotic Production by Bacterial Biocontrol Agents, *Anton van Leeuw.*, 81: 537-547.

Radjacommare. (2000): *Pseudomonas fluorescens* meidiated Systemic Resistance in Rice against Sheath Blight Disease and Leaf Folder Insect, *M. Sc. (Ag.) Thesis,* Tamil Nadu Agric. Univ., Coimbatore, India.

Raijmakers, J. M. and Weller, D. M. (1998): Natural Plant Protection by 2,4-diacetylphloroglucinol Producing *Pseudomonas* spp in Take-all Decline Soils, *Mol Plant Microbiol.*, 11: 144-152.

Rajalaxmi, K., Naik, M. K., Amaresh, Y. S., Sunkad, G., Patil, M. G. and Hosamani, A. C. (2012): Shelf Life of Two Indigenous Isolates of Fluorescent Pseudomonads as Bioagents in Different Carrier Materials, *J.Mycopathol.Res.*, 50(1): 85-88

Ramamoorthy, V. and Samiyappan, R. (2001): Induction of Defense Related Genes in *Pseudomonas fluorescens* Treated Chilli Plants In Response to Infection by *Colletotrichum capsici, J. Mycol. Pl. Pathol.*, 31: 146-155.

Ramamoorthy, V. R., Viswanathan, T., Raguchander, V. Prakasam and R. Samiyappan. (2001): Induction of Systemic Resistance by Plant Growth Promoting Rhizobacteria in Crop Plants Against Pests and Diseases, *Crop Protec.*, 20: 1-11.

Sarvanakumar, D. (2002): Rhizobacteria Induced Systemic Resistance against Biotroph (*Exobasidium vexans*) and Necrotroph (*Macrophomina phaseolina*) Pathogens in Tea and Green Gram, *M.Sc. (Agri.) Thesis*, Tamil Nadu Agric. Univ., Coimbatore, India.

schnider, U., Keel, C., Blumer, C., Troxler, J., Defago, G. and Haas, D. (1995): Amplification of the Housekeeping Sigma Factor in *Pseudomonas fluorescens* CHA0 Enhances Anti-biotic Production and Improves biocontrol Abilities, *J Bacteriol.*, 177: 5387–539.

Senthilkumar, T. and Ramakrishnan, S. (2004): Studies on the Compatibility of *Pseudomonas fluorescens, Trichoderma viride* and Carbofuran 3G and their Influences on *Meloidogyne incognita* in okra, *Annu. Pl. Protec. Sci.*, 12(1): 140-142.

Sharma, K., Sexena, A., Dak, G., Sharma, R. and Agarwal, A. (2007): Isolation and Assay of Antifungal Activity of Siderophore Producing *Pseudomonas aeruginosa, J. Mycol. Pl. Pathol.*, 37: 251-253.

Sivakumar, G. and Sharma, R. S. (2003): Induced Biochemical Changes Due to Seed Bacterization by *Pseudomoans fluorescens* in Maize Plants, *Indian Phytopathol.*, 56: 134-137.

Sivakumar, G., Josephrajkumar, A. and Dhanya, M. K. (2012): Evaluation of Bacterial Antagonists for the Management of Rhizome Rot of Cardamom, *J. of Spices and Aromatic Crops*, 21(1): 9-15.

Sivakumar, G., Sharma, R. C. and Rai, S. N. (2000): Biocontrol of Banded Leaf and Sheath Blight of Maize by Peat Based *Pseudomonas fluorescens* Formulation, *Indian Phytopathol.*, 53: 190-192.

Smirnov, V. V. and Kiprianova, E. A. (1990): *Bacteria of Pseudomonas genus*, Naukova Dumka, Riev, Ukraine, 100-111.

Sundaramoorthy, S., Raguchander, T., Ragupathi, N. and Samiyappan, R. (2012): Combinatorial Effect of Endophytic and Plant Growth Promoting Rhizobacteria against Wilt Disease of *Capsicum annum* L. Caused by *Fusarium solani, Biol. Control.*, 60: 59-67.

Takase, H., Nitanai, H., Hoshino, K. and Otani, T. (2000): Impact of Siderophore Production on *Pseudomonas aeruginosa* Infections in Immunosuppressed Mice, Infection and Immunity, 1834-1839.

Takeda, R. (1958): *Pseudomonas* Pigments. I. Pyoluteorin, A New Chlorine-containing Pigment Produced by *Pseudomonas aeruginosa, Hako Kogaku Zasshi.*, 36: 281-290.

Thomashow, L. S. and Weller, D. M. (1996): Current Concepts in the Use of Introduced Bacteria for Biological Disease Control: Mechanisms and Antifungal Metabolites, Stacey G, Keen M. (eds). *Plant-microbe Interac.*, 1:187-235.

Upadhyay, A. and Srivastava, S. (2010): Evaluation of Multiple Palnt Growth Promoting Traits of an Isolate of *Pseudomonas fluorescens* Strain Psd, *Indian J. Exptl. Biol.*, 48: 601-609.

Van Loon L. C., Bakker, P. A. H. M. and Pierterse, C. M. J. (1998): Systemic Resistance Induced by Rhizosphere Bacteria, *Annu Rev Phytopathol.*, 36: 453–483.

Van Loon L. C., Bakker, P. A. H. M. and Pierterse, C. M. J. (1998): Systemic Resistance Induced by Rhizosphere Bacteria, *Annu Rev Phytopathol.*, 36: 453–483.

Van Peer, R. and Schippers, B. (1988): Plant Growth Response in Bacterization with Selected *Pseudomonas spp.* Strains and Rhizosphere Microbial Development in Hydrophonic Cultures, *Canadian J. Microbiol.*, 35(4): 456-463.

Velusamy, P. and Gnanamanickam, S. S. (2003): Identification of 2, 4-diacetyl-phloroglucinol Production by Plant-associated Bacteria and Its Role in Suppression of Rice Bacterial Blight in India, *Curr. Sci.*, 85(9): 1270-1273.

Velusamy, P., Immanuel, J. E., Gnanamanickam, S. S. and Thomashow, L. (2006): Biological Control of Rice Bacterial Blight by Plant Associated Bacteria Diacetylphloroglucinol, *Canadian J. Microbiol.*, 52(1): 56-65.

Vidhyashekaran, P., Rabindra, R., Muthamilan, Ubramaniyan, N. and Vasumathi, K. (1997): Development of Powder Formulation of *Pseudomonas fluorescens* for Control of Rice Blast, *Pl. Pathol.*, 46: 291-297.

Visca, P. A., Ciervo. and Orsi, N. (1994): Cloning and Nucleotide Sequence of the pvdA Gene Encoding the Pyoverdine Biosynthetic enzyme L- Ornithine N5-Oxygenase in *Pseudomonas aeroginosa*, *J. Bacteriol.*, 1128-1140.

Viswanathan, R. (1999): Induction of Systemic Resistance Against Red Rot Disease in Sugarcane by Plant Growth Promoting Rhizobacteria, *Ph. D. Thesis*, Tamil Nadu Agric. Univ., Coimbatore, India.

Walker, R., Rossall, S. and Asher, M. J. C. (2001): Compatibility with Seed Treatment Chemicals of Rhizobacteria Antagonistic to the Sugarbeet Damping-off Pathogen *Aphanomyces cochlioides*, *Bulletin-OILB/SROP*, 24(3): 243-246.

Wienberg, E. D. (1970): Biosynthesis of Secondary Metabolites: Roles of Trace Elements, *Adv. in Microb. Physiol.*, 4: 1-44.

Yeole, R. D. and Dube, H. C. (2000): Siderophore Mediated Antibiosis of Rhizobacterial Fluorescent Pseudomonads against Certain Soil Borne Fungal Plant Pathogens, J. Mycol. Pl. Pathol., 30: 335-338.

Zdor, R. E. and Anderson, A. J. (1992): Influence of Root Colonizing Bacteria on the Defense Responses of Bean, Plant Soil, 140: 99-107.

Zhang, Y., Fernando, W. G. D., Keivit, T. R., Berry, C., Daayf, F. and Paulitz, T. C. (2006): Detection of Antibiotic Related Genes from Bacterial Biocontrol Agents with PCR, Canadian J. of Microbiol., 52: 476-481.

Index